HUMAN EMOTIONS AND THE ORIGINS OF BIOETHICS

This book provides a unique phenomenological dialogue between psychology and philosophy on the origin of bioethics that shows the importance of bringing emotions into bioethical discourse.

Divided into two parts, the book begins by defining bioethics and explaining the importance of emotions in making us human, allowing us to consider life holistically. Ferrarello argues that emotions and bioethics are better served when they are combined, and that dismissing emotions as nothing more than a nuisance to our rationality has created a society that does not fit our human nature. Chapters explore how ethics relate to intimate life and how ethical agents determine themselves within their surrounding world, uniquely and interrogatively using "bioethics" to consider not only medical dilemmas but also issues concerning environmental and individual well-being. By addressing personal, interpersonal, and societal problems as dynamically interconnected in bioethical problems she helps us to renew our sense of responsibility toward a good quality of life.

This interdisciplinary book is invaluable reading for students of health science, psychology, and philosophy, as well as for those interested in the link between emotions and bioethical discourse from both a psychological and philosophical perspective.

Susi Ferrarello is assistant professor at California State University, East Bay, USA. She has a Ph.D. in Philosophy from the Sorbonne in Paris, and an MA in Human Rights and Political Science from the University of Bologna. She is the author *Phenomenology of Sex, Love, and Intimacy* (Routledge, 2019), and is also a philosophical counselor.

HUMAN EMOTIONS AND THE ORIGINS OF BIOETHICS

Susi Ferrarello

Routledge
Taylor & Francis Group

NEW YORK AND LONDON

First published 2021
by Routledge
2 Park Square, Milton Park, Abingdon, Oxon OX14 4RN

and by Routledge
52 Vanderbilt Avenue, New York, NY 10017

Routledge is an imprint of the Taylor & Francis Group, an informa business

British Library Cataloguing-in-Publication Data
A catalogue record for this book is available from the British Library

Library of Congress Cataloging-in-Publication Data
Names: Ferrarello, Susi, author.
Title: Human emotions and the origins of bioethics / Susi Ferrarello.
Description: 1 Edition. | New York : Routledge, 2021. | Includes
bibliographical references and index.
Identifiers: LCCN 2020031280 (print) | LCCN 2020031281 (ebook) |
ISBN 9780367427283 (hardback) | ISBN 9780367427313 (paperback) |
ISBN 9780367854638 (ebook)
Subjects: LCSH: Emotions. | Bioethics.
Classification: LCC BF531 .F47 2021 (print) |
LCC BF531 (ebook) | DDC 174.2--dc23
LC record available at https://lccn.loc.gov/2020031280
LC ebook record available at https://lccn.loc.gov/2020031281

ISBN: 978-0-367-42728-3 (hbk)
ISBN: 978-0-367-42731-3 (pbk)
ISBN: 978-0-367-85463-8 (ebk)

Typeset in Bembo
by MPS Limited, Dehradun

To Severino, Martino, and the forest in Bubendorf

CONTENTS

INTRODUCTION

Why do we experience anxiety, restlessness, or fear? Why do we cheat, lie, or act in a selfish way? Are we all alone, or are we all caught up in a web of interconnections? How can we make decisions that improve the quality of our personal and social lives? And, most importantly for this book, what does bioethics have to say about all of this?

This and my forthcoming book (The Role of *Bio*-Ethics in Emotional Problems) will address these questions and show their relevance in bioethics. Starting from the idea that bioethics, as its etymology shows, studies the value systems (ethics) regulating our reflective life (bios), this book will discuss the main philosophical biases that have lead to a *Lebensphilosophie* which undermines societal as well as personal well-being. This book is divided into two parts. The first one (Chapters 1–3) defines bioethics, explains the importance of emotions—specifically how they make us human and capable of considering life as a whole—and illustrates how the two are better served when they are combined as opposed to unnecessarily divorced from each other. The second section, consisting of Chapters 4 and 5, tackles the problems of reductionism, dualism, and scientism. Here, we will see how these concepts have created the main theoretical biases that have led to a consideration of life that is fragmented, individualistic, and mechanistic. In The Role of *Bio*-Ethics in Emotional Problems, consisting of four chapters, I will discuss how this worldview has enhanced psychological problems such as anxiety, narcissism, restlessness, and emotional numbness which are becoming increasingly common among the younger population.

A global society that is currently considering property rights on off-world commerce[1]—such as on the Moon and Mars—without having solved the problems of its on-world commerce (the use of fossil fuels, for example) clearly shows that there is an urgent need to rethink the role that human beings have in maintaining the health and well-being of our planet. Coming to peace with the finitude of human existence; changing some basic structures of human thinking; and measuring growth based not on destructive illusory categories, but on actual possibilities, are just some of the necessary steps human beings need to take. A bioethics that takes into account emotions can help us here.

But bioethics must also take into consideration the choices that we, as individuals and interconnected texture of society, make in our daily lives. In my analysis, which I will elaborate on in this book, it has become apparent that many of the psychological issues affecting our society come from a way of looking at life that promotes the separation of individuals from their environment under the promise of an easy fix to complex problems due to a hypertrophic trust in technology.

With this and my forthcoming book, I intend to address personal, interpersonal, and societal problems as dynamically interconnected with each other, with the goal of renewing our sense of responsibility toward maintaining a good quality of life. I believe the starting point to doing so is to reconsider the role of emotions in every level of our life. Dismissing emotions as nothing more than a nuisance to our rationality has made many of our rational choices inhuman. We have created a society that does not fit humans: our cities have become a place to host lonelier and lonelier people (Chapter 3), our doctors are getting emotionally sicker (Chapter 2), and our environment has been exploited in a mindless, and often heartless, way (Chapters 3–5). It is no surprise that emotional disorders are becoming a growing concern, with one of more troubling symptoms being the increasing suicide rates among young adults.

To make our lives better, we need to make our lives fit for living beings. To do so, we must cleanse from our view of living beings all those biases that reduce human beings to machines, spirits disconnected from their bodies, islands far from each other. The continuity of life, and its innumerable ramifications, is a fact that needs to be observed, respected, and taken into account when making decisions conducive to a good life.

As I will explain in more detail in this book, the idea of bioethics that I defend comes from its founder, Van Rensselaer Potter. I use the word *bioethics* as an integrative[2] discipline that does not consider only medical dilemmas but also issues concerning environmental and individual well-being. I tried to avoid, as much as possible, an anthropocentric point of view in order to defend the dignity of living beings as an interconnected dynamic system that nurtures the multitude of ways in which we recognize life. Hence, I used notions such as place and nature to loosely indicate the space hosting this life, while using environment—being a relative concept itself—to indicate the space that is "around" (from French, *environ*) any subjective expression of life.

This book will build upon my previous work, *Phenomenology of Love, Sex, and Intimacy,* by expanding on the problem of emotions and their intentional roots.

Both this book and my forthcoming The Role of *Bio*-Ethics in Emotional Problems will try to find an answer as to how we can live a healthy emotional life capable of nurturing ourselves and our relationships within a healthy environment. I used phenomenology as a method of investigation, although I tried to make the book accessible to readers who are not interested in engaging with the phenomenological tradition.

This book will be structured in two parts. First, it will lay the foundation for a new bioethics capable of conceiving life (*bios*) as an intersubjective and inter-intentional space where we can be emotionally co-responsible. Second, it will cover the analysis of ego, intersubjectivity, and the dichotomy that separates ego's internal and external life along with the theoretical biases that accompany this separation. The goal of the volume is to raise the readers' awareness of their emotional life within their environment. Hence, the book will delineate an ethics that looks at life as a dynamic interconnection of lived experiences. In particular, in the forthcoming book, The Role of Bio-Ethics in Emotional Problems, I will focus on the lived experiences of anxiety, emotional numbness, and restlessness to see from a closer view how this (bio)-ethics would fit in human emotional lives.

In the first chapter, I examine the different angles of bioethics, from its foundation to its contemporary application. I describe bioethics from a historical and conceptual point of view and examine the biases that, even today, still harm the effectiveness of bioethics. From a historical point of view, Potter founded bioethics with the intent of bringing together biological and medical science with philosophy. Originally, bioethics was meant to develop a wise approach to guarantee the survival of the Earth and its organisms. The bi-local birth of bioethics and the cogent need to find an answer to medical cases transformed bioethics into a sort of medical ethics from which, at times, philosophical reflection on moral principles was excluded. The historical atrocities of Nazi eugenics and the Tuskegee experiment led to a need for an agreement on how to handle the violation of human dignity and the inviolability of the patient. Principlism and the human rights system emerged as a form of bioethics that was supposedly independent of philosophical thinking, but in fact at times just as a poorly organized philosophical reflection. This provided bioethics with a beneficial ground for compromise and agreement above religious, regional, and political particularism, yet this often lacked coherence. As a suggestion, I promote here the idea of accepting the instability of bioethics as its strength and not as its weakness. A bioethics that views situations on a case-by-case basis, specifically through a reflective equilibrium and the presuppositionless approach, has a real chance to produce rigorous and life-adherent results. An important bias, in fact, that has prevented bioethics from applying its full potential has been the reductionist attitude in science that, on the basis of a dualistic view of the world, oversimplified the way we look at the complexity of the organisms in a dualistic manner, hence reinforcing a cosmetic application of science. Bringing together biology and philosophy was, according to its founder, a way to recompose this painful gap between life and its vital principle. From the analysis I conducted, it emerged that the historical reasons that led to the need for founding a bioethical discipline took its origin from these theoretical biases which fostered a view of science as superior than any living being and at the same time detached from life in virtue of its being objective. We do not want to promote this idea of science; rather, we want to defend a participated and descriptive idea of science capable of questioning and renewing itself at each of its endeavors.

In the second chapter, I present four reasons why emotions are important in bioethics:

1. Unhealthy people generate an unhealthy environment.
2. We need to care if we want to receive good care. Empty empathy might be harmful.
3. We need emotionally intelligent AI to avoid corrupting our daily lives in new ways.
4. Emotions are engaging and make us human.

In the second part of the chapter, I discuss the philosophical and psychological sources that led to a disparaging attitude toward emotions. Emotions, in fact, were often read as that biological component of our body that clouded our reasoning from functioning correctly. It is interesting to see how two recurrent themes of the theory of emotions emerged both in philosophy and psychology: on the one hand, emotions are considered as the language that nature uses to speak to us; on the other, there has always been the strong belief that we need to control emotions in order to be fully human. What makes us better than animals, and accordingly above nature, is our will to say No to certain emotions. Yet, given the knowledge we have today about the limbic system and the under-standing of its interaction with the environment, we have no reason to encourage an inhuman split between reason and emotions since emotions are reasons as well. Negating that system means to negate our right to be.

The third chapter is an investigation of the theoretical and practical implications of emotions in our intentional life. In the first part of the chapter, I discuss the meaning of intentionality and argue that emotions are intentional through and through. After discussing weak (Crane, 1998) and strong (De Sousa, 1987) in-tentionalism in relation to emotions and the two strategies proposed by strong intentionalism—perceptual and evaluative—I lay out a third alternative (Husserl, 1901; Teroni and Deonna, 2012): emotions should be seen as fully intentional. In his *Logical Investigations*, V, Section 15 (1900/01), Husserl took a position in relation to his masters, Stumpf and Brentano, concerning the problem of the intentionality of sentiments such as pleasure or pain. According to Husserl, especially in his later works (1926), emotions can be intentional because their sensory qualities animate the directedness expressed by the way in which the emotion appears to the ob-server. The way in which Husserl explained the intentional essence of emotions invites us to avoid any reductionist and psychologistic approach in that he kept the sensuousness and the meaning, the real and ideal, as two different temporal substances which instantiate themselves in the appearance of the phenomenon. The fact that emotions can be considered intentional through and through means that we can track the direction of our emotional life and tend to it in a responsible and aware manner. To facilitate the understanding of the complex intricacy of the intentional web, I have organized the different forms of intentionality mentioned by Husserl into three groups: passive, active, and practical. While the passive intentions belong to sensory affections and lower feelings (instincts, pulsions), practical intentions (wisdom, care) define that moment of awakening in which the given content is considered in an attentive way by the volitional body which decides whether to accept that content as an object and assign a meaning or value to it or to reject it and push it back to the passive layer. Active intentionality, instead, indicates a meaning- and value-assigning act which operates on the content of that lived experience that has been approved by the volitional body. Epoché and reduction are two theoretical devices introduced by Husserl to facilitate the eidetic process of looking at the essential structure of the intentional content and eliciting an ethically balanced way of looking at the multifaceted reality that unfolds from the intentional contents.

In the second part of the chapter, I examine practical cases in which an implied refusal to tend to the intentional power of emotions and a lack of aware participation in one's intentional life can severely impact the well-being of individuals and society. In medicine, the examples of pain treatment management and misdiagnosis in women shows how strongly implied personal biases against emotions can harm the life of individuals. Similarly, examples of neutral emotionless architecture serve as a showcase to prove how impoverishing an emotionless planning can be for the quality of our daily lives, both at home and at work.

In the fourth chapter, I argue against reductionism and substance dualism by showing the continuity of life as an organism in physics, biology, and psychology. Using Husserl's theory of parts and whole, and its complex application of ontological and epistemological foundation, I explain how the structural difference of time constitutes one's notion of identity that is vitally interconnected with the notion of environment. Ultimately, I discuss a provisional definition for what it means to feel alive and expound on its causality. More specifically, the epistemological and ontological foundations of parts and whole with which we recognize that something *is* and we sense its being there proves to be an alternative way of thinking about life in a relational way. In fact, individuals, defined as nodes of systemic truth, are not dichotomic islands who occasionally connect with each other, but are organisms whose parts are interwoven with the environment in which they express their liveliness as a functioning cooperating system.

Understanding the fluidity and continuity of the boundaries between individuals and their environment helps to overcome a dualistic view of the distance that separates our bodies from what we recognize as external. The formal property of environmental sets puts in question the traditional distinction between subject and object that is central to traditional scientism and a certain reification of living beings. This object or that body that I recognize as separate from others is in continuity with them; there is no space for a strict separation because, as I show with Aristotle and others, the notion of space itself involves a continuity between entities. Speaking of individual organisms or objects is an abstraction (Dupré and Maureen O', 2007, 842). Objects are no more than "temporarily stable nexuses in the flow of upward and downward causal interaction" (Dupré and Maureen O', 2007, 842) that we use to facilitate our understanding of reality. Most importantly, this chapter shows the continuity between organism and environment, parts and whole, self and identity. Our sense of self and identity is often so dualistically biased that we cannot perceive any continuity between the two, to the point that the world appears to us as an external being from which we feel completely detached, like remote islands that struggle to communicate with each other. Thinking of our being as an isolated island separated from the rest of the environment would mean to miss the full picture of what we are and lose the concrete terrain of passive intentionality from which we can produce meanings and values. A living being is part of the components produced by the system, and it is the realization of this system in a concrete unity in time and space that can produce meanings and values understandable for itself and others. Survival depends on the ability to transform this interdependence into meanings so that the merely physical surroundings can continuously become a set of meanings and values available for us. Being a person does not consist of adhering to a mental construct, it is being part of experiential facts and the way in which they interact with the environment. If we impoverish the environment, we impoverish our chance to be ourselves.

The fifth chapter argues against a worldview that proposes a strict distinction between internal and external reality. Since substance dualism encourages a view of the body as impermeable and strictly separates the self from the body, and accordingly from its environment, this chapter discusses the notion of permeability of the body in order to show the continuity between the self and the environment. In preparation for the next three chapters, the goal of this chapter is to reduce the space between the two in order to overcome psychological disturbances coming from the separation of the body from its own mind and of the individual from its own environment.

Hence, I discuss the constitution of selfhood as it arises from kinesthesia, that is, our ability to perceive our movement and build meanings according to the way in which we relate to our senses. Accordingly, I examine the case of pregnancy to show how difficult it is to draw a line between the internal space of the self and the external space of otherness. I explain how a pregnancy changes the body of the mother and how much the mother contributes to the constitution of the body of their children. In a similar fashion, I describe how this form of mutual constitution takes place in the vegetative life of plants and trees. I will then criticize the Aristotelian idea of the passive life of plants in favor of a humbler effort that should be made by us to understand their dynamic and intersubjective interactions. To this purpose, I describe what is interaffectivity for human beings and how its lack can lead to psychological and ecological problems. Human community is built on interaffectivity and when our ability to interact with each other and with our environment is missing, we have problems with our feelings; we might not feel anything or feel too much, we might isolate ourselves from others and our real self hence risking being affected by psychological disorders that I am going to describe in the next three chapters. This lack of a systemic view of life has led to an impoverished notion of well-being, which, even in public health, is described as isolated care administered to the individual separated from others and the environment. Clearly, this also leads to the systemic lack of care in medical fields such as epidemiology.

In general, the goal of the book will be to show the importance of emotions in bioethics and the urgency to think bioethics in integrative terms.

Notes

1 See Outer Space Treaty and Space Settlement Prize Act.
2 I am not alone in this. For a bibliographic review of this point, see Sodeke and Wilson (2017). Integrative bioethics is a bridge builder worth considering to get desired results. *The American Journal of Bioethics: AJOB*, 17(9): 30–32. https://doi.org/10.1080/15265161.2017.1353174.

Bibliography

Crane, T. (1998). "Intentionality as the mark of the mental". *Royal Institute of Philosophy Supplement*. Cambridge: Cambridge University Press, 229–251.

De Sousa, R. (1987). *The Rationality of Emotion*. Cambridge, MA: MIT Press.

Deonna, J., Teroni, F. (2012). *The Emotions: A Philosophical Introduction*. London: Routledge.

Dupré, J., Maureen O' M. (2007). "Metagenomics and biological ontology", *Studies in the History and Philosophy of Science C: Biological and Biomedical Sciences*, 28: 834–846.

Ferrarello, S. (forthcoming). *The Role of Bio-Ethics in Emotional Problems*. London: Routledge.

Ferrarello, S. (2018). *Phenomenology of Love, Sex, and Intimacy*. London: Routledge.

Husserl, E. (1901/1984). *Logische Untersuchungen*. U. Panzer (Éd.), Den Haag: Martinus Nijhoff.

Sodeke, S. O., Wilson, W. D. (2017). "Integrative bioethics is a bridge-builder worth considering to get desired results", *The American Journal of Bioethics: AJOB*, 17(9): 30–32.

1

BIOETHICS: WHAT ARE WE MISSING?

Introduction

In this chapter, I will discuss the difficult genealogy of bioethics in order to give justice to the original aspirations of its founding father, Van Rensselaer Potter (1911–2001). First, the chapter will focus on the story of the main protagonists behind the creation of bioethics, as well as how this story evolved over the first few decades. Second, I will explain the theoretical reasoning that led to the foundation of bioethics. To do so, I offer a brief excursus of Husserl's interpretation (1936) of Galileo's and Descartes' foundation of science so as to explain the roots of the reductionist attitude that has led science to dismiss the value of human and natural life in favor of technological findings. Third, I will discuss what the scope of bioethics is today and what attempts bioethics has made to overcome political, religious, and geographical particularism. Last, I will raise the question of what kind of characters a universally applicable bioethics should have in order to function as the bioethics that its founder had in mind.

I. Coining a Word

In 1970, a deeply human reflection on moral qualities such as humility, dignity, love, and commitment[1] led to a book that launched a new discipline: bioethics. The author, Van Rensselaer Potter, wrote *Bioethics: Bridge to the Future* (1970) under the auspices of improving the quality of life of "living systems"—meaning, not limited to humans (Potter, 1975, 2299)—through an interdisciplinary integration of life sciences, philosophical reflection, and moral choices.[2] The term "bioethics" was coined by Fritz Jahr[3] in 1927 and was inspired by the Kantian categorical imperative according to which all living beings have the right to be treated not as a means to an end but as ends in themselves—that is, as unique individual agents that possess the sanctity of life. Although Potter did not openly cite Fritz Jahr, he was similarly inspired. In continuity with Jahr's program, Potter writes:

> I chose bio- to represent biological knowledge, the science of living systems; and I chose ethics to represent knowledge of human value systems. On the one hand we are concerned with biological evolution, and on the other we are concerned with cultural evolution.
>
> *(Potter, 1975, 2279)*

The decision of Potter and Jahr to use the two Greek words *bios* and *ethos* points to an intersubjective and, so to speak, transhuman framework in which this new discipline was meant to function. The word ήθος (ethos) points to "an accustomed place" (Herodotus, 2, 142; Plato, Phaedrus, 277a) and "habits" (Plato, the Laws, 792e; Aristotle, Eudemian Ethics, 220a,39) that a person develops through time. The use of the ancient Greek word *bíos* (βíος) instead of *zoé* (ζωή) speaks to the distinction concerning the reflective quality of human life. While *zoé* indicates the *essence* of life that universally belongs to all living beings (whose opposite is not death but extinction, as death belongs to individuals only), *bíos* (βíος) indicates the conditions of possibilities for our life not just to be but also to thrive if we so choose. *Zoé* is the life that flows in us whether we pay attention to it or not; it refers to the boundless facticity of life (ζωή comes from Greek ζάω, "I live"). *Bíos*, on the other hand, is the way we choose to live; that is, the decisions we make to express the living biological principle that animates our being. For this reason, in Greek the word *bíos* is generally accompanied by qualifying adjectives such as practical (πρακτικός), contemplative (θεωρητικός), or political (πολιτικός). A *zoé*-ethics would not have reason to exist because life just is; as such, no philosophical reflection or moral considerations can be implied. But bioethics does involve these forms of reflections in order to improve the quality of our unreflective (ζωή) life and reflective (βíος) biological life. For this reason, Potter continues:

> I wish to characterize humility with responsibility as the basic bioethic. The reason for this categorization stems from the fact that this basic bioethic emerges from a consideration of what bioethics is all about, namely, an understanding of how our thinking brain can combine biological knowledge with a social and philosophical consciousness. (1975, 2297)

Basic bioethics—in contrast to the separate branches cybernetic-, techno-, and digital-ethics—concerns the ongoing effort of humanity to combine wisdom with scientific knowledge as it emerges from "consideration" and "understanding"; that is, consciously considering how best to combine biological and technological knowledge with philosophical and social knowledge. This means that bioethics should not be an extension of just medical ethics but, instead, should globally refer to all the sciences of well-being, namely, environmental, political, psychological, and social well-being. These latter intellectual pursuits must be included in bioethical research in order to improve the quality of life and to contribute to cultural and biological evolution. Moreover, the all-encompassing nature of this improvement equally concerns all living systems. Bioethics, as its founder conceived it (see Figure 1.1), encourages us to think in terms of interconnection rather than in terms of individualistic functioning.

This book and the forthcoming one (The Role of *Bio*-Ethics in Emotional Problems) want to come back to bioethics as its founder, Potter, conceived it (see Figure 1.2); for this reason, the books' structure follows Potter's theoretical map. In addition, I have expanded on the theoretical drifts—reductionism, scientism, and individualism—that contributed to the rise of psycho-sociological problems, since these negatively impact the well-being of our organism as individuals and environment.

I.1 Bilocal Birth of Bioethics

According to the theologian W. T. Reich, bioethics originated from a bi-located birth (1995). In fact, a little after Potter coined this new discipline, a group of professionals extensively contributed to its growth in different directions. Independently of Potter, psychiatrist Gayling and philosopher Callahan founded the Hastings Center, a center that is still very actively caring for one's well-being in relation to new technologies. In a similar direction, the Dutch obstetrician

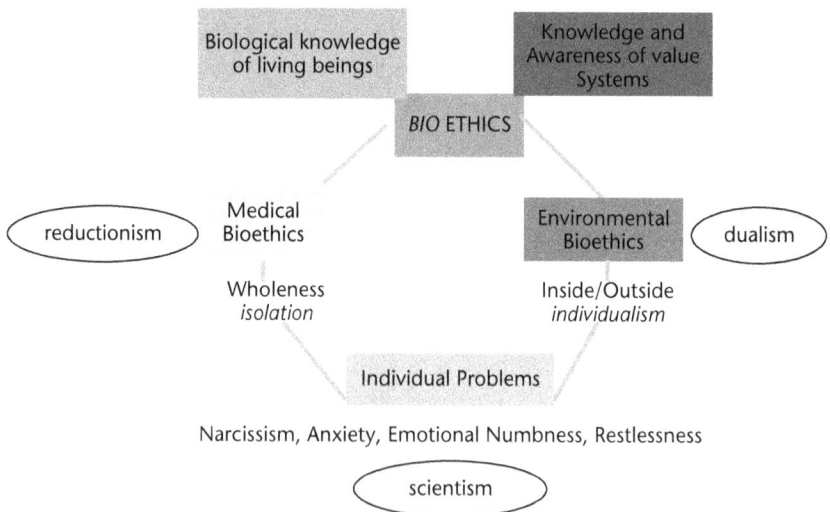

FIGURE 1.1

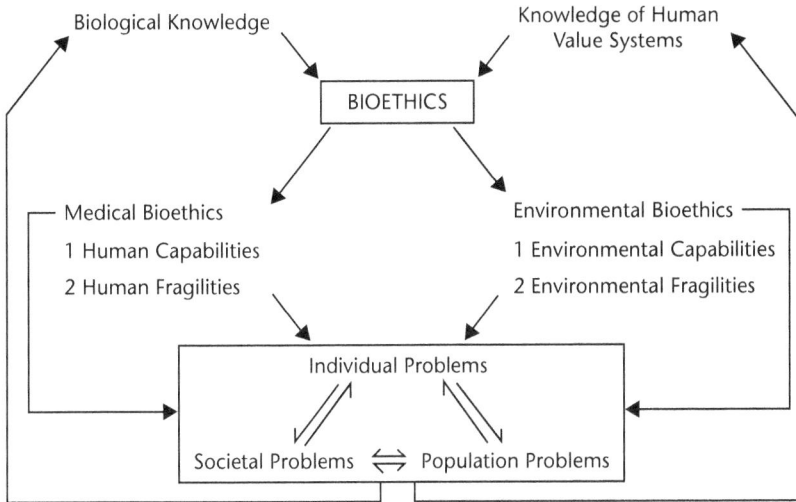

FIGURE 1.2   Potter, R. *Global Bioethics*, 72.

Andre Hellegers (1926–1979) and the political activist Sargent Shriver (1915–2011) used the term *bioethics* in 1970 when they inaugurated the Joseph and Rose Kennedy Institute for the Study of Human Reproduction and Bioethics.[4] For them, bioethics was "the ethical scrutiny of specific problems raised by medicine and the biological sciences" (Reich, 1995, 71). Most importantly, Reich's project of an *Encyclopedia of Bioethics*,[5] with himself as editor-in-chief,[6] and the publication of Daniel Callahan's philosophical essay "The Roots of Bioethics" led to a definition of bioethics that connected it mainly to the medical field. According to Hellegers-Reich's view, as it emerges from their Encyclopedic project, bioethics is a "systematic study of human conduct in the field of human science and health care as this conduct should be examined according to moral values and principles" (Reich, 1978, xix). Hence, at the very beginning, there were two bioethics: one which would appear as a sort of medical ethics (Reich's) and another one (Potter's) which was conceived as an ethical reflection on and for the survival of Earth.

It is worth noting that this bi-located birth impacted the meaning of bioethics only at its birth; in fact, during its second wave in 1995, bioethics seems to have stabilized its scope within the range of medical ethics. Potter complains that "the focus of attention to the problems of medical ethics has led us to forget the original spirit of bioethics as I imagined it in reference to the global pattern of sciences of life" (Russo and Potter, 1995, 24). Considering his original goal in bioethics anticipated a much wider range and involved an ongoing search for wisdom whenever new discoveries in the sciences of life and biotechnologies emerged, Potter regretted the fact that bioethics became mainly a medical ethics focused on the problems that take place in hospitals and health care systems.

For this reason, in 1995 Reich decided to revise his definition of bioethics in the entry of his *Encyclopedia* toward Potter's direction. In a 1995 interview with Spinasanti, he affirmed that, "Bioethics is not a wider form of medical ethics. We extended bioethics to include social and environmental problems as well as those problems related to the health and life sciences" (Spinsanti, 1995, 219). In the revised version of the *Encyclopedia,* Reich wrote, "[Bioethics] is the systematic study of human conduct in the area of *the life sciences and health care,* insofar as this conduct is examined in the light of moral values and principles" (Reich, 1978, xix).

The need to care for survival on a larger scale seems to be the most compelling goal of bioethics for both groups; Bateson's later book, with the title *Steps to an Ecology of Mind* (1972/2000), proposed as well a definition of bioethics that accented the importance of the environment and respect for a variety of biological intelligences. This respect is what truly regulates, according to Searle (1992), environmental survival.

Thus, at the end of the second wave of bioethics, a general consensus gathered around the idea of bioethics as a complex, interdisciplinary subject. There was a realization that American bioethics focused more on individual autonomy and dignity of life brought to extend bioethics: "to consider not only human communitarian values but also to include communities of other living creatures. (...) The moral status of non-human life forms demands re-evaluation" (Whitehouse, 2003). The decisions that such a discipline has to make are based on a systematic interconnected character of living systems which are part of the ecosystem as a whole.

Unfortunately, today a tendency still persists to limit bioethics to the field of medicine, as if medicine itself could be individualized and detached from the environment (Morris and Saunders, 2017). As we will soon see, the original demand for wisdom that characterized bioethics in its foundation seems, today, to be either strongly questioned or outright replaced by practical demands.[7] The philosophical and intersubjective character of bioethics seems again to be endangered in favor of practical choices that bioethicists are called on to make every day in their area of work (Baker et al., 1993; Baker, 2002; Rose, 2007).

1.2 Philosophy and Bioethics

As a consequence of this difficult agreement concerning the scope of bioethics, the role of philosophy in bioethics has been intermittently disregarded as "not only useless, but also dangerous. (...) Medicine must not be contaminated by philosophy. It would be a mixture of chocolate and garlic" (Bleuler, 1921, 9). With similar elegant eloquence, the German psychiatrist Bleuler continued by stating that "philosophy has produced nothing else but a cemetery of theoretical systems which are haunting us like ghosts. Half of the philosophers are engaged in trying to kill these ghosts again and again; the other half is busy to revive the same ghosts. The best strategy is to ignore philosophy and to separate it as strongly as possible from medicine." Although it would go against the original spirit of the founders of bioethics, Bleuler is, unfortunately, not alone in proposing this division.[8]

The ambition of combining philosophy and science, as mentioned above, was the core goal of Potter's work (1974, 2279). Contrary to what Bleuler stated, I believe that both medicine and philosophy were not born perfect but have improved themselves through a long chain of trial and error. The cemetery of theoretical systems is merely a sign of human growth. For both disciplines, the creation of new "systems" was not happenstance but originated from strong commitment to a positive and sustainable evolution. The cure for ebola, polio, hepatitis, and cholera did not come out of one single attempt. Similarly, in philosophy, productive systems to enhance the quality of life—the democratic system, for example—are the improved work of many previous attempts.

Another example is the cure that philosophical bioethics had to find against reductionism. The foundation of bioethics, in fact, has helped philosophy and medicine get rid of the shackles of reductionism by looking at the human being as a whole (Potter, 1988) and not as a disconnected combination of body and mind. Although I will dedicate more space later in this chapter to explain what I mean by reductionism, for the sake of this argument I will briefly define *reductionism* as any attempt to reduce a complex phenomenon to the functioning of its individual parts; most notably, psychophysical reductionism, as Nagel named it (2012), is the attempt to reduce psychological phenomena to physics and chemistry. Looking at the human being not only as a physical machine but as a complex whole brought positive changes to how medicine and health sciences administered care to patients. It encouraged, for example, the introduction of concepts such as empathy or the use of literature and arts as a means to lift the spirit of the patient. Philosophical critique of reductionism (Nagel, 2012) has allowed us to see the human body not just as an assemblage of its components but as a unique combination of spirit and mind in which, following the Aristotelian argument, the resulting whole is bigger than the mere combination of its parts. I believe that separating philosophy from bioethics and giving in to the irritation that one might feel toward something whose use is not immediately understandable would involve a tremendous loss for bioethics, as well as a betrayal of its original spirit.

I.2.1 Short Reflection on Utility

The word *utility* comes from Latin *utor,* make use of, profit by, take advantage of. To some extent, I do agree with Heidegger when, in his *Introduction to Metaphysics* (2000, 12), he wrote that *philosophy is useless*. It is true: philosophy cannot be reduced to any consumeristic goods. In this sense, philosophy does not have to serve any immediate disposable purpose in our daily ordinary life. Philosophy is not a technique that one applies for immediate commodity; it is not a consumable good of which one can take advantage. Philosophy is a reflection for life (meant both as bios and zoé) which should hopefully prepare us to face the new challenges of our technological progress.

I do not want to say that we cannot make use of philosophy or that philosophy is useless per se; I want to emphasize the difference between the usefulness of a philosophical investigation and that of something like a phone application. The latter is certainly more pragmatic and situated than the former. An example of the effectiveness of philosophy was the seminal report of the Warnock Committee on embryo research in 1984; a team of philosophers was appointed to design a new policy on embryo research which was, at the time, still in its early stages. Thirty years later, this report contributed to the foundation of the Human Fertilisation and Embryology Authority (HFEA) also producing the policy re-commendations, by the HFEA's own consultation, on mitochondrial replace-ment. Although the effects of this philosophical work were not immediately visible when they were designed, through time, this philosophical reflection led to a legislation that improved the quality of choices available for future parents.

The theoretical reasoning produced by philosophy is what informs the theoretical content of our laws and, accordingly, the shape we decide to give to our society. The theoretical content of an ought on which a law is based cannot come from the practical life itself; otherwise, it would lose its universal effectiveness in the particularism of each singular case. As Kelsen and Radbruch noticed, the *Sollen* (ought) cannot come from a reaction to the events of factual life but from its essence; if that happened, it would just repeat the factual event itself. Each ought requires a reflection and an interpretation of factual events according to a casuistry of possible consequences ensuing the application of that interpretation. For this reason, Potter's idea to create a discipline that combines philosophy with science can only be beneficial if it provides life sciences with ought-contents that can serve policy- and law-making processes applicable for a wider range of situations. Consequently, an effective bioethics meant as an ought-based discipline, a branch of practical ethics or applied philosophy, can help to orient one's action within non-ordinary situations as it "must primarily be concerned to address a practical 'ought' question" (Sheehan and Dunn, 2013, 56). Bioethics might not appear immediately useful because it is not an instantly consumable good. Fortunately, I would say, its lasting results structure the future of our society and are not devoured by immediate consumption.

Hence, the useless succession of theoretical systems lamented by Bleurer is part of the history of our progress. I believe that separating philosophy from bioethics would be not only a loss but also a lie. If such a separation occurred, reflection on practical cases would be impoverished or, worse, replaced by empty slogans. Moreover, exiting philosophy from bioethics would mean a betrayal of the original foundational spirit of the discipline and a forgetfulness of the philosophiae doctor[9] (PhD) title that is assigned to any profession which involves a certain degree of reflection.

II. Events Behind the First Codes in Bioethics

The Nuremberg Tribunal in 1946 represented a wake-up call for humanity; the abuses in experimentation on human subjects and the war crimes committed by high-ranking Nazi officials and doctors shed light on how poorly human life was valued and how devoid of meaning it had become. The decisions taken at the Nuremberg trial were systematized in the Nuremberg Code (1947) which recognized the need and legitimacy of human experiment but established a number of ethical conditions under which the scientific experiments must be pursued. This code was the model for subsequent codes such as the Declaration of Helsinki,[10] issued by the World Medical Association at its 18th General Assembly in June 1964, that deepened and expanded the Nuremberg Code, namely in what concerns the autonomy of the subject of experimentation. Unfortunately, these codes did not prevent other dehumanizing actions from taking place. It was, in fact, with the Belmont Report[11] (1978) issued by the American National Commission for the Protection of Human Subjects that other caveats were imposed on medical research on humans.

Bioethics was born in reaction to a scientific reifying attitude that treated human beings as objects of science and not subjects of their life. In his *Global Bioethics* (1988), Potter advocated against a science that *reduces* life to a functioning mechanical body whose parts are considered mostly as instrumental and more important than the whole; he advocated against a reductionist science. He cited Leopold (1887–1948) when he wrote "the reductionist approach used by specialists in the university system 'dismemberment;'" they examine "plants, animals, and soils as instruments (...) without looking at the harmony" (Leopold cited in Potter, 1988, 15). As mentioned in the previous section, the imperative of immediate utility as something consumable that serves an immediate purpose in our daily life was extended to whole living beings: trees to produce paper, earth minerals to get gas, human beings to exploit for their labor, and so on, higher and higher in the chain of production. Reducing the system of living beings to particular objects of science reduced life to a commodity, that is, a consumable good with a goal that was supposed to be higher than the worth of life itself. Reducing science to its utility reduced its objects to disposable goods.

II.1 Tuskegee

One of the more infamous examples of reductionism applied on living beings was the Tuskegee experiment (1932–1972). The Belmont Report (1978) was written to denounce and condemn the behavior of scientists who valued this experiment more than human life. This experiment involved 600 African-Americans who had been deprived of actual therapy against syphilis so that scientists could follow the natural course of the disease and its effects. Even after the events were made public, the scientists involved, Heller, for example, did not see any reason why the experiment should have been considered unethical.

Two days after the story broke, Dr. Heller, by then a special consultant to the National Cancer Institute and its former head, declared, "there was nothing in the experiment that was unethical or unscientific" (Reverby, 2009, 87). Science was simply more useful, more human than humans, more alive than life. Even after the public expressed their horror in knowing about this cruelty, most of the leaders of the experiment did not see their behavior as ethically troubling. There was nothing unethical because it was conducted under the hieratic umbrella of science. In the letters that Dr. Vonderlehre and Dr. Clarke exchanged on April 8, it was clear that even if a treatment against syphilis was found they were not willing to end the experiment. In their minds, the scientific curiosity to discover the effects of untreated syphilis was nobler and worthier than the life of the people involved in the experiment (Gray, 2000, 53). This immoral use of science led to considering the life of 600 human beings as worth nothing in comparison to the scientific goal behind the project.

III. How Did We Arrive Here?

How is it possible that life itself started having less worth than science? How did living beings come to be considered objects and means of scientific research and not its end and the purpose to serve?

In *Crisis of European Science* (1936), Husserl explains in great clarity the cultural steps that led to this demeaning behavior toward living beings. When he presented his talk in Prague in 1934, he was in his late seventies, struggling with declining health, and in the midst of the political crisis imposed by the German National Socialist Regime that had come to power the year before. In a letter dated August 30, 1934, the organizing committee of the international congress in Prague had asked Husserl to comment on "the mission of philosophy in our time."[12] The ideas gathered around that theme became the core of Husserl's last project, the most engaging one for the large audience.

In this project, he declared that he wanted to understand "the origin of the modern spirit" (C 57; K 58), and, in particular, the nature of "bestowal of meaning" or "sense bestowal" (*Sinngebung*, C 58; K 58). According to Husserl, Galileo and Descartes were the main protagonists of an age that shaped a new idea of science and modern spirit that led humanity into an irrational disconnect. "*Menschentum* is being human within human organisms (Menscheiten) generatively and socially connected. A human being can be rational only if humanity is rational" (Husserl, 1936, 44). The modern notion of science separated humanity into particular functioning pieces generatively and socially disconnected, that is the source of its growing irrationality. What were the steps that led to it?

III.1 Galileo Galilei

Motivating Galileo's project was his ambition to free science from biblical interpretations in favor of a rationalization of Nature. In his *Saggiatore* (1623),

Galileo defined nature as a book whose pages are written in a mathematical language and whose characters are expressed in geometrical shapes (Section 9, 53). The finalism of nature is not per se understandable by human beings, though the scientist can observe its laws and read its structure through mathematics and geometry, that is objective nonhuman languages. In search of objective principles to describe nature, science became τέχνη (*techne*), a technology, and no longer the realization of human spirit (Section, 33, 150). The root *tek-*, which in Latin becomes *ars* or Art, indicates a process of production and reproduction. Differently from science, technology does not involve any investigation of nature because technology's goal is to reproduce the object of its activity in an unquestioned manner. According to Husserl, it is under this unconditional and unquestioned validity that living beings became objects of reproductions and no longer subjects-objects of research. The meaning of their being grew smaller and smaller, almost insignificant (Husserl, Section 14, 97). For this reason, Husserl sees at the genesis of the modern spirit the growing contrast and ensuing defeat of the world of life (*Lebenswelt*) against the world of science. According to Husserl, the Galilean world is populated by spatio-temporal forms whose contents are established by measurements of their extensions (Section 8, 56). The meaning of these beings exists in force of their possibility to be measured. Hence, in the Tuskegee experiment or the Nazi's eugenic experiments, for example, the possibility of measuring results on the human body is seen as the *via regia* to unlocking the secrets of Nature and for this reason this goal is more alive than any living creature and more worthy of respect than any individual life.

While in Husserl's *Lebenswelt* measuring means *inventio* (from Latin, finding), that is discovering the meaning in the given moment of the intersubjective interconnection of that living being in the system of nature (Husserl, 1936/1970, Section, 8, 57); in Galilean science,[13] measure becomes an objectivating tool that transforms natural beings into objective forms. Behind the number, human beings, animals, and organic systems disappear and become technological objects, that is, reproducible—Benjamin would say, technological (1935)—pieces of the language of nature. As nothing more than a number, life loses its meaning. The reduction of living being[14] to object originates here, from a need for conclusive answers which dissolves the systemic harmony of beings (*plena, Fuelle* to use Husserl's language) and breaks it into disconnected forms. For Husserl, "the world is not just totality but it is a whole (*Allenheit*)" whose interconnected contents and forms cannot be discarded without risking a significant loss of meaning and values.[15] For this reason, Chapters 4 and 5 of this book will be dedicated to the description of the way in which this harmonic totality of human beings has been disrupted, and what the consequences of this disconnection are in our ecological and psychological life. Husserl continues: "True nature does not lie in the infinite in the same way that a pure straight line does; even as an infinitely distant 'pole' it is an infinity of theories and is thinkable only as verification; thus, it is related to an infinite historical process of approximation"

(Husserl, 1936, 42). No final and immediately useful answer can be given in science because the prerogative of science is to not give anything for granted; the conclusiveness and usefulness of an answer would limit the horizon of the infinite line of nature and the scientific attitude with which we try to interpret it.

III.2 Rene Descartes

Descartes, the father of modern philosophy, was the one to bring Galilean intuitions into a system.[16] In *The Passion of the* Soul (1649), he wrote: "We think we see the torch itself and hear the bell itself, rather than simply having the sensation of movements they have caused" (2015, 205). Descartes' rationalist meditative approach toward the systemization of human knowledge into a rational form was inspired by both the experience of the fragility of human science and Teresa D' Avila's meditative approach (Mercer, 2017).[17] According to Husserl's reading of modern science, the naturalization of the psychical sphere and the origin of the dualism between mind and body passed through this Cartesian rationalistic foundation of science; Husserl's explanation is the following:

> After Galileo had carried out, slightly earlier, the primal establishment of the new natural science, it was Descartes who conceived and at the same time set in systematic motion the new idea of universal philosophy: in the sense of mathematical or, better expressed, physicalistic, rationalism—philosophy as "universal mathematics."
>
> *(Husserl, 1936, 74)*

After Galileo, philosophical thinking became a reflection on the "numbers" of nature as they were expressed in geometrical forms; philosophy was universal mathematics. For Husserl, Descartes systematizes Galileo's empirical understanding of nature by assigning an organizing function to the mind as if the mind was the main processor through which the natural findings are ordered and stored in what we call knowledge. Descartes recognized, in fact, the importance of the mind in this scientific process, but, according to Husserl, in the rush of providing a solid ground for Galileian objectivism, he did not question the contents of the mind and its thoughts. The mind is there to give a foundation of validity for what is essentially graspable.

According to Husserl, Descartes was on the verge of finding a truly meaningful ground for objectivism capable of integrating meanings with measures, values with data (Section 17, 103) but he used the evidence of the *ego cogitans*, the thinking mind, to prove that there are two distinct categories of objects of knowledge, a spiritual and a material one. With Descartes, the human soul (*res cogitans*), too, became a natural object among many, detached from its body (*res extensa*) and isolated from other souls. The isolated pole of the *res cogitans* is what provides the rational ground for modern science and its enlightened spirit.

It is in reaction to this understanding that empiricists explained how important the role of bodily human senses is in the process of knowledge since our senses might deceive us in anything we come to know. Assailed by the uncertainty that such a discovery evoked, Descartes sought for a way to find a stable scientific and measurable knowledge capable of overcoming the biases of our senses. To use the Cartesian example cited before, how do we know that our human senses do not trick us into perceiving something different than a torch? When we look at a torch, we think we see the torch but in fact we have the sensation of it as it is caused by the movement of our eyes. How do I know that this sensation is telling me something accurate? The answer he gave was that the *ego cogitans,* the mind, has an innate self-evident idea that proves the certainty of anything that is vetted by it. This self-evident idea is the idea of an *ego cogitans*: I can question anything, but I cannot question the fact that I am questioning because that act is itself an act of thinking. According to Husserl, this self-evidence has the merit to have been unveiled by Descartes' application of epoché, that is, the suspension of judgment in order to apply radical skepticism on all that is gathered by human senses and to accept only self-evident knowledge grounded on apodictic truth. Philosophical knowledge is, according to Descartes and Husserl, absolutely grounded knowledge; it must stand upon a foundation of immediate and apodictic knowledge whose self-evidence excludes all conceivable doubts. Every step of mediate knowledge must be able to attain the same sort of self-evidence (Husserl, 1936, 74).

In Descartes' system, the emerging self-evidence is the *ego cogito* itself.[18] I can doubt everything but not my own doubting. "I, the ego performing the epoché, am the only thing that is absolutely indubitable, that excludes in principle every possibility of doubt" (1936, 78). What resists my radical attempt to question my sensuous knowledge and put in parenthesis my beliefs is in fact my same questioning.[19] According to Husserl, the problem emerging from this radical suspension was a cogito whose contents remained unexplored. The apodictic evidence that Descartes unveils remained a pole useful to justify, to a certain extent, Galileo's physicalism, but it remained, according to Husserl, in itself empty. "Thus the ego becomes determined, for Descartes, as mens sive animus sive intellectus" (1936, 83). Therefore, even if the world of the senses as governed by our body, *res extensa*, might be deceiving the world of our thoughts, the truthfulness of the *res cogitans* resists any doubt and assures us that what we think of the world of the senses is true: "Cogito, existo (I think, I am)."[20] The evidence of a *res cogitans* is the first ground for a dualistic distinction between mind (*res cogitans*) and body (*res extensa*) which envisions reality as an object of thoughts (*cogitata qua cogitata*).

III.2.1 What Kind of Dualism?

What kind of dualism can we attribute to Descartes' "cogito, existo"? The literature concerning Descartes' dualism is quite rich. According to Hart (1996, 265–267),

Descartes introduced a form of substance dualism which is not to be confused with the property and predicate dualism that are its consequences. Property dualism asserts that the properties of the mind and those of the matter are substantially different; for this reason, consciousness cannot be reduced to neurobiology. This dualistic way of categorizing matter/mind properties generates a predicate dualism according to which while there is only one ontological category of substances and properties of substances (usually physical), the predicates that we use to describe mental events remain mental representations. Substance dualism separates the substance of mind and body as irreducible to each other.

The thinking ego becomes the object of its body as the thought experienced by this machine. Similarly to the scientific world of nature, the human world is a thought (*cogitatum*) with the difference that the lifeworld is the *cogitatum* of the mind while nature is the *cogitatum* of the body. The *ego cogito* reduces the human psyche to a mechanical piece or a theater, to use Dennett's expression; the pineal gland, located inside the bigger machine of the human body, has the duty to regulate the exchange between the two. As mentioned before, Husserl's main criticism goes toward the apodictic acceptance of the truthfulness of the *ego cogito* and its contents.

> He does not see that, by being convinced of the possibility of the goal and of this means, he has already left this radicalism behind. (…) The ego is not a residuum of the world but is that which is absolutely apodictically posited.
>
> *(Husserl, 1936, 80)*

The *ego cogito* emerging from the epoché is taken as the unquestioned self-evident truth of an omniscient God that puts in the machine-body a self-evident idea of perfection,[21] which explains why humans know what they are sensing in a consistent way.[22] What seems to interest Husserl in Descartes' substance dualism is the temporal structural difference between *res cogitans* and *res extensa*. The temporal experience of *having* a body (res cogitans, in Husserl's terms Leib) is quite different from the temporal experience of *being* a body (res extensa, in Husserl's terms Koerper). Acknowledging the high difficulty involved from this problem, he wrote, "The same Body which serves me as means for all my perception obstructs me in the perception of itself and is a remarkably imperfectly construed thing" (Husserl, 1989, 167).

Having a body means to be able to sense our own limits (Grenzen) in the space we occupy as a thing among other things. The main difference between these two modalities of being is temporal because it is in time that things (our own body included) appear to us. A temporal extended object will never appear to us if it exists only in the here and now, as a living presence. For something to be,[23] a temporal horizon or field should be present. The celebre example that Husserl gave is that of the melody: we would not be able to retain the melody if the tones in which it is expressed were not retained, anticipated in a "constantly gradated coming" (Husserl, 1968). This ability does not belong to our being a thing among other things because in that sense we are a living presence without any skill to anticipate or retain what has just been; that ability belongs to our mind. Having a body, being a *res cogitans*, means being able to figure in time the appearance of the life-world; as Zahavi remarks (2003), the two are not distinguished only in an object-relation way but in a temporal way. On the one hand, the temporal experience of being a body opposes to the pre-reflective presupposition of having a body. Having a body is the phenomenological presupposition for the body to be perceived and described in scientific terms.

According to Wilson (2014), Descartes' dualism can be expressed in temporal terms. In Principles II. 23, for example, Descartes used time as a means to describe bodies as individuals since he claimed that "any variation in matter or diversity in its many forms depends on motion." For Waller, Descartes used two temporal attributes: (1) successive duration and (2) an innate idea of time (2004, 8). The former characterizes the *res cogitans* in the way in which it organizes the knowledge pertaining to its *res extensa* and the world it comes into contact with; the latter indicates the temporal quality in which the *res extensa* is. Differently from the sense of time in Plato's philosophy which Julia Annas described as a "mysterious cosmic entity or container" (Laws, 818c), both to Descartes and Husserl time is a constitutive quality that allows to distinguish the dual nature of our being as a thing among other things (being a body or res extensa) and as a reflecting subject (having a body or res cogitans). The substantial difference is not determined by a point of discontinuity between the two but by the nature of the time that constitutes every single fiber of both. Descartes and his followers did not conceive the mind-body dualism as a disconnection between the two. Their interaction and its laws, in fact, were conceived according to regular relations that inform the domain of natural philosophy and physics. Regis, one of his followers, named these regular interactions between brain states and resulting sensory experiences as laws of mind-body relations (see Hatfield, 2004).

III.2.2 Science of Spirit and Science of Nature

Unfortunately, this dichotomy between mind and body was often interpreted in a compartmental way to the extent that gave rise to a compartmental way of doing science. According to Husserl's reading, it was Dilthey (1833–1911) who systematized sciences on the basis of the Cartesian substance dualism: science of nature (Naturwissenschaft) and science of the spirit (Geisteswissenschaft). Husserl wrote, "Dilthey, one of the greatest humanists, devoted the energies of his whole life to a clarification of the relation between nature and spirit" (Husserl, 1936, Appendix 1, 1).

It is still not clear what position Husserl held in reference to Dilthey. In fact, Husserl seems to be very critical of Dilthey's worldview as leading up to relativism (1910) but then, after an epistolary exchange between the two, it seems that Husserl denied his attacks and celebrated his work (Carr, 1925, 1936, xxxvi).[24] In any case, the substance of Husserl's analysis of Dilthey's contribution to the evolution of science revolved around the criticism of having organized science in two separate groups reflecting the Cartesian distinction of *res extensa* and *res cogitans*: natural science as the study of the *res extensa* and human sciences as the study of *res cogitans*. While natural sciences have the task to arrive at law-based causal explanations, the task of human sciences is to understand and describe the organizational structures of human and historical life. While Descartes, Kant, and many other brilliant minds who came before Dilthey's time mastered both groups of sciences, after this division a professionalizing compartmental trend started creating a drift between humanists and scientists. Following this separation philosophy became a science of the spirit somewhat distant from the science of nature; one was cultivating the knowledge of the mind, the other observing the body and often the two did not talk to each other. They treated human beings and their environment according to the same distinctive mark of separation that still informs the course of our basic education and, accordingly, humors an unquestioned belief in the disconnection between mind and nature.

What Potter and Reich did with bioethics was to bring together what was originally separated. They tried to reintroduce a harmonious way to look at nature and the human being as a part of it. As I showed in the previous sections, the attempts to separate philosophy from bioethics reflect again this drift between human and natural science with the excuse of pursuing a more efficient practical way to handle medical problems; I hope that the irritation toward reflection and a questioning attitude toward life can be overcome in favor of a more holistic way to look at life.

III.3 Bioethics Against the Recurrent Malaise of Reductionism

In his essay on reductionism, Reich defined *reductionism* as "a recurrent malaise that distorts the meaning of bioethics and its methods" (1990, 141). At its inception, both for Potter and Reich,[25] bioethics was supposed to recompose the gap between science and values, life, and philosophy. Potter cited Novikoff as follows:

> Equally essential for the purposes of scientific analysis are both the isolation of parts of a whole and their integration into the structure of the whole. The consideration of one to the exclusion of the other acts to retard the development of biological and sociological sciences (…) to achieve a truly holistic or eco-systematic approach, not only ecology but other disciplines in the natural, social, and political sciences as well must emerge to new hitherto unrecognized (…) thinking and action.
>
> *(Novikoff, 1945, 209)*

Reich, Potter, Novikoff, and other prominent bioethicists expressed the necessity to place the Galieian method[26] within a comprehensive perspective that integrates science of the spirit and science of nature. Reflecting on the whole and its parts (more on this point in Chapter 4) is the way in which bioethics can "give back morality to science" (Engelhardt and Caplan, 1987, 7–27), meaning to life. In October 1971, the Society for Health and Human Values, and its closely affiliated Institute on Human Values in Medicine, formed the national reference group known as the Burns's Committee on Medical Humanities. Its goal was to resolve "the dilemma of creating an educated person and a technically trained one … attitudes that make it possible for health professionals to understand and to deal with the human environment in a more effective way" (Minutes, archives in W. T. Reich, 1990). When Al Vastyan, founding chairman of the Department of Humanities at the Hershey Medical Center of Pennsylvania State University, was asked, "[w]hy are people now interested in adding the humanities to medical education?" Vastyan answered:

> I think that our era has been one of movements towards participatory democracy, of racial justice, towards radical criticism of existing institutions—all in order to counter the technological momentum. I think that we are beginning to realize that technology itself does not build its own sense of values. How can we harness these dramatic achievements for human ends?
>
> *(Minutes, Medical Humanities Committee, 3/1/1972, IMH Records, RG9, Box 2, Folder 18, UTMB archives)*

The technological and scientific progress that Western society made from Galileo to today is undeniable; it is also true that psychosocial problems such as depression or anxiety are currently experiencing unprecedented growth (WHO report, 2020). These problems might be the sign for which a synergy between human and life science is needed in order to evolve toward a wiser society, or as Potter would put it, in order to survive. Remaining loyal to Dilthey's organization of sciences and to a reductionist view of knowledge would increase a "dilemma oriented, problem-solving, deductive, rationalistic, individualistic and rights-focused enterprise" (McCormick, 1994, 149) that would put our society into more and more danger, both emotionally and environmentally.

III.4 Scientism

Scientism is one unfortunate aspect of reductionism. By scientism, I mean here the unquestioned belief according to which science and its "cosmetic" application is the only reliable answer to complex problems and the unique source of knowledge (Sorell, 1994, 1 ff). Cosmetic indicates here any ad hoc intervention to fix a part that is considered broken without considering the whole organism to which the cosmetic intervention is directing. By doing so, the scientist attitude tends to devalue the wide array of intelligences that living beings and organisms have to offer for the survival and improvement of the environment (Rosenberg, 2011) while emphasizing a false belief in final measurable answers to complex problems. Hence, scientism promotes the idea of science as a useful instrument that measures unquestioned truths (Husserl, 1936), which are true as far as they remain crystallized in that given measurement.

Scientific education should treasure an understanding of science as never-ending research for a truth whose essence is never exhausted in any fixed measurement (Husserl, 1936). That is, life-changing discoveries such as those around the nature of gravity, the physics of light, and medical cures against polio did not result from a one-time ingenious attempt but were encased in a long-standing chain of intuitions and attempts to translate these intuitions into fruitful answers. Portraying science as an instrumental mode of reason (Carson, 2010a) often allowed for an immoral use of technology. As Heisenberg noticed (1969), the instrumentalization of science via technology triggered a process of persuasion to perform unethical atrocities against life, the effects of which our Earth is still suffering. The marvel of technology and immediate utility of science were a sufficient reason to silence any moral objections and conflicts of interest.[27]

In that sense, Heidegger's aforementioned critique of the utility of reason (2000) and Habermas'(1962) description of the public sphere as the ideal realm for reasonable confrontation represented a necessary significant reaction against an instrumental use of reason and technologization of science. I will describe more in detail the impact that scientism had on the well-being of our society and environment in the chapters dedicated to emotional numbness, anxiety, and narcissism (forthcoming book, The Role of Bio-Ethics in Emotional Problems). The thesis I will defend in those chapters is that a science of cosmetic applications for immediate utility has treated emotional problems as "anti-aesthetic" issues. Thus, science has often pursued an easy fix that relied mostly on ad hoc medications without looking at the problem in its entirety within the organismic whole "human being-environment."

III.5 Dualistic Disconnection

As we saw in Section II, one of the interpretations of the Cartesian dichotomy leads to a consideration of the body as substantially separate from the mind; this substantial separation, systematized by Dilthey's organization of science, has had a high impact on the way in which we organized our knowledge, our education at school, and later on the organization of our professional life (Alsop, 2005). We became objects of our own mind, objects for each other to consume. The meaning of life is pursued in other objects and goods because only objects are effectively real: a newer smartphone, a fancier car, or a more expensive piece of clothing is a fitter depository of one's own life-meaning and accordingly, joy.

Our profession, too, must be objective and almost objectual. For example, in the workplace we are asked to not be ourselves but the objectivation of our profession. This means that we are asked to behave as a universal body of guidelines that preferably do not include who we really are as a whole person because behaviors, at work, must not be personal. The result is that we live more than half of our lives as objects avoiding to be persons and unable to connect with ourselves as a whole; we are promised that by doing so we will be rewarded with career promotions and wealth. Yet, this reward is mostly objectual (wealth expressed in expensive objects) generating often a behavior that drains our vitality and without vitality happiness is lost (more on this point in Chapter 2, Section II).

In the *Quest for Certainty* (1929, 20), Dewey remarked how this way of organizing our knowledge has impacted how humans relate to each other, to their own body, and to their own environment; since the mind is disconnected from the body, the biological continuity between the two is lost and the mind is either reified in an organ or isolated in the spiritual realm. Dewey wrote, "We are so accustomed to the separation of knowledge from doing and making that we fail to recognize how it controls our conceptions of mind, of consciousness and of reflective inquiry" (Dewey, 1929, 22).

The disconnection between body and mind reflects an image of the world that is not real as the world is not a distinct realm detached from the efficacy of our thinking.[28] Our life in the world is one with our learning from and our thinking of our life-world. Breaking the continuity between the biological and the reflective life of the individual undermines one's sense of reality and the choice one makes in relation to what is believed to be real, as well as increasing one's sense of isolation. Perceiving oneself as incapable of making any difference in a world that is placed in a dimension so ontologically different from one's own sphere of action leads to the loss of a sense of purpose and meaning in life.[29]

One way to overcome this disconnection and its nefarious consequences is, in fact, to defend the continuity between body and mind, environment and self—a strategy that I will pursue in Chapters 4 and 5. A similar strategy has been proposed by Fuchs (2017), who attempted to overcome the Cartesian dichotomy by demonstrating the continuity of the self from first (self-experiencing subject) to third perspective (living being) which reveals the self as "an organismic" self-preserving and self-reproducing being and not as a unit separated from its own body. Training this double perspective on the self as "subjective self-experience" and as living being allows us to see the nature of the two as continuous (as it seems it was according to the temporal interpretation of Descartes' dichotomy); consequently, the self is "a manifestation of the life process as a whole (and not a product of the brain only)" and any "thought experiments of a possible translocation of the mind via brain transplantation or by other means" (Fuchs, 2017, 133) would be simply inconceivable. Fuchs' strategy can be reinforced by Searle's observation against neurobiological reductionism:

> Common sense tells us that our pains are in physical space within our bodies, that for example, a pain in the foot is literally inside the area of the foot. But we now know that is false. The brain forms a body image, and pains, like all bodily sensations, are parts of the body image. The pain-in-the-foot is literally in the physical space of the brain.
>
> *(Searle, 1992, 63)*

The practice of reducing our knowledge of our concrete being to one substance only, whether it is material (neurology, genetic) or spiritual (animism, theology), inevitably reduces the complexity of our being to a thin superficial layer and detaches our sense of being to the point that we feel isolated even from ourselves as if something will always be missing. This disconnection leads to a mindless way of relating to each other and to the environment because the mind, *res cogitans*, has no significant part in the actual world, *res extensa*; it is just one of its attributes. A binary way of living is conducive to seeing reality according to an internal-external dichotomy for which internal mental processes do not necessarily correspond to or engage with the external world (Westerman and Steen, 2007).

I will dedicate more space to this problem in Chapter 5. For now, it is important to prepare the ground for the theoretical challenges that Potter's bioethics needs to overcome in order to be applicable.

IV. The Imperative of Bioethics and Its Field of Application

When medicine encountered ethics, it was said that the two saved each other. There were those like Toulmin who wrote that "medicine saved ethics from its dryness, philosopher geographer of values and concepts" (Toulmin, 1982, 740) and others, such as Potter, who thought that philosophy gave medicine its much needed wisdom to overcome its dilemmas in a considerate way (Potter, 1988). The medical codes, such as the Declaration of Helsinki and all its subsequent revised and amended versions (Tokyo, 1975; Venice, 1983 and Hong Kong, 1989, also known as, respectively, Helsinki II, III, and IV), stemmed from the ethical reflection on the medical profession and its goal for self-improvement and professionalization in the application of biotechnological discoveries on living beings. Yet, as we saw from Sections I and II, bioethics' scope of action is not limited only to medical problems. For instance, when the inaugural Congress of the International Association of Bioethics in Amsterdam in 1992 required the term "bioethics" to be defined in order to be integrated into the Constitution of the Associations, upon invitation, the philosopher Peter Singer defined bioethics as "the study of the ethical issues raised in health care and in the biological sciences," including, "the study of social, legal, and economic issues related to these ethical issues" (2009, 11). Baker wrote, the role of the bioethicist is not that of watchdog, policing and protecting the boundaries of morality, but rather of facilitator, assisting society to reflectively articulate, interpret, and specify our common morality in the context of the rapidly evolving world of biomedicine.

(Baker, 2002, 50–51)

The ethical component of bioethics is not a definitive one, in the same way as ethics, medicine, and physics are not definitive disciplines; their space for improvement is infinite. In that sense, ethical intuitions are important for laying down a foundational and referential ground on which one can reason on complex cases. As Chan remarked:

The role of moral intuitions in bioethics is a contested one, and being led by the 'moral nose' is often looked upon as being a poor method of 'doing bioethics.' Yet, bioethical reasoning often relies first on appeals to intuition to establish the basic premises from which axioms can be abstracted and against which more complex problems can be compared and analysed. (2015, 18)

The problem with bioethics is that sometimes we have to bend accustomed moral principles into new imaginative forms because of the far-fetched results of current bio-technological discoveries. Hans Jonas (1903–1993),[30] for example, was one of the first philosophers who started thinking in terms of scarcity and, accordingly, in terms of the responsibility that older generations have in respect to future ones. He formulated, thus, an imperative of responsibility whose goal is the preservation of a world fitting for present and future generations when he wrote,

"Act so that the effects of your action are compatible with the permanence of genuine human life"; or expressed negatively: "Act so that the effects of your action are not destructive of the future possibility of such life"; or simply: "Do not compromise the conditions for an indefinite continuation of humanity on earth"; or, again turned positive: "In your present choices, include the future wholeness of Man among the objects of your will." (1984, 11)

This self-preserving ethics proposes an idea of human beings as capable to take care of existence as a wholeness in the present and in the future. Each human choice has to be considerate of the integrity of humans and their environment. In that sense, "one can indeed say that bioethics and environmentalism have risen from common grounds" (Cascais, 1997, 15).

Hottois (1946–2019), another important pioneer in bioethical discussions, proposed the criteria of freedom, beneficence, and responsibility[31] as main principles to regulate wisely the use of techno-scientific discoveries. According to Hottois, bioethics is neither a new techno-scientific discipline, nor a new universalistic ethics, but a field covering medical ethics, deontology, and environmental ethics; the core of bioethics is anthropocosmic solidarity, close to a philosophy of nature attentive to evolutionary dimensions. In that sense, in accordance with Hottois, I do believe that psychological, sociological issues should be as important as biotechnological ones. When reading cases concerning bioethical issues, one often has the impression that the persons involved are two-dimensional and their emotional depth seems to be completely absent. The complexity of one's character is reduced to very simple traits and one's intentions are rarely taken into consideration (more on this point in Chapters 2 and 3). For this reason, I think it is important to bring emotions and feelings into bioethics, in order to allow this "anthropocosmic solidarity" to happen.

V. Choosing Which Bioethics?

For all the reasons mentioned above, it is quite difficult to define which bioethics to choose, which criteria to follow, *which motives should move our final decisions, and which values should inform the meaning* of what is considered to be correct in the conduct of our life in relation to each other and the environment. In the next concluding sections, I will explore these points and what I think is the best direction to take.

V.1 A Democratic Bioethics?

> To ask a politician, let alone the person on the street, to make decisions about complex issues like nuclear power is said to be archaic. Neither the politician nor the everyday citizen has the information and sophistication to deal with such decisions. Albeit unpalatable to many, the technocratic solution is seen to be foreordained: political issues must be redefined in scientific or technical terms. It is the job of experts. They must be brought to the fore.
>
> *(Fischer, 1990, 22–23)*

The job of the bioethicist is to facilitate complex decisions for the well-being of the society from a social, environmental, medical, and psychological perspective. The decision-making activity changes, of course, its feature according to the political and geographical context in which it is practiced.

Michael Walzer affirmed that "it is a feature of democratic government that the people have a right to act wrongly" (1981, 385). If we apply this to the catastrophic environmental problems we are facing in the era that Crutzen and Störmer (2000) have called anthropocene, it is understandable why some thinkers have rejected the habit to treat environmental issues democratically (Heilbroner, 1974; Ophuls, 1977; Shearman and Smith, 2007). As early as 1873, the Italian geologist Antonio Stoppani acknowledged the increasing power and effect of humanity on the Earth's systems and used the expression "anthropozoic era" to remark this negative impact; it was in the 1980s that the biologist Stroemer coined the term *anthropocene* which was then adopted by the chemist Crutzen to emphasize the damage brought from the human beings on the environment. For this reason, Shearman and Smith believe that at this point human beings should not be given the freedom to choose how to affect the environment but they should be guided by strict policies regulating their relationship with the environment (2007, 162–163). In his work, Saxén has reasoned on this problem in bioethics and has proposed how diversity of thought and social inclusivity can represent a solution to the democratic use of common resources (2017, 136). He defines *bioethics* as a cultural giant that should be able to include and harmonize the different discrepancies that arise from different cultures and historical moments. White normativity, which establishes the dominance of white structures in bioethical academia (Karsjens and Johnson, 2003, 22–23), tends to reinforce existing biases.[32] Paul Farmer noted, for example, that bioethics tends to focus its attention on problems that arise from "too much care" for patients in industrialized nations, while giving little or no attention to the ethical problem of the poor (Farmer, 196–212). Farmer characterizes the bioethics of handling morally difficult clinical situations, normally in hospitals in industrialized countries, as "quandary ethics." He does not regard quandary ethics and clinical bioethics as unimportant; he argues, rather, that bioethics must be balanced and give due weight to the poor (Farmer, 192–193).

V.2 A Religious or Lay Bioethics?

The situation becomes even more complex if we reflect on the impact that religious values can have on different bioethical issues. While Western bioethics seems to be focused on individuals' rights and obligations, Islamic bioethics, for example, is more focused on religious duties and obligations. Hence, in disputes concerning medical treatment and preserving life problems, it is possible that the two bioethics will hold opposing points of views and suggest decisions that would be labeled as unethical from each other's points of view (Chamsi-Pasha and Albar, 2013, 8–14). Muslim bioethics is heavily influenced by the teachings of the Qur'an and accordingly by Shariah or Islamic law, and the sanctity of life is seen as a value to be preserved and preferred over its quality. Thus, euthanasia and abortion are interpreted in opposing ways from Islamic and lay bioethics so that it is almost impossible to find a conciliatory answer concerning these issues. From a Catholic point of view, the debate is impossible to recompose as well. When bioethics was imported in Italy in 1973, the deontological and teleological character of nature was emphasized against the arguments of the quality of life (Fornero, 2005). Theologians, such as Sgreccia, defended the importance of preserving the worth of every form of life against arguments in favor of the quality of life to which every human being has a right (arguments defended, for example, by Engelhardt and Singer). While for these latter, a fetus, for example, is not yet an autonomous individual capable of choice and will, for the former a person begins at the moment of conception. Similarly to this latter, Muslims believe that all human life, even one of poor quality, needs to be given appreciation and must be cared for and conserved (Shomali, 2008, 1).

Although religion is always present to make its opinions heard, according to Rachels, life has a sanctity that does not necessarily have to be interpreted in a religious way. Having a life (bios) with projects, aspirations, and decisions is more important than being alive (zoe). For this reason, killing a life does not imply a denial of its sanctity if that life has lost its biographical characteristics. According to Dworkin, something is sacred, when "its willing destruction would dishonor what should instead be honored" (1994, 98). The problem is that although all of us can agree on the "sovereign commitment to the sanctity of life," there is no agreement on what is considered sacred in reference to human life, even less regarding natural life. This disagreement would, at best, lead to a regional bioethics whose decisions are made on the basis of the level of religiosity of the places in which it is practised; at worst, it would lead to a tyrannical way to exert one of the two views on the other.

For this reason, the theologian Kueng wrote in *Menschenwuerdig Sterbe* (1996) that it is not possible to impose religious worldviews on one another. Kueng, whose young years were shaken by the illness of his brother dying from brain cancer, decided to take some distance from a traditional way of interpreting God in order to leave some freedom to be with God according to one's own sense of responsibility and need. "Is it really God who decides how human life is reduced to mere biological life?" (1995, 24–26). He wants to believe in a God that supports the dignity of a dying human being or a suffering mother and allows these humans to take the responsibility of their own lives without needing others to decide on their behalf. In that sense, the reference to human rights and to Beauchamp and Childress' principlism are two adjacent approaches that seem to leave that space of freedom and respect open.

V.3 The System of Human Rights in Bioethics

The Universal Declaration on Bioethics and Human Rights adopted by the United Nations Educational, Scientific, and Cultural Organisation (UNESCO) on October 19, 2005, was an important step in the search for global minimal standards in bioethics. The principles proposed by Beauchamp and Childress[33] sought to extend over the regionalism of different cultures: beneficence, non-maleficence, autonomy, and justice (more on this in the next section). Similarly, in 2005, De Castro (Philippines) and Berlinguer (Italy) chaired the working group for the international bioethics committee. On that occasion, they both agreed that "a worldwide common sense to foster understanding and cohesion in relation to new ethical categories and new practical possibilities emerging from science and technology" was needed (UNESCO IBC Report on the possibility of elaborating a universal instrument on bioethics, June 13, 2003. 2 UNESCO 33rd General Conference, Paris). What emerged in that encounter was that since "omnis definitio in jure periculosa est" (Every definition in law is perilous), it was good to draw a chart of principles capable of including the main pillars of human rights existing in different countries[34] without the need to redefine new principles. This guideline would have guaranteed an equal respect of living beings according to the level of tolerance proper to each different custom. Another important characteristic, in line with UN agencies, was the nonbinding nature of the code: although principles are considered sacred, each country could maintain its autonomy when deciding bioethical matters. The main agency appointed to guide the process was the World Health Organization (WHO).[35] International policy documents relating to bioethics over the past two decades have been written according to a rights-based approach, which, in its turn, was based on the important notion of human dignity.

Important criticisms have been raised, though, against this human rights version of bioethics. One of them relates to the problem of boundaries. For example, Andorno[36] noticed (2007, 150–154) that the Council of Europe's Convention on Human Rights and Biomedicine ("Oviedo Convention") has perhaps exceeded "its mandate by drafting such bioethical instruments. In particular, the charge is that it is trespassing on a topic that lies in the responsibility of the World Health Organization. The second criticism is that UNESCO's reliance on international human rights norms is inappropriate." In fact, even though principlism and human rights can represent a common denominator useful for overcoming their differences and finding a democratic arena in which to meet, especially when decisions relating to common resources need to be made, they are still not the final answer for each of the countries involved since human rights do not have the same importance everywhere. For now, the human rights system is the best crossroad of ethics, legislation, and politics we have to enforce the respect for intersubjective values. "There are few mechanisms available other than human rights to function as a global ethical foundation, a Weltethik" (Thomasma, 2001, 299–303). In other words, "the human rights framework provides a more useful approach for analysing and responding to modern public health challenges than any framework thus far available within the biomedical tradition" (Mann, 1996, 924–925).

V.4 Principlism

The human rights system in bioethics goes hand in hand with the four principles proposed by Beauchamp and Childress. Tom Beauchamp and James Childress published *Principles of Biomedical Ethics* in 1979, the content of which was reflected in the *Belmont Report* (1979) issued by the National Commission for the Protection of Human Subjects of Biomedical and Behavioral Research. Both documents reinforced the belief that the following four principles should be essential to any moral code in bioethics: respect for autonomy, beneficence, non-maleficence, and justice. Philosophy is explicitly excluded from it:

> Although inspired by Kant's deontological ethics and Bentham's and Mill's consequentialist ethics, this approach wants to be a practical approach for decision-making. For this reason, it considers itself as based on "*unphilosophical common sense and tradition.*"
>
> *(emphasise mine, Beauchamp and Childress, 1994, 100)*

In the *Belmont Report,* the National Commission described these principles as "comprehensive:" they are "stated at a level of generalization" that should prove helpful to investigators, human subjects, and interested citizens, and together they "provide an analytical framework that will guide the resolution of ethical problems" (Belmont Report, 256). From the National Commission's view, these principles are "general prescriptive judgments" that provide "a basic justification for the many particular ethical prescriptions and evaluations of human actions" (Ibid.). Instead of a singular moral theory or a universal abstraction, a bottom-up approach was chosen as a guiding moral principle for the National Commission's deliberations. Yet, contrary to Potter's bioethical spirit, principlism appeals to particular cases and tries to reach consensus without appealing to philosophy and any humanistic disciplines. Common sense and tradition are the explicit references of this framework.

This choice has not come without consequences. In fact, the lack of theoretical unity is one of the main criticisms raised against principlism as it makes principlism comparable to a dangerous form of moral relativism. Clouser (1995), for example, asserted that the principles, chosen by Beauchamp and Childress, lack a systematic consistency because they are drawn from conflicting moral theories (i.e., Kant's deontological ethics and Betham's consequentialist ethics), hence leading to contradictory conclusions even when used on a case-by-case basis. Clouser states: "It is a kind of relativism espoused (perhaps unwittingly) by many books (usually anthologies) of bioethics. They parade before the reader a variety of "theories" of ethics—Kantianism, deontology, utilitarianism, other forms of consequentialism, and the like—and say, in effect, choose whichever of the competing theories, maxims, principles, or rules suits you for any particular case. Just take your choice! They each have flaws—which are always pointed out—but on balance, the authors seem to be saying, they are probably all equally good!" (Clouser, 1995, 224). I find this way of espousing unphilosophical thinking to biomedical discoveries irresponsible. Moreover, it seems, once again, to go against the original spirit upon which bioethics was founded to bring together a comprehensive view on life. While I do understand the need for finding a common ground from which to start an informed reasoning on problems, I believe that we should raise the bar instead of lowering it. Winkler, for example, objects to how the mid-level principles are often in an unresolvable conflict with each other because there is no unified moral theory from which they are all derived (1993). "There is no priority ranking, even including the sophistication of reflective equilibrium theory, [the principle-based approach] remains open to the charge of being seriously mistaken. It can be said to leave out of account the very complex processes of *interpretation* that constitute our moral understanding both of cases and of principles. Most importantly, within the complex realities of practice, it is dominantly the interpretation of cases that informs our understanding of principles rather than principles guiding the resolution of difficult cases. All or most of the real work in actual moral reasoning and decision-making is case-driven rather than theory-driven" (cited in Takala et al., 2014, 44–45). There are roads that we can take to stay loyal to a case-driven approach without inviting relativism and excluding philosophical reflection. For example, the method of wide reflective equilibrium (WRE), first introduced by John Rawls in his "The Independence of Moral Theory" (1974), could be a way to find a common ground from where to start an informed bioethical dialog without excluding philosophical reflection on the case. WRE is described as a method that attempts to produce coherence "in an ordered triple of sets of beliefs held by a particular person, namely (1) a set of considered moral judgments, (2) a set of moral principles, and (3) a set of relevant (scientific and philosophical) background theories." So, WRE can be defined as a coherent method of justification in ethics that, even though it does not stick to any specific normative ethics, avoids mixing contradicting normative ethics with each other.[37] In the very last section, I will present a model of ethics that allows the application of this method in a very organic way while maintaining the depth of cautious moral reflection that should be applied on each bioethical case.

V.5 Dignity and a Collective Labor

Yet, even if Rawls recognized that moral choices can be based on a democratically agreed upon set of moral principles, he considered human dignity—which in the human rights system holds a key orienting role for bioethical choices—incapable of providing a grounding base for bioethics because we do not know what dignity is. He wrote, "Each person possesses an inviolability founded on justice that even the welfare of society as a whole cannot override" (Rawls, 1971, 586; 1). The medical ethicist Ruth Macklin also wrote that "dignity[38] is a useless concept in medical ethics and can be eliminated without any loss of content" (Macklin, 2003, 20–28). A wide debate started around this relevant problem. Martha Nussbaum disagrees with Rawls and Macklin. She believes, in fact, that dignity is part of the world's nature as it involves an exercise of practical reason (*phronesis*) which allows humans to make moral rational choices (Nussbaum, 2008, 351–380). Yet, according to Nussbaum, we need some help from our society in order to develop this functioning and make it effective. A life worthy of human dignity is a life in which one can exercise its own capabilities.[39] According to the philosopher, bioethics is a shared intellectual labor on cases which are in every circumstance different. Each case requires capabilities that we do not yet possess, but we could if we developed the right context in which they could flourish. Our "dignity" ultimately derives from our capacity to act upon the dictates of our own reason—i.e., from our autonomy as moral agents (2008, 339). "What do I mean, then, by saying that a life that does not contain opportunities for the development and exercise of the major human capacities is not a life worthy of human dignity? I mean that it is like imprisoning or raping a free thing whose nourishing (based on these capacities) consists in forms of intentional activity and choice" (Nussbaum, 2008, 379). The task of the bioethicist is to individuate the areas in which these capabilities are impeded and, when possible, improve them. So, it is not the mere application of principles that can help us to understand the right solution to a case but a long and close study of the new case, asking both how the principles developed so far, and also whether the case itself poses any challenge to the practical principles so far articulated—even when the definition of a concept is not clear.

From my point of view, meanings have a genetic aspect that makes their content sometimes elusive and difficult; that is why we educate and praise experts in words, writers, and scholars, for example, because they help us to learn from this elusiveness. Etymological studies of words often show how far we went with the use of a certain meaning and how much history has impacted its structure over time. The innocuous word "demon," for example, originally referred to a provider (daiomai) or even to a positive inner principle (as in Hesiod, *Op.* 122; Aristotle, *Av.* 544; Plato, *Phaedrus*, 107d), but, with the advent of Christianity, the word came to signify exactly the opposite, an evil tempting spirit. The rich and sometimes elusive nature of our words should not defeat us and lead us to abandon them or, worse, consider them as useless. As Wittengstein explains: "the ostensive definition explains the use—the meaning—of the word when the overall role of the word in language is clear. Thus, if I know that someone means to explain a color word to me the ostensive definition "That is called 'sepia' will help me to understand the word. (…) One has already to know (or be able to do) something in order to be capable of asking a thing's name. But what does one have to know?" (Philosophical Investigations, Section 30). The use of ostensive categories that inform about the criteria of applicability of a defined term (Kotarbinska, 1960) could help to control the elusiveness of a meaning when this arises. The concept of dignity has the same problem as the words "sepia" or "demon:" we are not always sure what this word signifies for us today in the place where we live and what it will mean in the future in this same place. Yet, this does not mean that dignity has no meaning; rather the opposite, it has plenty of meanings. We can make these meanings accessible and fruitful by operationalizing them into ostensive categories and by assuming a patient, humble attitude toward the reference that each time the ostensive categories will express.

V.6 Choosing an Unstable Bioethics?

From what is discussed above, it seems that bioethics is destined "to be unstable from the beginning" (Evans, 2011, 114). Each case is so unique that ethical rigidity might lead to mistakes and involuntary harm. Given the ongoing novelty inherent in bioethical issues, the scientific and rigorous traits of bioethics can be connected more to its being presuppositionless rather than its being rigidly fixed in a one-way oriented solution. If bioethics' theoretical core remains based on a reflective equilibrium (WRE) resulting from open presuppositions and a questioning attitude for which nothing is taken for granted and each case is studied as bearer of a new meaning, then, I believe, bioethics can retain a scientific rigorousness free from simplistic reductionistic attitudes.

> There is no comprehensively shared understanding of what bioethics really is even among those who are one way or another involved in the discipline. Further, there is no clear agreement on who "does" or "practices" bioethics, or indeed who should do or practice it. "Bioethicists" themselves also have different ideas on what it is that they actually do—or are supposed to do. There are debates concerning whether bioethics is—or should be—descriptive or prescriptive, what methodology is to be used in bioethical inquiry, and about what the goals of "bioethics" are.
>
> *(Chambers, 2001, 25)*

I do think that reflective instability is the strength of bioethics and not its weakness. Any attempt to make bioethics simpler and more stable would lead to a reductionistic and scientistic attitude, the results of which we have already painfully experienced in Tuskegee, for example. While I think that the instability and absence of an unquestioned basis is the strength for a scientific approach to bioethics, I am strongly against the attempt to erase reflection from bioethics, reject shared foundational values (such as dignity), and reduce bioethics to a list of practical principles which at times might even be conflicting with each other. Being presuppositionless is different from giving in to relativism; in fact, instability here refers to the absence of personal assumptions around the validity of a given experience while relativism would imply an acceptance of any assumption as valid until otherwise proven. It is important to ground the most important choices we make in our ethical life on questioned, justified, and proven criteria. For this reason, I think that the experience-based character of phenomenology can help bioethics to thrive in more than one context, as phenomenology welcomes intersubjective investigation of practical cases and human rights values, while avoiding the mistake of entertaining normative ethics that are conflicting with each other as is Beauchamp and Childress' principlism.

V.6.1 Phenomenological Bioethics

As Svaeneus wrote in his book dedicated to phenomenological bioethics, although we cannot yet talk of a phenomenological bioethics it is true that phenomenology has already informed parallel fields such as care, nursing, narrative, and feminist ethics, each one of them informing medical ethics and medical humanities (1999, 2017). Since phenomenology is based on the study of the bodily lived experience, its application on the study of illness, pain, and disability has revealed itself to be particularly insightful (Toombs, 2001; Moazam, 2005). Being able to switch from the first to the second perspective is what allows adequate descriptions of the lived experience to emerge. In that sense, according to Svaeneus (2017), phenomenology operates as a philosophical anthropology that can explain thorny bioethical lived experiences according to a reflexive equilibrium. As the author put it:

> Phenomenology is not a theory about other theories, but rather a theoretical enterprise which tries to take a step *back* from other theories in order to free itself from prejudices and be able to study 'the things themselves' as they become manifest in their 'self-showing.' (2007)

As I will show in this book and in other places (2021, 2022), phenomenology can provide bioethics with tools, such as epoché and reduction, to ease the medical encounter and increase the quality of care toward each other and the environment (Chapters 3 and 5). Moreover, it can give everyone a way to access different ways of conceiving reality and understanding the emotions attached to it through intentional analysis and its contents (forthcoming, The Role of *Bio*-Ethics in Emotional Problems and Chapter 3 of this book). Finally, it can structure the ethical reasoning within a flexible scientific model because its theoretical foundations are continuously renewed by the questioning attitude of the phenomenological method.

In particular, phenomenological ethics is a relatively new approach to ethics whose emphasis is put on the description of the lived experience and the ethical phenomenon. Its origin can be traced back to Brentano's "The Origin of the Knowledge of Right and Wrong" (1889), but it is with the development of Husserl's phenomenological ethics (1908, 1914, 1920) that its themes started inspiring a long line of thinkers whose influence reached the fields of philosophy, psychology, theology, gender studies, bioethics, and political science. The main themes of phenomenological ethics focus, on the one hand, on the epistemological understanding of the highest practical good and its ethical demand (Husserl, Reiner, Pfänder, Sartre, Løgstrup, and Levinas) and, on the other hand, on the description of what we do when we behave in a moral way (Scheler, Hildebrand, Hartmann, Levinas, and Simone De Beauvoir).

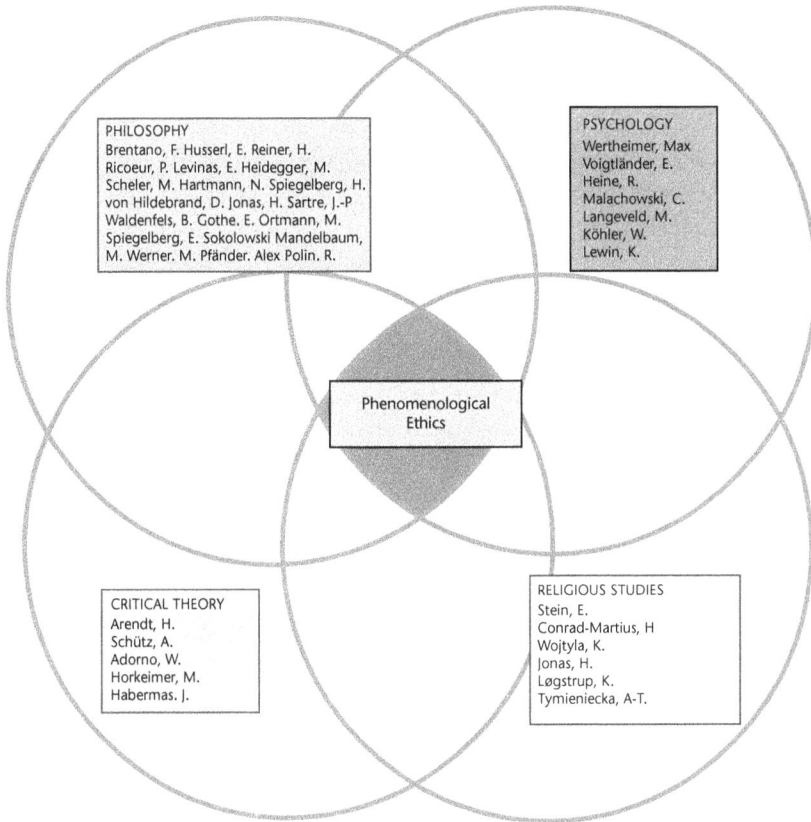

PHILOSOPHY
Brentano, F. Husserl, E. Reiner, H.
Ricoeur, P. Levinas, E. Heidegger, M.
Scheler, M. Hartmann, N. Spiegelberg, H.
von Hildebrand, D. Jonas, H. Sartre, J.-P
Waldenfels, B. Gothe. E. Ortmann, M.
Spiegelberg, E. Sokolowski Mandelbaum,
M. Werner. M. Pfänder. Alex Polin. R.

PSYCHOLOGY
Wertheimer, Max
Voigtländer, E.
Heine, R.
Malachowski, C.
Langeveld, M.
Köhler, W.
Lewin, K.

Phenomenological
Ethics

CRITICAL THEORY
Arendt, H.
Schütz, A.
Adorno, W.
Horkeimer, M.
Habermas. J.

RELIGIOUS STUDIES
Stein, E.
Conrad-Martius, H
Wojtyla, K.
Jonas, H.
Løgstrup, K.
Tymieniecka, A-T.

FIGURE 1.3

In this sense, phenomenological ethics lends itself well to the discussion of bioethical problems and their solutions. In fact, its bifocal attention to the epistemology of good and its experiential normative demand has brought leading phenomenologists, such as Levinas and Scheler, to abandon the primacy of epistemology to favor the importance of moral experience and its practical adherence to the experiential reality. They argued, in fact, that cognitive performance is grounded in prior moral experience and not the other way around. Moreover, phenomenological ethics emphasizes the role of emotions in meaning-making as we can see in Brentano's and Scheler's axiology.

Although this experiential approach might induce us to consider ethical phenomenology as a nonsystematic ethics, psychology (Lewin, Koehler, Wertheimer, and Langeveld) and theology (Wojtila and Stein) used this approach for a methodological investigation of a variety of ethical themes: the centrality of values, empathy, intersubjectivity, otherness, responsibility, I-thou, embodiment, affectivity, and interaffectivity. These are all themes that I believe are important for a full-rounded bioethics.

Finally, the presuppositionless of phenomenology can increase the flexibility and at the same time the rigor of bioethics as free from any Zeitgeist and personal bias. According to Chatterjee (1973), there are at least four forms of presuppositions. First, the *material presupposition* assumes the veracity of an external world and considers its events as causally ordered. Second, the *cognitive presupposition* indicates that it is possible for us to gather valid knowledge about the object of our investigation. Third, *formal presupposition* relates to the predicative idea according to which the subject copula and predicate scheme of judgment will lead us to substance. The fourth presupposition consists in the acknowledgment of the authority *of predecessors* such as for example Descartes' "cogito, existo" as rooted in St Augustine's contention regarding the credibility of the existence of the ego. Chatterjee (1973) pointed out that Husserl rejects all these presuppositions, but not the *presuppositions of natural science*. In fact, the departure point for any phenomenological investigation is the concreteness of life and the way in which this is experienced. The reason why Husserl would reject the other forms of presuppositions has not only theoretical but also historical roots according to Embree (1997). After the First World War, in fact, a good number of Universities were funded by the Catholics; this means that all professors had to take the Oath against Modernism and Affirmation to the Church in order to get funds. The Church's doctrines on Infallibility of the Pope, immaculate birth of Mary, and purgatory were a part of the Oath. And, the Church had no qualms about punishing those who opposed or criticised them.[40] Husserl's claim of presuppositionless came as a wise deception to free his philosophy and phenomenological method from this Zeitgeist while giving it the flexibility to be continuously questioned and proved. Hence, being presuppositionless does not mean to give up on the rigorousness of science; on the contrary, it means to devote one's knowledge to its truth without being trapped inside the moods of the time or the biases of one's own point of view. Phenomenological descriptions are presuppositionless in the sense that they do not allow a presupposition to remain a presupposition even when it is devoid of its meaning.

For this reason, I encourage a bioethics that overcomes reductionism and its scientist features; allows a due acknowledgment of emotions in case descriptions and decision-making processes; and takes into consideration the psycho-physiological and metaphysical biases that reductionism generated, all this in order to promote a harmonious relationship between human beings and their environment. For this relationship to be harmonious, the substance dichotomy that separates the body from mind has to be integrated within an experience-based and presuppositionless approach capable of valuing every form of intelligence and making consistent decisions according to the uniqueness of life (more on this point in Chapter 3).

Conclusion

In this chapter, I have examined the different angles of bioethics from its foundation to its contemporary application. I described bioethics from an historical, conceptual point of view and examined the biases that, even today, still harm the effectiveness of bioethics. From an historical point of view, Potter founded bioethics with the intent of bringing together biological and medical science with philosophy. Originally, bioethics was meant to develop a wise approach to guarantee the survival of the Earth and its organisms. The bilocal birth of bioethics and the cogent need to find an answer to medical cases transformed bioethics into a sort of medical ethics from which at times philosophical reflection on moral principles was excluded. The historical atrocity of Nazi eugenics and the Tuskegee experiment led to a need for an agreement on how to handle the violation of human dignity and the inviolability of the patient. Principlism and the human rights system emerged as a form of bioethics that, supposedly, was independent of philosophical thinking (but in fact at times just as a poorly organized philosophical reflection) and provided bioethics with a beneficial ground for compromise and agreement above religious, regional, and political particularism yet often lacking coherence. As a suggestion, I promoted here the idea of accepting the instability of bioethics as its strength and not as its weakness. A bioethics that uses the case-by-case effort through a reflective equilibrium and the presuppositionless approach to resolve bioethical issues as they arise has a real chance to produce rigorous and life-adherent results. An important bias, in fact, that has prevented bioethics from applying its full potential was the reductionist attitude in science that, on the basis of a dualistic view of the world, oversimplified the way we look at the complexity of organisms in a dualistic manner, hence reinforcing a cosmetic application of science. Bringing together biology and philosophy was, according to its founder, a way to recompose this painful gap between life and its vital principle. From the analysis I conducted, it emerged that the historical reasons that led to the need for founding a bioethical discipline took its origin from these theoretical biases which fostered a view of science as superior than any living being and at the same time detached from life in virtue of its being objective. We do not want to promote this idea of science; rather, we want to defend a participated and descriptive idea of science capable of questioning and renewing itself at each of its endeavors.

Notes

1 Potter (1975, 2299): "Idealistic survival: the purpose of human existence is what we make it, yet it is deep within us. For individuals it is enjoyment through healthy function, love, and commitment, growth, and development, identity, and maintenance of species; as a society, it is to provide an environment in which people of all races can develop their individual abilities to discover, examine critically, preserve and transmit the knowledge, wisdom, and values that will help ensure the survival of the present and future generations with improvement in the quality of life and in human dignity."

2 Potter (1975, 2279): "I have regarded bioethics as the name of a new discipline that would combine science and philosophy."

3 See also on this point Lolas, F. (2008). "Bioethics and animal research: a personal perspective and a note on the contribution of Fritz Jahr," *Biological Research*, 41(1):

119–123; Sass, H. M. (2007). "Fritz Jahr's 1927 concept of bioethics," *Kennedy Institute Ethics Journal*, 17(4): 279–295.

4 The Georgetown Institute was named after Joseph and Rose Kennedy, the parents of Shriver's wife, Eunice Kennedy Shriver, as well as President John F. Kennedy and Senators Robert and Edward Kennedy. In an interview with Warren Reich, Shriver claimed "none of us had ever heard of Potter. (...) I was not familiar with the word [bioethics]." See Reich (1994), Le Roi (2003, 215–231).

5 "It was an exciting task I had set for myself—the task of determining what bioethics should become—on the basis of the elements that had already emerged, those that were just beyond the horizon, and the old and new cultural developments that were shaping them. What cluster of issues was bioethics beginning to confront, and what types of issues would it be likely to address? To which disciplines and areas of knowledge should bioethics create links in order to address those issues properly? What sort of moral methodologies already existed in all the major cultures of the world? How have they responded to moral issues in health and life, and how would they be likely to respond to the newer problems of the life sciences? Briefly put: what intellectual resources would bioethics require, and to which publics would it be likely to address itself?" (Reich, 2003, 14).

6 See Cascais, 2014, available online: "That was publicly announced in 1973, eventually published in 1978 and would become the reference work in the field, with a new completely revised five-volume edition in 1995."

7 On the international growth of bioethics and its definition, see Fox and Swazey (2008, 215–285). For specific examples, see Diaz-Amado (2011), Reubi David (2010), Moazam and Jafarey (2005), Gross and Ravitsky (2013, 247–255), and Macer Darryl (2001, 70–77).

8 On the relationship between philosophy and bioethics: "Bioethics has at least some of its roots in philosophy, but we do not, by and large, have an explicitly-developed 'philosophy of bioethics'" Brassington (2013), Archard (2011), Gesang (2010).

9 From an etymological point of view, the word *doctor* indicates the one who is guided and educated (from Latin, e-doceo) in its own discipline. Educating, in fact, means *e-ducare,* to guide someone out of their own ignorance. For that to be possible, theoretical reflection is needed.

10 Revised and extended versions: Tokyo (1975), Venice (1983), and Hong Kong (1989), also known as, respectively, Helsinki II, III, and IV.

11 See Cascais (1997, 25): "For more experiments on this kind: the notorious Tuskegee experiments, carried out between 1932 and 1972 in the state of Alabama, involved about 600 destitute afro-Americans who were given placebo treatments and deprived of actual therapy against syphilis, so that the natural course of the disease and its effects could be followed, in spite of the discovery of a cure from it through penicillin in 1954; the Willowbrook State School (New York) experiment on mentally retarded children was conducted between 1956 and 1971 and involved chidren who were injected with the hepatitis virus for the research of an effective vaccine. Moreover, immunotherapy experiments, sponsored by the US Public Health Service and the American Cancer Society, were also performed on senior citizens who were injected with cancer cells in 1963, at the Jewish Chronic Disease Hospital and Medical Centre of Brooklyn. Also, psychotropic drugs were trialed in the American military and various kinds of experiments that combined the safeguard of national defence and the advancement of medical knowledge were carried out in the United States during the cold war, on both military personnel and civilians, such as the injection of plutonium in 18 human subjects, already in 1945, but namely the now well-known human radiation experiments, sponsored by the US Department of Defence and by the Atomic Energy Commission, this latter having inherited the contracts and projects of the former Manhattan Project. Unfortunately, the list would still be quite long."

12 On the genesis of this book, see Carr (1980, x–xi): Husserl's letter was read in the session bearing that title. The letter contains many ideas and language similar to the first parts of the *Crisis* and states that "the grounding which would give effective force to what I have to say [on this subject] would require a substantial treatise." (1) *Acmelte Werke* is edited by Herman L. van Breda and is published at The Hague by Martinus Nijhoff. Subsequent references to this series will be by volume numbers and dates and thereafter by titles of individual volumes. (2) The letter, which will be quoted more extensively below, is found in the Actes du huitieme Congres Internationale de Philosophie ä Prague, 2–7 September 1934 (Prague, 1936, XLI–XLV). According to the recently published correspondence with Roman Ingarden, Husserl actually wrote a lengthy essay at this time to accompany his letter to Prague, but the essay was not read. Husserl described it as a "hurriedly written (two weeks) outline of a historical inter-pretation of the origin of our guiding idea [Zweckidee] of philosophy." He writes that it has "given me to think" and that it "led to deep problems in the philosophy of history which truly disturb me." (3) Then, in May 1935, Husserl lectured in Vienna, following an invitation by the Vienna Kulturbund, on "Philosophy in the Crisis of European Mankind." (4) In November of the same year, he lectured in Prague on "The Crisis of European Sciences and Psychology," and it was this series of lectures that served as the basis for the projected work. As a Jew who was denied any public platform in Germany, Husserl had to publish, as he had lectured, outside his own country. An international yearbook called *Philosophia*, edited by Arthur Liebert in Belgrade, arranged to publish the crisis in installments. After his return from Prague, Husserl worked feverishly on the essay, and the first two parts of the present text were published in *Philosophia* in 1936. By the time Husserl became ill in 1937, the text of the third part was longer than that of the first two parts combined and was still not completed. Eugen Fink, who was Husserl's research assistant and worked closely with him during this period, had produced a typed version of Husserl's stenographic manuscript of Part III, and Husserl had gone over it, perhaps public reading of the letter is reported in the "Feuilleton" of the Frankfurter Zeitung, October 2, 1934, and is confirmed by personal recollections of Professor Herbert Spiegelberg. (5) Edmund Husserl, Briefe an Roman Ingarden (The Hague: Nijhoff, 1968, 89) (Letter LXXIII of 26 November 1934; see also Letter LXX, 88). (6) For the rest of this account, unless otherwise indicated, see Walter Biemel's editor's introduction to the posthumous German edition of the *Crisis* (Die Krisis der europäischen Wissenschaften und die transzendentale Phänomenologie: Eine Einleitung in die phänomenologische Philosophie, Husserliana, vol. VI (1954; 2nd printing, 1962).

13 According to Husserl, Galileian science was mostly organized around mathematics, geometry, and physics. Mathematics was assigned the task to recognize the pure forms of nature, to geometry the duty to measure them, and to physics to acknowledge the causality through numerical forms. None of these sciences took into consideration the role of scientist in science nor the sensuous interconnected content of these forms (Husser, 1936, 67).

14 "In his view of the world from the perspective of geometry, the perspective of what appears to the senses and is mathematizable, Galileo abstracts from the subjects as persons leading a personal life; he abstracts from all that is in any way spiritual, from all cultural properties which are attached to things in human praxis. The result of this abstraction is the things purely as bodies; but these are taken as concrete real objects, the totality of which makes up a world which becomes the subject matter of research. One can truly say that the idea of nature as a really self-enclosed world of bodies first emerges with Galileo" (Husserl, 1936, 60).

15 "The difficulty here lies in the fact that the material plena—the 'specific' sense-qualities—which concretely fill out the spatiotemporal shape-aspects of the world of bodies cannot, in their own gradations, be directly treated as are the shapes themselves. Nevertheless, these qualities, and everything that makes up the concreteness of the

sensibly intuited world, must count as manifestations of an 'objective' world. Or rather, they must continue to count as such; because (such is the way of thinking which motivates the idea of the new physics) the certainty, binding us all, of one and the same world, the actuality which exists in itself, runs uninterrupted through all changes of subjective interpretation" (Husserl, 1936, 33).

16 Although his co-eves considered Descartes not an original philosopher except for his physics (Digby, 1644; Sturm, 1686, 161–165), the historian Kuno Fischer (1824–1907) was the first one to name Descartes the father of modern philosophy (1878, 1, 147–150, 440) following Cassirer's (1874–1945) reconstruction of pre-Kantian philosophy and acknowledging Descartes as the one who introduced the rationalist Geist necessary for both empiricism and rationalism to grow.

17 See Descartes, Discourse (1637, 6:4), "I found myself beset by so many doubts and errors that I came to think I had gained nothing from my attempts to become educated but increasing recognition of my ignorance."

18 "Then, examining attentively what I was, and seeking that I could pretend that I had no body and there was no world or place that I was in, but that I could not, for all that, pretend that I did not exist, and that, on the contrary, from the very fact that I thought of doubting the truth of other things, it followed very evidently and very certainly that I existed; while, on the other hand, if I had only ceased to think, although all the rest of what I had ever imagined had been true, I would have no reason to believe that I existed; I thereby concluded that I was a substance, of which the whole essence or nature consists in thinking, and which, in order to exist, needs no place and depends on no material thing; so that this 'I', that is to say, the mind, by which I am what I am, is entirely distinct from the body, and even that it is easier to know than the body, and moreover, that even if the body were not, it would not cease to be all that it is" (Descartes, 1639, retrieved online https://www.marxists.org/reference/archive/descartes/1639/meditations.htm).

19 "While we thus reject all of which we can entertain the smallest doubt, and even imagine that it is false, we easily indeed suppose that there is neither God, nor sky, nor bodies, and that we ourselves even have neither hands nor feet, nor, finally, a body; but we cannot in the same way suppose that we are not while we doubt of the truth of these things; for there is a repugnance in conceiving that what thinks does not exist at the very time when it thinks. Accordingly, the knowledge, *I think, therefore I am*, is the first and most certain that occurs to one who philosophizes orderly" (Descartes, 1639, retrieved online https://www.marxists.org/reference/archive/descartes/1639/meditations.htm).

20 "In the *Discourse on Method*, Descartes formulated the first principle of his philosophy as 'je pense, donc je suis.' (1) The famous formula 'cogito, ergo sum,' which has been traditionally attributed to Descartes himself, originated actually not in his writings, but in the Latin translation of 'je pense, donc je suis.' Etiennne de Courcelles, the translator of the *Discourse on Method* into Latin, translated it into the formula 'Ego cogito, ergo sum, sive existo.' Descartes himself did not write the phrase 'cogito, ergo sum' anywhere in his writings except the *Search after Truth*, so far as we can trace his writings" (Suzuki, 2012, 73–80).

21 In a dialog from his *Gelassenheit* (1959), Heidegger writes: "If thinking is what distinguishes man's nature, then surely the essence of this nature, namely the nature of thinking, can be seen only by looking away from thinking" (from *Discourse on Thinking: A Translation of Gelassenheit* by Anderson et al., 1966). By "thinking," Heidegger refers to representational thinking in that sense distinct from contemplative or profound awareness.

22 "Now we consider all the above as things or qualities or modes of things. When, however, we recognize that it cannot happen that something is made from nothing, then the proposition 'nothing is made from nothing' is considered, not as if it were

some thing that exists or even as a mode of a thing, but as some kind of eternal truth that is present in our mind, and it is called a common notion or an axiom" (Descartes, 1639, retrieved online https://www.marxists.org/reference/archive/descartes/1639/meditations.htm).

23 I do not imply here any Meinongian or Heideggerian difference between being and existing. More simply, I use this term to express the concreteness of the phenomenon.

24 See Moran (2012, 9): "Dilthey's philosophy of worldviews (Weltanschauung Philosophie) as denying the objective validity of cultural formations. The elderly Dilthey was put out that he was the focus of Husserl's attacks and wrote to Husserl denying the charge of relativism. He died shortly afterwards in 1911, but, years later, in his 1925 lectures, Husserl made amends, acknowledging Dilthey's important contribution to descriptive psychology. It is clear that Husserl continues to engage with Dilthey in the Crisis, and not just because of the Berlin philosopher's importance for Heidegger."

25 Reich (1978). Preface (xi–xiv): "(1) the recurrent bioethics malaise that is traceable notably to an expanding reductionism in the methods and scope of bioethics; (2) how both the malaise that nestles in the community of bioethicists and the reductionism that is its cause distort the meaning of bioethics as it has been shaped by cultural factors; and (3) how a corrective might be achieved by taking seriously a consideration of three sorts of cultural forces that shaped bioethics from its origins." (See also the impact of reductionism on the health professions, in Wear and Kuczewski, 2004; Farmer and Campo, 2004.)

26 Galileo's steps (1) make an observation that describes a problem, (2) create a hypothesis, (3) test the hypothesis, and (4) draw conclusions and refine the hypothesis) refined by Descartes' points: (1) Accept as true only what is indubitable. (2) Divide every question into manageable parts. (3) Begin with the simplest issues and ascend to the more complex. (4) Review frequently enough to retain the whole argument at once. The parts that Galileo enumerates and Descartes divides should be seen as they interconnect within the systemic whole in which they are placed.

27 For example, in 1971, Heisenberg raised the issue of conflict of interests in science: scientists who struggle for financial support from the government cannot be considered objective advisors when it comes to expressing their technical opinion about acquiring a new 300-GeV accelerator. Or, even more cogent, how do we reintegrate German science and technology in the post-war era? Also, on this point, Carson's book (2010), *Heisenberg in the Atomic Age,* is very interesting because it tackles these and even more cogent questions while defending the thesis of a duplicitous Heisenberg who did not try to stop the construction of the atomic bomb and did not argue against the immoral use of technology during the Nazi regime.

28 I am well aware that I am not the first one to state this critique of Marx (1818–1883) and the critical theory inspired by his work. Fraser (1947) and Jaeggi (1967), for example, shed light on this problem and its implications in the political and economic texture of our society.

29 On this point, the interesting book of Regenia Gagnier [*Individualism, Decadence and Globalization. On the Relationship of Part to Whole,* 1859–1920, Palgrave Macmillan (2010)] retraces the story of individualism in biology, economics, philosophy, and social sciences.

30 We can initially refer to the results of ecological and philosophical biology and their main protagonists, von Uexküll (1920), Plessner (1970), and Jonas (1966). At the same time, we can draw on biological system theories put forward by Bertalan (1968) and Maturana and Varela (1987), and on enactive approaches to life, as represented in particular by Varela et al. (1991), Thompson (2005, 2007), and Di Paolo (2005, 2009).

31 See Cascais (1997, 11): "Informed consent being the touchstone of the free pursuit of research, beneficence (not to attempt anything that is not to the well-being of

individuals and humankind at large), and responsibility (according to which any ethical claim is grounded in what he calls an anthropocosmic solidarity - man is a product of natural evolution, non-human and human phases of the evolutionary process are not inimical or incommensurable, but, instead, they're inextricable; only an evolutionary ethics can account for the openness and unpredictability that characterises human condition as a set of both natural and cultural possibilities; pragmatism, prudence and responsibility should therefore be the guiding lines to approaching the sense of complexity and ambivalence of all human enterprise)."

32 See, for example, a case discussed in Roscoe and Schenck (2017). A Chinese mother who was giving birth to an infant affected by down syndrome expressed the clear decision to not allow a simple surgery that would have saved the life of the child. The husband of the woman (himself Chinese, too) agreed with her because both wanted to spare the unhappy life that the child would have had as soon as she would have been brought to China. Their decision was not considered acceptable. Chinese costumes were ignored by American laws because the couple was having the child in an American hospital which is, in the end, ruled by American laws.

33 Andorno (2005, 151): "The UNESCO declaration on Human Genome and Human Rights of 1997 includes and further develops some of these principles: Rights of 1997, or are regional but not global instruments, such as the European Convention on Human Rights and Biomedicine of 1997. It is important to indicate that the Declaration includes in its section II important substantive principles relating to bioethics, such as: Respect for human dignity and human rights (Article 3.1) Priority of the individual's interests and welfare over the sole interest of science or society (Article 3.2) Beneficence and non-maleficence (Article 4) Autonomy (Article 5) Informed consent (Article 6) Protection of persons unable to consent (Article 7) Special attention to vulnerable persons (Article 8) Privacy and confidentiality (Article 9) Equality, justice and equity (Article 10) Non-discrimination and non-stigmatisation (Article 11) Respect for cultural diversity and pluralism (Article 12) Solidarity and co-operation (Article 13) Access to healthcare and essential medicines (Article 14) Benefit sharing (Article 15) Protection of future generations (Article 16) Protection of the environment, the biosphere and biodiversity (Article 17). Section III ('Application of the principles') is devoted to principles of a more procedural nature such as: The requirement for professionalism, honesty, integrity and transparency in the decision-making process regarding bioethical issues (Article 18) The need to establish independent, multidisciplinary and pluralist ethics committees (Article 19) The call for an appropriate risk assessment and management in the biomedical field (Article 20) The need for justice in transnational research (Article 21)."

34 This choice was criticized by some based on the idea that human rights were brought by Western society. Yet, it has to be noted that, paradoxically, some of the most severe criticisms of the universality of human rights come from Western scholars (Sen and Drèze, 1989). According to Amartya Sen (1999, 15), these views are often based on a misconception of non-Western (largely Asian) societies, as if people in these countries had little or no interest in their rights and were only concerned with issues of social order and discipline (misconception which is of course well exploited by authoritarian regimes). In this connection, it is revealing that the only two papers written by non-Western authors that appear in a journal special issue on the declaration openly contradict the pessimistic view of the journal editorial and have a favourable opinion of the human rights approach adopted by UNESCO.1 (see Sen and Drèze, 1989, 15; Sen, 1998, 20; and Asai and Oe, 2005).

35 See Taylor (1999): "Although many experts noticed that this agency could not be prepared for this task for the following reasons: The field is growing, rapidly encompassing more diverse and complex concerns, due to its interdisciplinary nature. WHO has very limited experience in international health lawmaking. Such a task

would deplete the organisation's limited resources and undermine its ability to fulfill its well established and essential international health functions. Member states are highly unlikely to limit their autonomy and freedom by granting to WHO alone such an expansive new mandate. Decentralisation of the international lawmaking enterprise presents great advantages that cannot be ignored" (Taylor, 2004).

36 See, for example, Andorno (2005). "The Oviedo convention: a European legal framework at the intersection of human rights and health law," *Journal of International Biotechnology Law*, 2:133–143.

37 For students who are introduced for the first time to normative ethics, Aristotle's virtue ethics, Kant's deontological ethics, and Mill's consequentialist ethics provide the main criteria to guide the norms according to which we decide our actions. These schools of thinking propose principles whose outcomes are often in conflict with each other because, for example, Aristotle's virtue ethics has as a goal to reach the medium between extremes in front of a specific choice, while for Kant the right thing to do is an inner voice, a moral ought that we cannot ignore and for Mill the rightness of a choice is based on the positive consequence that that choice would have for the largest amount of people. Mixing up these different schools brings an internal contradiction that by its nature cannot be solved.

38 On the notion of dignity, the collection of essays commissioned by Edmund Pellegrino, president of the Council on Bioethics is a must read as he put together the opinions of leading philosophers, political scientists, and theologians on the topic of dignity. See https://www.thenewatlantis.com/docLib/20091130_human_dignity.pdf.

39 See Cascais (1997): At the end of her essay, she presents a long list of capabilities central to the human being worthy of dignity: "(1) Life. Being able to live to the end of a human life of normal length; not dying prematurely, or before one's life is so reduced as to be not worth living. (2) Bodily Health. Being able to have good health, including reproductive health; to be adequately nourished; to have adequate shelter. (3) Bodily Integrity. Being able to move freely from place to place; to be secure against violent assault, including sexual assault and domestic violence; having opportunities for sexual satisfaction and for choice in matters of reproduction. (4) Senses, Imagination, and Thought. Being able to use the senses, to imagine, think, and reason—and to do these things in a "truly human" way, a way informed and cultivated by an adequate education, including, but by no means limited to, literacy and basic mathematical and scientific training. Being able to use imagination and thought in connection with experiencing and producing works and events of one's own choice, religious, literary, musical, and so forth. Being able to use one's mind in ways protected by guarantees of freedom of expression with respect to both political and artistic speech, and freedom of religious exercise. Being able to have pleasurable experiences and to avoid non-beneficial pain. (5) Emotions. Being able to have attachments to things and people outside ourselves; to love those who love and care for us, to grieve at their absence; in general, to love, to grieve, to experience longing, gratitude, and justified anger. Not having one's emotional development blighted by fear and anxiety. (Supporting this capability means supporting forms of human association that can be shown to be crucial in their development.) (6) Practical Reason. Being able to form a conception of the good and to engage in critical reflection about the planning of one's life. (This entails protection for the liberty of conscience and religious observance.) (7) Affiliation. A. Being able to live with and toward others, to recognize and show concern for other human beings, to engage in various forms of social interaction; to be able to imagine the situation of another. (Protecting this capability means protecting institutions that constitute and nourish such forms of affiliation, and also protecting the freedom of assembly and political speech.) B. Having the social bases of self-respect and non-humiliation; being able to be treated as a dignified being whose worth is equal to that of others. This entails provisions of non-discrimination on the basis of

race, sex, sexual orientation, ethnicity, caste, religion, national origin. (8) Other Species. Being able to live with concern for and in relation to animals, plants, and the world of nature. (9) Play. Being able to laugh, to play, to enjoy recreational activities. (10) Control over one's Environment."

40 It may also be noted that Husserl's teacher, Franz Brentano, a Catholic priest was defrocked from the priesthood, dismissed from the church, and forced to resign his teaching position from the University of Vienna because he questioned and criticized the Church's teachings on the infallibility of the pope.

Bibliography

Alsop, S. (2005). *Beyond Cartesian Dualism*. Dordrecht: Springer.

Andorno R. (2005). "The Oviedo convention: A European legal framework at the intersection of human rights and health law", *Journal of International Biotechnology Law*, 2, 133–143.

Archard, D. (2011). "Why moral philosophers are not and should not be moral experts", *Archard D Bioethics*, 25(3): 119–127.

Asai, A., Oe, S. (2005). "A valuable up-to-date compendium of bioethical knowledge", *Developing World Bioethics*. Special Issue: reflections on the UNESCO draft declaration on bioethics and human rights, 5, 216–219.

Baker, R. (2002). "From meta-ethicist to bioethicist", *Cambridge Quarterly of Healthcare Ethics*, 11, 369–379.

Baker, R., Porter, D., and Porter, R. (1993). "Introduction". In R. Baker, D. Porter, R. Porter (eds.). *The Codification of Medical Morality: Historical and Philosophical Studies of the Formalization of Western Medical Morality in the Eighteenth and Nineteenth Centuries*. Dordrecht: Kluwer Academic Publishers, 1–14.

Bateson, G. (1972). *Steps to an Ecology of Mind*. Chicago: Chicago University Press.

Beauchamp, T. L., Childress, J. F. (1994). *Principles of Medical Ethics*. New York: Oxford University Press.

Beauchamp, T. L., Childress, J. F. (2001). *Principles of Biomedical Ethics*. Oxford: Oxford University Press.

Bleuler, E. (1921). *Naturgeschichte der Seele und ihres Bewußtwerdens. Eine Elementarpsychologie*. The Netherlands: Springer.

Brassington, I. (2013). "What's the point of philosophical bioethics?", *Health Care Analysis*, 21(1): 20–30.

Carson, C. (2010a). "Science as instrumental reason: Heidegger, Habermas, Heisenberg", *Continental Philosophy Review* 42(4): 483–509.

Carson, C. (2010b). "Method, moment, and crisis in Weimar science". In E. Peter, Gordon, and John P. McCormick (eds.). *Weimar Thought: A Critical History*. Princeton: Princeton University Press, 179–199.

Cascais, A. F. (1997). "Bioethics: History, scope, object", *Global Bioethics*, 10(1-4): 9–24.

Chambers, T. (2001). The Fiction of Bioethics: A Precis, *The American Journal of Bioethics: AJOB*, 1, 40–43.

Winkler, E. R., Coombs, J. R. (eds.) (1993). *Applied Ethics: A Reader*. London: Blackwell.

Chamsi-Pasha, H., Albar, M. A. (2013). "Western and Islamic bioethics: How close is the gap?", *Avicenna Journal of Medicine*, 3(1): 8–14.

Chatterjee, M. (1973). *The Existential Outlook*. Orient Longman: New Delhi.

Chattopadhyaya, D. P., Embree, L. E., and Mohanty J. (1992). *Phenomenology and Indian Philosophy*. Indian Council of Philosophical Research. New Delhi: Motilal Banarsidass Publishers.

Clouser, K. D. (1995). "Common morality as an alternative to principlism", *Kennedy Institute of Ethics Journal*, 5(3): 219–236.

Crutzen, P. J., Störmer, E. F. (2000). "The anthropocene", *Global Change Newsletter*, 41, S.17–S.18.

Dennett, D. (2003). *Freedom Evolves*. New York: Viking Books.

Descartes, R. (1649/2015). *The Passions of the Soul and other late philosophical writing*. Moriarty, M. (trans.) Oxford: Oxford University Press.

Dewey, J. (1929/1930). *The Quest for Certainty*. New York: The Putnam.

Diaz-Amado, E. (2011). *Bioethicization and Justification of Medicine in Colombia in the Context of Healthcare Reform of 1993*. PhD thesis. University of Durham.

Dworkin, R. (1994). *L'impero del diritto*. Milano: Il Saggiatore.

Embree, L. (1997). "What is phenomenology", *The Encyclopedia of Phenomenology*, 18, 1–10.

Evans, J. H. (2011). *The History and Future of Bioethics: A Sociological View*. Oxford: Oxford University Press.

Farmer, P., Campo, N. G. (2004). "New malaise: Bioethics and human rights in the global era", *The Journal of Law, Medicine & Ethics*, 32(2): 243–251.

Fischer, F. (1990). *Technocracy and the Politics of Expertise*. Newbury Park, CA: Sage Publications.

Toombs Kay (ed.), (2001). *Handbook of Phenomenology and Medicine*. Kluwer Academic Publishers.

Fornero, G. (2005). *Bioetica Cattolica e bioetica laica*. Milano: Mondadori.

Fox, R. C., Swazey, J. P. (2008). *Observing Bioethics*. Oxford: Oxford University Press.

Fuchs, T. (2017). "Self across time: The diachronic unity of bodily existence", *Phenomenology and the Cognitive Sciences*, 16: 291–315.

Fujiki, N., Sudo, M., and Macer, D. J. (2001). "Bioethics and the impact of human genome in Japan and East Asia", *Turkish Journal of Medical Ethics* 9, 70–77.

Gagnier, R. (2010). *Individualism, Decadence and Globalization. On the Relationship of Part to Whole, 1859–1920*. London: Palgrave Macmillan.

Gesang, B. (2010). "Are moral philosophers moral experts?", *Bioethics*, 24(4): 153–159.

Gray, F. (1998). *The Tuskegee Syphilis Study: The Real Story and Beyond*. Montgomery: Black Belt Press.

Gray, F. (2000). "The Lawsuit," in Tuskegee Truths. In *New Zealand the Accident Compensation Commission Paid Compensation*, 473–488.

Gray, F. (2015). The lawsuit. In Tuskegee Truths. In Reverbery , S. M. (ed.). *New Zealand the Accident Compensation Commission Paid Compensation*. Chapel Hill: Michigan University Press.

Gross, M. L., Ravitsky, V. (2013). "Israel: Bioethics in a Jewish-Democratic state", *Cambridge Quarterly of Healthcare Ethics*, 12(3): 247–255.

Habermas, J. (1962). *Strukturwandel der Öffentlichkeit: Untersuchungen zu einer Kategorie der bürgerlichen Gesellschaft*. Luchterhand, Darmstadt.

Hart, W. D. (1996). "Dualism", *A Companion to the Philosophy of Mind*. In Samuel Guttenplan, (ed.). Oxford: Blackwell, 265–267.

US Dept of Health, Education, and Welfare, (1973). *Final Report of the Tuskegee Syphilis Study Ad Hoc Advisory Panel*. Washington, DC: US Government Printing Office.

Hart, J. (1998). "Genesis, instinct, and reconstruction: Nam-In Lee's Edmund Husserl's Phänomenologie der Instinct", *Husserl Studies*, 15, 101.

Hatfield, G. (2004). Sense-data and the mind–body problem. In Ralph Schumacher (ed.), *Perception and Reality: From Descartes to the Present*. Mentis, 305–331.

Heidegger, M. (1969). *Discourse on Thinking: A Translation of Gelassenheit.* In J. M. Anderson E. A. Freund (eds.). New York: Harper.

Heidegger, M. (2000). *Intro to Metaphysics.* Yale: Yale University Press.

Heilbroner, R. (1974). *An Inquiry into the Human Prospect.* London: Calder & Boyars.

Heisenberg, W. (1969). *Der Teil und das Ganze: Gespräche im Umkreis der Atomphysik.* Munich: Piper.

Husserl, E. (1936/1954). *Die Krisis der europäischen Wissenschaften und die transzendentale Phänomenologie: Eine Einleitung in die phänomenologische Philosophie,* Biemel, W. (ed.). Dordrecht: Kluwer.

Husserl, E. (1936/1970). *Crisis of European Sciences and Transcendental Phenomenology,* In Carr, D. (ed.). Evanston: Northwestern Press.

Husserl, E. (1968). *Briefe an Roman Ingarden, Letter LXXIII of November 26, 1934; see also Letter LXX,* p. 8 The Hague: Nijhoff, 1968.

Husserl, E. (1989). *Ideas Pertaining to a Pure Phenomenology and to a Phenomenological Philosophy, Second Book. Studies in the Phenomenology of Constitution.* In collected works of Edmund Husserl, vol. 3. Trans. R. Rojcewicz, and A. Schuwer. Dordrecht: Springer.

Jing-Bao N. (2005). "Cultural values embodying universal norms: A critique of a popular assumption about cultures and human rights", *Developing World Bioethics,* 5(3): 251–257.

Karsjens, K. L., Johnson, J. M. (2003). "White normativity and subsequent critical race deconstruction of bioethics", *The American Journal of Bioethics,* 3(2): 22–23.

Engelhardt Jr., H. T., Caplan A. (eds.) (1987). *Scientific Controversies: A Study in the Resolution and Closure of Disputes Concerning Science and Technology.* New York: Cambridge University Press.

Kotarbinska, J. (1960). On ostensive definitions, *Philosophy of Science,* 27(1): 1–22.

Kueng, H. (1996). *Menschenwuerdig Sterbe.* Munchen: Piper.

Le Roi, P. (2003). "The birth and youth of the Kennedy Institute of Ethics". In J. K. Walter, K. Eran (eds.). *The Story of Bioethics: From Seminal Works to Contemporary Explorations.* Washington, DC: Georgetown University Press, 215–231.

Lolas, F. (2008). "Bioethics and animal research: A personal perspective and a note on the contribution of Fritz Jahr", *Biological Research,* 41(1): 119–123.

Macer Darryl R. J. (2001). "Bioethics in Japan and East Asia", *Turkish Journal of Medical Ethics,* 9, 70–77.

Macklin R. (2003). "Dignity is a useless concept", *BMJ,* 327, 1419–1420.

Mann J. (1996). "Health and human rights. Protecting human rights is essential for promoting health," *BMJ,* 312, 924–925.

McCormick, R. (1994). "Blastomere separation: Some concerns", *The Hastings Center Report* 24, 14.

Mercer, C. (2017). "Descartes' debt to Teresa of Ávila, or why we should work on women in the history of philosophy", *Philosophical Studies,* 174(10): 2539–2555.

Minutes, Medical Humanities Committee. (3/1/1972). IMH Records, RG9, Box 2, Folder 18, UTMB archives. Cited (2016) In Garner, Jotterland, Ranson (eds.), *The Development of Bioethics in the United States.* Holland: Springer.

Moazam, F., Jafarey A. M. (2005). "Pakistan and biomedical ethics: Report from a Muslim country", *Cambridge Quarterly of Healthcare Ethics,* 14(3): 249–255.

Moran, D. (2012). *Husserl's Crisis of the European Sciences and Transcendental Phenomenology. An Introduction.* Cambridge: Cambridge Press.

Morris, G., Saunders P. (2017). "The Environment in Health and Wellbeing", *Oxford Research Encyclopedia of Environmental Science.*

Naaman-Zauderer, N. (2015). "Passions of the soul". In L. Nolan (ed.), *The Cambridge Descartes Lexicon*. Cambridge: Cambridge University Press, 569–572.

Nagel, T. (2012). *Mind and Cosmos: Why the Materialist Neo-Darwinian Conception of Nature is Almost Certainly False*. Oxford: Oxford University Press.

Novikoff, A. B. (1945). The concept of integrative levels and biology, *Science* 101, 209–215, 10.1126.

Nussbaum, M. (2008). Human dignity and political entitlements. In *Human Dignity and Bioethics: Essays Commissioned by the President's Council on Bioethics*, online Retrieved from here: https://repository.library.georgetown.edu/handle/10822/559351 Publisher: The President's Council on Bioethics.

Ophuls, W. (1977). *Ecology and the Politics of Scarcity: Prologue to a Political Theory of the Steady State*. San Francisco: W.H. Freeman.

Potter, V. R. (1964). "Models as aids to communication", *National Cancer Institute Monograph*, 13, 111–116.

Potter, V. R. (1971). *Bioethics, Bridge to the Future*. Englewood Cliffs, NJ: Prentice Hall, Inc., 24.

Potter, V. R. (1972). "Bioethics for Whom?", *Annals of the New York Academy of Sciences*, 196 (Art. 4), 200–205.

Potter, V. R. (1975). "Humility and responsibility-A bioethic for oncologist: Presidential address", *Cancer Research*, 35, 2297–2306.

Potter, V. R. (1988). *Global Bioethics*. Ann Arbor, Michigan: Michigan University.

Rawls, J. (1971). *A Theory of Justice*, Cambridge, MA: Harvard University Press.

Reich, W. T. (1978). "Preface" (xi–xiv) and "Introduction," (xv–xxii). In *Encyclopedia of bioethics*, vol. 4, 1st ed, ed. W.T. Reich. New York: Macmillan/Free Press.

Reich, W.T. (1990). "La Bioetica negli Stati Uniti: Orientamenti e Tendenze". In *Vent'anni di Bioetica: Protagonisti, idee, istituzioni*, ed. C. Viafora, 141–175. Padua: Fondazione Lanza and Gregoriana Libreria Editrice.

Reich, W. T. (1994). "The word "bioethics": Its birth and the legacies of those who shaped it", *Kennedy Institute of Ethics Journal*, 4(4): 319–335.

Reich, W. T. (1995). "The word "bioethics": The struggle over its earliest meanings", *Kennedy Institute of Ethics Journal*, 5(1): 19–34.

Reich, W. T. (2003). "Shaping and mirroring the field". In Walter J. K., K. Eran (eds.), *The Story of Bioethics: From Seminal Works to Contemporary Explorations*. Washington, DC: Georgetown University Press; 165–196.

Reubi, D. (2010). "The will to modernize: A genealogy of biomedical research ethics in Singapore", *International Political Sociology*, 4, 142–158.

Reverby, S. M. (2000). "Tuskegee syphilis study legacy committee" *Tuskegee Truths: Rethinking the Tuskegee Syphilis Study*. Chapel Hill: University of North Carolina Press, 559–566.

Reverby, S. M. (2009). *Examining Tuskegee. The Infamous Syphilis Study and Its Legacy*. Chapel Hill: University of North Carolina Press.

Roscoe, L., Schenck, D. P. (2017). *Communication and Bioethics at the End of Life Real Cases, Real Dilemmas*. Holland: Springer International Publishing

Rose N. (2007). *The Politics of Life Itself: Biomedicine, Power and Subjectivity in the Twenty-First Century*. Princeton, NJ, and Oxford: Princeton University Press.

Rosenberg, A. (2011). *The Atheist's Guide to Reality: Enjoying Life without Illusions*. New York: W.W. Norton.

Russo, G., Potter, V. R. (1995). *La prima idea di Bioetica*. Torino: Sei, 5–18:11.

Sass, H. M. (2007). "Fritz Jahr's 1927 concept of bioethics", *Kennedy Institute Ethics Journal*, 17(4), 279–295.

Searle, J. (1992). *The Rediscovery of the Mind*. Cambridge and London: The MIT Press.

Sen A. (1998). "Universal truths: Human rights and the westernizing illusion", *Harvard International Review*, 5, 216–219. 17.

Sen, A. (1999). *Choice, Welfare, and Measurement*. Cambridge, MA: Harvard University Press.

Sen, A., Drèze, J. (1989). *Hunger and Public Action*. Oxford, England and New York: Clarendon Press Oxford University Press.

Shaheen, B., Stearns, J. M. (1998). "The philosopher is not always right: A comment on "the customer is not always right", *Journal of Business Ethics*, 17, 1, 39–44.

Shearman, D. J. C., Smith, J. W. (2007). *The Climate Change Challenge and the Failure of Democracy*. Westport, CT: Praeger.

Sheehan, M., Dunn, M. (2013). "On the nature and sociology of bioethics", *Health Care Analysis*, 21(1): 54–69.

Shomali, M. A. (2008). "Islamic bioethics: A general scheme", *Journal of Medical Ethics and History of Medicine*. 1, 1.

Sorell, T. (1994). "The customer is not always right", *Journal of Business Ethics*, 13, 913–918.

Sorell, T. (2013). *Scientism: Philosophy and the Infatuation with Science*. London/New York: Routledge.

Spinsanti, R. (1995). "Incontro con Warren Reich", *L'Arco di Giano*, 7, 219.

Suzuki, F. (2012). "The Cogito Proposition of Descartes and characteristics of his ego theory", *Bulletin of Aichi University of Education*, 61, 73–80.

Svenaeus, F. (2017). *Phenomenological Bioethics: Medical Technologies, Human Suffering, and the Meaning of Being Alive*. London, United Kingdom: Routledge.

Svenaeus, F. (2017). *Phenomenological Bioethics*. London: Routledge.

Takala, J., Hamalainen, P., Saarela, K. L., Yun, L. Y., Manickam, K., Jin, T. W., Heng, P., Tjong, C., Kheng, L. G., Lim, S., Lin, G. S. (2014). Global estimates of the burden of injury and illness at work in 2012, *Journal of Occupational and Environmental Hygiene*, 11, 326e33.

Taylor A. (1999). "Globalization and biotechnology: UNESCO and an international strategy to advance human rights and public health", *American Journal of Law & Medicine*, 4, 479–542.

Taylor A. (2004). "Governing the globalization of public health", *The Journal of Law, Medicine & Ethics*, 32, 500–508.

Thomasma D. (2001). "Proposing a new agenda: Bioethics and international human rights", *Camb Q Healthc Ethics*, 10, 299–310.

Toulmin, S. (1982). "How medicine saved the life of ethics", *Perspectives in Biology and Medicine*, 25 (4): 736–750.

Walzer, M.L. (1981)."Philosophy and democracy", *Political Theory*, 9, 379–399.

Wear, D., M. Kuczewski. (2004). "The professionalism movement: Can we pause?", *The American Journal of Bioethics*, 4(2): 1–10.

Westerman, M. A., Steen, E.M. (2007). "Going beyond the internal-external dichotomy in clinical psychology: The theory of interpersonal defense as an example of a participatory model", *Theory and Psychology*, 17(2): 323–351.

Whitehouse, P. (2003). "The rebirth of bioethics: Extending the original formulations of Van Rensselaer Potter", *The American Journal of Bioethics, AJOB*, 3, W26–W31.

Wilson, D. (2014). *The Making of British Bioethics*. Manchester: Manchester University Press.

Zahavi, D. (2003). Inner time consciousness and pre-reflective self-awareness. In D. Welton (ed.), *The New Husserl: A Critical Reader*. Bloomington: Indiana University Press, 157–180.

2

EMOTIONS IN BIOETHICS

Introduction

In this chapter, I am going to defend the following argument: a successful bioethics needs to integrate emotions in its discourse in order to thoroughly think through the problems commonplace in the field and to guarantee the "decent survival" that Potters, its founder, envisioned as its main goal (1964, 1971, 1972, 1975, 1988).

In the first part of this chapter, I am going to present four arguments in defense of my thesis, and in the second, I will present a short excursus on the history of emotions so as to understand the still persisting disparaging attitude toward them and to clarify what we normally mean by emotions. I believe that if bioethics could better integrate emotions in its discussions, it would lessen the reductionistic dualism with which human beings relate to each other and to other organisms.

I. A Quick Overview

What are emotions? How much do they affect the constitution of healthy values in one's personal and intersubjective life? To what extent does a poor emotional constitution of values impact the political and social well-being of the community? The human being is not intellect only, and yet the curiosity about human emotional life has been belittled since the dawning of the modern age (Descartes, 1984–1991; Herbart, 1906; Spinoza, 2001). The increasing number of Nobel Prizes in economics that have been granted to scholars who highlight the importance of emotions in economic behavior and support a disciplinary paradigm shift is a sign of the current change;

(Davidson et al., 2003). The onset of mental health disorders,[1] such as depression, social anxiety, or panic, that are exponentially affecting the population worldwide should be a sign of a change that we need to make and should encourage us to include a serious consideration of emotions in every discipline, bioethics included (Blum and Nelson-Mmari, 2004, 402–18). According to the WHO, depression affects, each year, 340 million people worldwide (in my forthcoming, *The Role of* Bio-*Ethics in Emotional Problems* Chapter 3, I will discuss in detail one of its components, i.e., emotional numbness).[2] Given the immense variety of problems caused by emotional distress (Blum and Nelson-Mmari, 2004, 402–418), it is timely to address emotions in an interdisciplinary way in order to promote functional organizations (Fredrickson, 2000) and a healthy society;[3] bioethics can point us in the right direction.

While Descartes discarded emotions as mere agitation of the animal spirits in the pineal gland, Spinoza considered emotions fluctuations of the vital stream, and Herbart, as well, counted them as the waste in the up-building of the mind. The heart, translated in modern philosophy with Gemüt,[4] was believed to be the center of human understanding; mastering the heart knowledge equated to achieving real wisdom (Σοφία). Such a mastery was considered in Plato's (1997, a–c) philosophy as the soul's highest yearning, while in Aristotle's (1984, a–c) as the perfect balance between reason and desire (Ruckmick, 1929). With the rise of Neo-Platonism and Christianity, a disparaging attitude toward the body also arose, viewing the body as a pale vestige of celestial perfection. This contributed to a declining interest in humans' view of their emotions (James, 1997). It was this decline that directly fostered the dismissive Enlightenment attitude toward emotions which still informs the social stigma around emotional disorders (Ruckmick, 1929). In his *History of Insanity in the Age of Reason*, Foucault (2016) elucidates the steps that during the Enlightenment led people with mental disorders to be confined to the margins of the society—a condition that, unfortunately, still persists.

Darwin's *Origin of the Species* (1859) moved the focus of the research to the natural sciences. His work represented a stepping stone to renew biological interest in emotions and gave new impulses to study them, now meant as serving habits and neuromuscular responses. The rise of biology and psychology as disciplines separated from philosophy determined a renewed, flourishing interest in emotions which, unfortunately, reinforced the social stigma around emotional disorders because now scientific physiological proofs were used to prove the sickness and danger of emotionally disordered persons (Foucault, 2016). The separation between "Geisteswissenshaften" (human sciences) and "Naturwissenshaften" (natural sciences) theorized by Dilthey (1833–1911) and put in practice by Wundt (1832–1920) through the foundation of experimental psychology led to the breach that is still being reflected in the way in which professions and disciplines are organized to date.

II. Reasons Why Emotions Should Be Brought into Bioethics

There are at least four reasons why I believe that professionals whose work relates to well-being and environmental care (philosophers, doctors, nurses, environmentalists, biologists, politicians, etc.) should receive basic training so as to understand emotions and the way in which these emotions impact daily human lives. I believe that the multidisciplinarity of bioethics is conducive to this kind of training that would educate different forms of intelligence for a better social and environmental life. It is very important that people from different areas of work understand the role that emotions play in their private and professional lives; without this understanding, no serious and effective bioethics would be possible. Hereby, I present four reasons to justify my point, although throughout the book I will provide more arguments in its favor.

First, some of the individuals suffering from emotional disorders might encounter strong difficulties in being part of a healthy environment for themselves or others. Narcissists in different professions, for example, do not always have the emotional presence to actually care about the environment, the consequences of their technological inventions, or the people with whom they work. It is difficult to fight for a healthy environment at work or in nature if one is self-absorbed and emotionally unbalanced. How can we think that our society can make wise decisions if we are getting emotionally sicker and sicker?

Second, if human beings, in their personal and professional lives, understood how the intentions that move their emotions are structured, it would be possible to care better for each other. It would be easier to extend compassionate understanding toward each other's vulnerabilities. Instead, our professional life often asks us to be emotionally neutral at work. In order to be professional, we should not make things personal; instead, we should adhere to a prearranged policy that regulates our behaviors. I will discuss here only one implication of this requirement, that is, if half of our life has to be emotionally neutral, it is quite possible that we live half of our life without facing our emotions and consequently who we are. If an emotional problem hits us, we jump into work to forget about it as work provides for us a safe emotionally neutral space. Yet, we know that denial and repression lead to more serious emotional problems and to a progressive detachment from reality. True empathy and care do not equate to saying the right thing at the right moment, "sorry, sir, for your loss," but they require an emotional presence that truly accompanies the words as they are emotionally meant by the professional. In that mutual recognition, a true connection is possible in the professional environment. If the professional is detached from themselves, we risk nurturing an empty detached society in which to live and exchange services. This is what I am going to discuss with a second case in Section II.2.

Third, given the inventions emerging under the umbrella of artificial intelligence, in particular through machine learning technology, becoming aware of one's own emotional and ethical biases would prevent technological creations from reproducing our same human biases and exploiting human emotional weaknesses as a means of control. An emotionally biased and unintelligent artificial intelligence would be useless and damaging for human beings and the environment.

Fourth, emotions are important components of human decisions and behaviors. Understanding their structure would allow us to engage more positively with our environment and to make more sustainable choices to improve it. We are the environment and what we do affects the environment in each moment of our life; living a life detached from ourselves undermines the quality of our life and the chances of our survival as parts of our ecosystem.

In what follows, I will discuss cases connected to these reasons in order to show the necessity for a thoughtful consideration of emotions in bioethics.

II.1 Unhealthy People Unhealthy Environment: The Case of Depressed Doctors

There is a growing literature on the problem of depression in medical professions which reflects the increasing importance of taking care of this issue (Miles, 1998; Schwenk et al., 2008). The current social stigma around the problem of depression, especially among medical professionals, makes a call to action all the more urgent, as the impact of this problem is deeply wounding for all involved, even if it is sometimes hard to see. Though it had the goal of treating mental diseases with the same dignity as physical ones, the approval of the Mental Health Parity and Addiction Equity Act (MHPAEA) of 2008 in the United States has not prevented plenty of problems from continuing to persist.

In 2004, Schwenk and colleagues mailed an anonymous survey, the Patient Health Questionnaire depression module (PHQ-9) and other Likert-style questions (Schewenk et al., 2004), with the goal of assessing the risk of depression and suicide among physicians and vetting how much depression had impacted their interactions with patients. Out of 5,000 randomly selected practicing physicians in Michigan, moderate to severe depression scores were reported by 130 (11.3%). "Roughly one quarter of respondents reported knowing a physician whose professional standing had been compromised by being depressed. Physicians reporting moderate to severe depression were 2 to 3 times more likely to report substantial impact on their work roles compared to physicians with minimal to mild depression scores, including a decrease in work productivity (57.7% vs. 18.5%; $p < .001$) and a decrease in work satisfaction (90.8% vs. 36.2%; $p < .001$). The same physicians were 2 to 3 times more likely to report a wide range of dysfunctional and worrisome approaches to seeking mental health care compared to physicians with minimal to mild depression scores, including a higher likelihood that they would self-prescribe antidepressants (30.0% vs. 9.9%; $p < .001$) and a higher likelihood that they would avoid seeking treatment due to concerns about confidentiality (50.7% vs. 17.3%; $p < .001$)" (2008, 17–20). Moderate to severe depression among Michigan physicians seemed to have an important influence on physician work roles and potential negative impact on licensing and medical staff status. As proved from this and other studies (Miles, 1998; Gold, 2013), the risk of being stigmatized and losing their license increased the risk of depression in physicians who felt forced to alter their approach to seeking mental health care in moments of distress, "including seeking care outside their medical community and self-prescribing antidepressants. Having a mental health diagnosis on their record" is perceived as a sure way to lose their license (Gold, 2013).

In another article,[5] a young physician tells us that while he was studying to become a psychiatrist he discovered that he met the criteria for depression. That realization was a turning point in his life. While everything seemed to be falling apart, this physician made the decision to seek help and admitted to his advisor that he had a problem. His decision was quite brave and unpopular among professionals who are incredibly determined to pursue a medical career. In the same article, for example, Leonard Su, a former cardiovascular surgeon, affirmed that he would have never taken that test himself, partly because he thought he could not be depressed and partly because he was scared about the possible result. "My inner voice was incredibly hateful and kind of spiteful so that no matter what I did, it was always negative," said Su. "I had this idea that depressed people didn't do anything, that they sat in a dark room or didn't get out of bed, so because I was doing so many things, I couldn't be depressed" (Andrews, 2008). In the end, after having served as a surgeon for ten years, Su left medicine and dedicated his life to speaking about his story and the importance of sharing mental health problems without stigmas.

Similarly to the average of other professionals, physicians can be affected by depression as much as the rest of the population, that is, 7% of U.S. adults; even more than other people they might experience some difficulty in acknowledging their own problems because of biases of their own and because of the external pressure they feel. For this reason, they need support from society. Yet, the stigma is such that they do not feel free to seek help because that would undermine their profession and their chance to make a living.

> Because physicians have access to and knowledge of the means to end their life, they have a suicide completion rate estimated as twice higher than the rest of the general population, according to a 2018 report published in *Medscape*. Students and physicians in training, new to their careers and in a highly competitive environment, are even less likely to admit that they have a problem.
>
> *(Karcz, 2018)*

How do we expect these professionals to make important decisions every day about care for other human beings if their own emotions are stuck and repressed under the heavy weight of shame? After two of his classmates committed suicide during an internship, Mata wrote an article (2016) in which he concluded,

> Depression during internship affects not only objective outcomes like medical errors but also how interns value the profession and themselves, with potentially profound consequences for their future career decisions. Residency programs should implement both reactive interventions targeting depression and proactive interventions promoting resilience and wellbeing to address the issues that lead to depression.
>
> *(Mata, 2015, 1244–1250)*[6]

How can these young doctors support a society of well-being if we do not make space in our society for them to also be well? I think that a bioethics that takes emotions into account can promote good decision making in this matter and can create a better environment for people suffering from these problems.

II.2 Care to Be Cared: The Awkward Silence Around Miscarriage

Another reason to introduce emotions into the bioethical discourse is connected to the better care that we can provide to each other if we understand the emotional currents that run underneath our daily lives and interactions. Today, empathy is considered one of the most important dispositions[7] when working in health care and social environments. Although I think that empathy is very important in our daily interactions, I do not think that it can replace all the emotions that one can experience in a normal day as a professional. At times, in fact, empathy seems to have absorbed all the emotions one is allowed to feel in order to make possible a machine-like professionalism. It has become a sort of emotional master key. As I showed in Chapter 1 (Section III.3), being professional has become a way to work according to a neutral disposition that leaves behind all of our personal feelings in favor of pre-agreed emotional guidelines; they become the actual emotional brain that tells us how to act in any given interpersonal situation. Especially in litigious societies, it is very important to adhere to a precise script even in very human-oriented professions, such as psychotherapists, doctors, teachers, and so on. Being one's own person and acting out against the script, and according to one's own emotional charge, is a risk that can lead to the end of one's own profession. Yet, with time, we have realized that a totally neutral disposition is not helpful when dealing, for example, with a terminally ill patient or with a difficult student at school. Because of this, empathy has become a middle ground that allows us to still be emotionally neutral at work while also allowing us to tune into the emotions of the person we have in front of us so that we may effectively deal with their problem.

Yet, often, if we exercise empty empathy, we recognize the emotions of the other person without making significant contact with our own. While I think that empathy is a very important dispositional quality to have in private and professional life and an emotionally neutral behavior helps to reach an agreement in the intersubjective space of our society, I also believe that this cannot excuse us from dealing with and understanding our own emotions. Despite the growing number of empathy trainings for health care professionals,[8] more still needs to be done in bioethics to provide adequate empathetic care in distressing situations. In fact, in order to be empathetic human beings, we cannot ignore and remain ignorant of our emotional life. We need to know our emotions and understand how they impact us; otherwise, any attempt to be empathetic toward others sounds like an empty "robot-like" way to relate to people. I can say: "I'm sorry, sir, for your loss" but I have no idea about the emotional charge of this sentence because I'm disconnected from that scene while I am saying it. Let us consider a case concerning maternity:[9]

> A woman who had been pregnant with twins told the story of how she discovered that in her 20th week one of her babies died. Besides the strong sense of loneliness and the sudden change of reality that the woman experienced all at once, she said that comfort seemed to come only from her husband who happened to be present for that routine check. In her narrative, doctors took good care of her body but in a sort of overwhelming way. They asked her questions that she was not prepared to answer; they explained the reasons why the baby died and answered her questions when they arose. They did their job; they adhered to what the policy required of them. Yet, it did not seem to be enough and it did not bring her any comfort. She narrated her story the day after the event, therefore the emotional tone of her words was still soberingly earnest, in particular in the last lines where she asks herself: "How much shock can a person take? How do you get past something like this?" Despair, disappointment, disillusion, sadness, these are some of the emotions and feelings that are still sitting inside her without anyone being able to address them. Women who experience spontaneous miscarriage (one out of three, Tulandi and Al-Fozan, 2009) are at high risk for depression and anxiety disorders (Leis-Newman, 2012; Blackmore, 2011). Yet, society seems to not consider early miscarriages as an actual loss (Swanson, 1999; Green et al., 2003) but more like a sickness to the point that health insurances tend to not cover the costs of first trimester of pregnancy because of the high risk for miscarriage during this period of time.

"Because it is medically common, the impact of miscarriage is often underestimated (...) But miscarriage is a traumatic loss, not only of the pregnancy, but of a woman's sense of self and her hopes and dreams of the future. She has lost her 'reproductive story,' and it needs to be grieved" (Jaffe and Diamond, 2011) even if it is an early loss (Woods-Giscombé et al., 2010). "Still, for women who miscarry early, their grief is less socially acceptable than the anguish of someone who miscarries later in their pregnancy," says Jaffe. "With later losses, people can have a funeral or memorial service. When it's an early miscarriage or even a failed IVF cycle, it is often unacknowledged by others, [yet] these are invisible losses that feel disenfranchised and not validated." Although our society is getting better at understanding these emotions and in creating policies that allow the space for acknowledging the loss and the pain involved—for example, until ten years ago when perinatal losses occurred, the corpses were not always shown to their parents and were to be disposed of by the hospital personnel—there is still not enough empathetic understanding to relieve the stigma of this pain and create a nurturing environment for the people who suffer from it. One out of three pregnant couples who go through the experience of a miscarriage "will spend enormous amounts of emotional energy trying to explain why it happened," Diamond says. "They often blame themselves, even when it is inaccurate, to help make sense of it. Women may torment themselves with guilt and blame, re-writing the story, so to speak: 'If I hadn't gone to the grocery store' or 'If I didn't stay up so late.' It's a way of coping with the loss. I've come to see this as part of the grief process" (2012, 56). This sense of guilt can become even stronger in women who felt ambivalent about the pregnancy. "It's very, very important that clients know that their ambivalence did not cause the loss," Diamond writes. She presented the story of a client of hers, a 16-year-old woman, who miscarried at 12 weeks. "Everyone around her was thrilled and relieved. It took three sessions for her to acknowledge that she was grief-stricken," Diamond writes, "Part of her was relieved, but she was already used to the idea. Nobody around her could validate her sadness."

When an early miscarriage occurs, the costs to recover from psychophysical damages are left to the private life of the individual or the couple. Comfort comes from the idea, it is often said, that the grievance will diminish with time, especially if followed by a successful pregnancy. Yet, it is clear that this is not enough to take care of such a traumatic experience. Often, doctors have to advise their patients to go and meet with a psychotherapist or a counselor to validate their sense of loss, but the expense in terms of money and time (especially when the couple or the individual already has other children) would be too costly. As a consequence, Heller and Zeanah showed how 45% of the mothers who delivered a child within 19 months after a perinatal loss have more chances to develop a form of unhealthy disorganized form of attachment with their new child (Zeanah et al., 1999). The embarrassed silence around a miscarriage does not encourage a psychophysical recovery for the mothers and their families (Blackmore et al., 2011; Obama, 2018). The interesting findings collected in this study[10] showed how many women who had problems during their pregnancy or suffered a pregnancy loss had experienced the following recurrent emotions:

- **Feeling different from other pregnant women.**
  One woman remarked:
  "Other than brief spurts, I couldn't get excited until the very end, and even that was guarded. I've had friends who've seemed to go through pregnancies with an air of expectation that everything will work out, and I'm envious of the joy they seem to have had. I felt like all the commercials and cards out there about the joys of pregnancy were written for someone other than me. It made me feel defective a bit, that I couldn't get into fully loving being pregnant, even though my pregnancy was easy."
- **Feeling like you don't belong.**
  "You may feel like the average pregnant woman can't understand your feelings, yet you may feel uncomfortable talking about your pregnancy with your infertile friends who are still undergoing treatments."
- **Obsessing over pregnancy symptoms, symptoms of miscarriage, or preterm labor.**
- **Finding it difficult to change.**
  Going from a reproductive endocrinologist's care to that of an OB or midwife can feel burdensome. You may feel your pregnancy is more vulnerable and fragile than a fertile woman's, and that a regular provider will provide fewer opportunities for procedures such as ultrasounds that can assure you the baby is okay.
- **Desiring more data or care.**
  You might want to schedule more appointments, request extra ultrasounds, or rent a home Doppler for reassurance that the baby is still alive.
- **Distrust of your body's ability to carry a pregnancy.**
  This may be particularly true if you have a medical condition (such as a blood-clotting disorder or uterine anomaly) that causes your pregnancy to be high-risk.
- **Guilt.**
  You may feel like your body is at fault for a previous loss or for putting the current pregnancy at risk.
- **Fear of acknowledging a pregnancy.**
  You may feel scared to openly recognize your pregnancy **until after the first trimester**, or until after the week when you experienced a previous loss, or, for some women, until you have grown big enough that you cannot disguise your pregnancy any more.
- **Fear of bonding or becoming attached to a child.**
  You might feel hesitant to become attached until you feel sure she or he will remain alive.
- **Fear of preparing for a birth.**
  You may put off buying maternity clothes or purchasing baby items so as not to jinx a pregnancy.

- **Fear of complaining.**
  You might be scared to complain about pregnancy symptoms or discomforts because you might seem ungrateful.
  (citing verbatim from "our body our selves project")

The emotional effects of infertility and/or pregnancy losses are numerous and they can undermine the well-being of the individual. The Cartesian mind/body split takes place first of all in these situations, in clinics, hospitals, and doctors' offices where we encounter the limits of our body in a shocking way. We are forced to swallow the tears, split ourselves from our body, and pretend that the overwhelming flow of emotions is not touching us. Caregivers are there to provide care for the patient's body, but sometimes they cannot reach the whole human being. The other part, the psychological one, is left to the hands of private therapists and mental care professionals. What is actually missing is an adequate education to be truly empathetic toward the various range of health problems. In this case, recovering trust in one's body is possible when there is an environment capable of acknowledging the problem, and for this to be viable, every member of this environment has to have adequate emotional education.

Basic care cannot be left to the private lives of the people involved because they might not have the education or the financial means to access that care and they might miss that necessary space in which to process the complexity of their emotions. I think the support that psychotherapists and counselors can offer is one of the many possible resources necessary for facing the problem. Bioethics should move us toward a systematic change in this direction so that adequate policies can be put in place to take adequate care of each other in the professional environment. Bioethics is not only about big technological dilemmas but also about improving the quality of our daily invisible lives with wisdom, care, and compassion. One woman out of three experiences at some point in her life this problem; not all of them can afford private psychotherapeutic support, but all of them deserve the opportunity to be understood and to find a truly empathetic ear. Saying "you can try to have another child soon" is not a sufficient form of support and yet is the one most commonly provided. There are maternity programs that invest more in this direction,[11] but they are still perceived as an eccentric, expensive alternative. Bioethics can educate to empathize with these sensitive issues and expand care in truly empathetic directions.

II.3 Emotionally Intelligent Artificial Intelligence

AI algorithms are playing a more and more important role in the growth of our society and in the management of our daily lives. When algorithms are employed to replace human work in social tasks, the risk is that they might inherit human social biases (race-based opinions, sexism, etc.) and/or our same disparaging attitude toward emotions. The following case on algorithms meant to study readmissions in hospitals can be a good example.

II.3.1 Early Readmissions

An important example in medical care comes from the algorithms that are being devised to guarantee better care during hospitalization. He et al. (2014) conducted a study to improve an administrative claim-based model capable of predicting 30-day readmissions to the hospital. The algorithm used administrative claim data as a basis to predict 30-day empirical risk factors; these administrative data included standardized billing codes and admission characteristics available before discharge. None of these data speak of the relational net and emotional support that the patient will receive once back home. The goal of the algorithm is to avoid the 17.6% of hospital admissions that will result in readmissions within 30 days of discharge, with 76% of these being potentially avoidable (M.P.A. Committee, Report to Congress: Promoting Greater Efficiency in Medicare, 2007).

Similarly, in another study (Kansagara et al., 2011), an algorithm meant to predict hospital readmission risk was employed for the purpose of identifying which patients would benefit the most from care transition interventions and, accordingly, risk-adjusted readmission. In this case, as well, data came from administrative hospital databases which provided information concerning the admission and discharge of the patient. In this study, though, they compared this model with six different readmission risk prediction models applied on the same population. Only two of these models, those that incorporated functional and social variables, were of actual help detecting the risk of readmission. As the authors asserted, the models available still performed poorly and needed to use more efforts to improve their performance as their use became more widespread (2013, 1688).

I believe that the planning of these algorithms is inheriting the dualistic attitude still lingering in medical care: hospitals take care of the body but not of its emotional and spiritual well-being (Broedner, 2019). Technology knows "what humans know, how and why they know" (Weizenbaum, 1976). Often, the administration data collected in hospitals fail to take into consideration the emotional state and the emotional support network of the patient (Zhan and Miller, 2003, 58–63). In predicting the relapse of a patient and the effectiveness of hospital services, the emotional quality of life is often not counted among the variables. Clearly, a patient who has undergone surgery has a better chance to recover if surrounded by an emotionally nurturing atmosphere.[12] There is a wide literature on statistical techniques (Foltz, 2001; Bouquet, 2015; Ryan et al., 2017) to assess patient readmission risk by using many types of available data; most of these data focus on the semantic level of the information. A wide spectrum of data sources includes patient demographics, social characteristics, medications, procedures, conditions, and lab tests (Choudhry, 2013); others collect only a single source of data, for example, administrative data (He, 2014); while still others propose "logistic regressions" on independent variables chosen by hand (Futoma et al., 2015). According to La Rochelle Bengio Louradour and Lamblin

(2009), multilayer neural networks that combine many levels of nonlinearity would allow the presentation of highly nonlinear and highly varying functions such as those implied by the emotional-related data from discharged and newly admitted patients.

Hinton (2006, 1527) proposed initiating "the parameters of a deep belief network" whose "generative model holds many layers of hidden causal variables based on the training algorithm of restricted Boltzmann machines." The downside of this proposal would be the ethical opacity of the programming outcome. In fact, even though this way of programming would allow for more complexity which would make the machine learning more intelligent, it would make its decisional route more difficult to detect; giving these machines more emotional intelligence would turn them into more ethically transparent beings. As Bostrom and Yudkowsky (2011) remarked, machine learning technology whose decisions are based on decision trees or Bayesian networks are much more transparent to programmer inspection (Hastie et al., 2004) and, accordingly, their inherited ethical biases are easier to detect. "It will become increasingly important to develop AI algorithms that are not just powerful and scalable, but also transparent to inspection—to name one of many socially important properties" (2011, 2). Therefore, even if as it happens, "changes in federal regulation of the healthcare industry together with the novel use of payment penalties based on quality of care metrics" (De Castro, 2015, 214) require the creation of AI models to measure the meaning of well-being and its costs on health care structures, we need to take into consideration two bioethical factors: (1) the risk of transferring epistemological and social biases onto machine learning technologies through which, as it is in this case, we predict the effectiveness of clinical and care services and (2) the risk of losing track of the bias transmitted and its ethical transparency in the event that more complex models are put in place.[13] Having electronic data concerning health information available is certainly a source for which emotional intelligence needs to be carefully considered in the creation of such algorithms.

II.3.2 AI to Manipulate Emotions

Those who understood the importance of emotions and technology in the public arena have often chosen to manipulate emotions in favor of economic winnings. I refer here to the recent scandal of Cambridge Analytica which showed us how segmentation of data can be used to target populations from different countries and interfere in sensitive political affairs, such as elections and referendums. Most notably, the collusion between Facebook and Cambridge Analytica seems to have been decisive in the 2016 presidential election in the United States and the passing of the referendum, in the same year, that saw the United Kingdom withdraw from the European Union ("Brexit"). Using data from 50 million Facebook users, as well as online quiz-like personality tests developed by

Cambridge professor Aleksandr Kogan which tracked data from another 270,000 users, Cambridge Analytica was able to create a curve on which it could predict the behavior of individual users and their friends, all of whom were unaware of how their data were being exploited. Strategic Company Laboratories (SCL), a parent company of Cambridge Analytica, has also used psychographics to target voters in more than 100 election campaigns in over 30 countries spanning five continents. This once small political consulting firm was originally founded by "a group of renowned academics and a consortium of international investors [who] collaborated to establish the first academic think-tank specialising in the Science of Communication" (Ghoshal, 2018). The fees for its services were in the range of $200,000 to $2 million, according to *The New Yorker*. Located in the Caribbean, the government of the island nation of Saint Kitts and Nevis used SCL's services to delay elections and to promote a seemingly fake "national pride" campaign in order to prolong its power during the late 2000s. This campaign, called the 'It's Working' campaign, aimed at reminding people that, despite the difficulties, they were doing well and were still in power. These forms of political and technological manipulations of voters' emotions leave us with the question of whether psychographics should be, in fact, considered as a weapon to manipulate a large mass of people in political affairs. On this question, *Tools and Weapons* is the very descriptive title of a book that Microsoft president, Brad Smith, has recently published together with his colleague, Carol Anne Browne, to denounce the ethical dangers of the data business. In this book, they urge companies to create responsible technology capable of caring for the future and encourage governments to generate legislative regulations that can keep pace with technological innovation.

"We need a new culture of technology and business development for the age of AI which we call 'rule of law, democracy and human rights by design,'" Nemitz wrote (2018). These core ideas should be baked into AI, because we are entering "a world in which technologies like AI become all pervasive and are actually incorporating and executing the rules according to which we live in large part." To Nemitz, "the absence of such framing for the internet economy has already led to a widespread culture of disregard of the law and put democracy in danger, the Facebook Cambridge Analytica scandal being only the latest wake-up call." For this reason, the European Union's GPDR (General Data Protection Regulation, 2018), and the CCPA (California Consumer Privacy Act effective since January 2020) proposed legislation to collect, process, and protect personal data from individuals. Although the lack of legislation in technology came from the intention to preserve the individual's negative freedom (freedom from the interference of the government), it is more and more evident today how the markets of data and AI need to be regulated. In "A Declaration of the Independence of Cyberspace," John Perry Barlow addressed the governments of the world with the following words:

Where there are real conflicts, where there are wrongs, we will identify them and address them by our means. We are forming our own Social Contract. This governance will arise according to the conditions of our world, not yours. Our world is different. (Retrieved from https://www.eff.org/cyberspace-independence)

To reinforce this message, the Declaration of Independence of Cyberspace states:

Human beings possess a mind, which they are absolutely free to inhabit with no legal constraints. Human civilization is developing its own (collective) mind. All we want is to be free to inhabit it with no legal constraints. Since you make sure we cannot harm you, you have no ethical right to intrude our lives. So stop intruding! (Retrieved from https://www. eff.org/cyberspace-independence)

I believe that such a declaration made sense at the time in which it was conceived. Today, the growing number of scandals shows more and more how harming the absence of a clear policy can be; therefore, an ethical code as well as legislation are needed to protect the users, the new citizens. In line with what was stated in the previous section, Nemitz wrote (2018) that automated decision-making processes must provide meaningful data on the processing of information and the logic with which decisions are made. Companies, designers, producers, and the like must be able to explain how their algorithms do what they do, providing not only the explanation and reasoning behind their actions, but also the motivation. Everything one does through technology must be explained and justified; otherwise, it becomes a dictatorship. Any act we take or factual thing we do must provide reasons that are controllable by judges and explainable to society (see Articles 22, 40, and 5 of GDPR). Despite the idealism behind the freedom from technological legislation, the Internet, this Cartesian space of the mind, has to start being held accountable for its actions in order to guarantee dignity and decency of and for its users.

II.4 Emotionally Engaging

In this section, I will show how emotions have an engaging quality that reveals itself to be very important when a sense of responsibility toward the Other or the environment is needed. In an article on emotions and values in medical decision making, the authors showed in great clarity how criteria for the evaluation of cases and important decision-making processes are not exclusively based on a cognitive approach (as Grisso and Appelbaum, 1995) but also on emotions (as suggested by Charland, 1998; Banner, 2013). While in the cognitive approach, decision-making criteria are based on understanding the situation, appreciating the alternatives that the situation involves (i.e., being able to reason on each implication), and being able to communicate a choice in relation to the given event, the emotional approach challenges these standards with noncognitive factors. These latter "advocate for fuller acknowledgment of emotional factors and values" (2016, 765) because emotions provide crucial information about the situation and exert the affective power of derailing cognitive factors; habitual patterns of the emotional process can, often, influence the way in which individuals perceive intra-individual norms, leading an individual to act out of character due to being overwhelmed or, oppositely, relieved by their own emotions (Freyenhagen and O'Shea, 2013).

Against this account, it is usually believed that emotions spoil the formality of a content-neutral decision and impact negatively the reflective process (Stoljar, 2000; Freyenhagen, 2009). This belief becomes even stronger when the decisions are made within the sphere of professional life. Professional life has to be as free from emotion as possible. Professionalism, in fact, involves a space of agreement in which not the person but the professional operates. An essential component of professionalism is the shared sense of purpose and responsibility. In that regard, the professional is not exactly a human being with their own emotions, goals, and purposes but is the result of an intersubjective agreement that the community can recognize as understandable and acceptable. Gauthier (1986, 68) in *Morals by Agreement* calls this a disposition of "constrained maximization" for which people are more likely to cooperate with those conforming toward a shared set of purposes and an agreed set of principles. Emotions cannot be taken into account in this disposition because they are too unpredictable and fleeting. Rawls' "veil of ignorance" (1971, 397) engineered to guarantee a well-ordered society can serve as a theoretical expedient for a well-ordered professional life, too (Rommes et al., 2015). Hence, as Kouchaki (2015, 379) remarked, "professionals are expected not only to be competent, knowledgeable, objective, highly rational (...) but also to be cool, distant, impersonal, unemotional (...)" As mentioned above, in our professional life, which spans through more than half of our actual life, we are asked to reduce as much as possible the space for our emotions and act as empathetic robots in order to be considered reliable and professional.

Besides the ethical and psychological implications of this problem, which I will examine in my forthcoming *The Role of Bio-Ethics in Emotional Problems* in which Chapters 1 and 2 are dedicated, respectively, to narcissism and anxiety, this approach seems to create a fake world in which not humans but machines interact with each other. While robotic interactions might be acceptable (but not always) in performing repetitive tasks, they become more problematic in delicate human interactions (e.g., in a classroom or at the hospital). If we accept to reduce the space for emotions and deny their values in one's working life, we might encourage a devaluation of the engaging power that emotions have with the environment in which one operates. This might also affect the growth of a schizoid attitude with which one distances one's self from their own place in the world—an attitude that often leads to forgetting the impact that one has on workplace and society. In this beautiful passage, Basaglia, the psychiatrist who contributed to closure of psychiatric institutes in Italy, wrote:

I have asked an English colleague of mine with some shame: "What does an institution mean?" He could not give me an answer. He was very surprised about my lack of conceptual elegance (…) so he replied in a very pragmatic way "an institution is …—looking around—this pointing with his hands around him. We were in the room of an asylum. In that moment I had the realization: the institution at that time was the two of us there, in that place that was the asylum, and so I started to understand that all those speeches that we did at that time were discourses that could make that institution an open or a closed one and that institution was the two of us. If our discourses would encourage an opening that the institution was an open place as well; if our dialogues were closed, then the institution was a closed institution. This is about talking, but then there was also doing; that is, if the institution's staff manage the institution in a mentally and practically closed way, then that institution is a closed-minded one; if it does the opposite it is an open institution."

(Basaglia, 2000)

The place where we work and the product of our work is often seen as something external to us because of the objectivist and reductionist perspective I discussed in the previous chapter. Especially in medical institutions, schools, and social environments, we need to be careful about how much distance we want to put between our personal and professional selves because this distance will affect ourselves, the environment, and the people with whom we interact. Transforming ourselves into emotionless professionals impacts the people with whom we work. That generates a chain of emotionless clients and professionals who operate in a remote environment devoid of nurturing.

To solve this problem, Hollenstein (2018) and colleagues have proposed using design thinking in hospitals. Design thinking is a new way of organizing the professional space and teamwork based on empathetic intersubjective simulations (Farny et al., 2019). Ewald and colleagues show how important emotions are in building teamwork and how they tend to shape the team and its thinking process. Tracking emotional dynamics is important for understanding the team and the way in which it works. The final goal of this method is to understand the emotional tone that underlines the team meeting; this does not mean that design thinking invites an atmosphere in which everyone feels free to vent their own emotional state, but it wants to cultivate a balanced expression of emotions that can enrich the space of each member while being conducive to an integrated way of living in it.

II.4.1 The Case of Pro-Environmental Work in Class

From the point of view of conservative psychology, studying the impact that a more sympathetic ecological thinking can have on our society is key to ensuring a better quality of life.[14] Schultz's and Kaiser's (2012) research on pro-environmental behavior emphasizes how emotions can shape the change of a person's actions in relation to adequate and sustainable care for the environment. Starting with child development, to the promotion of pro-environmental behavior such as water conservation and cooperation over environmental resources, there are studies that focus on the effects that occur at a societal level, through education, in thinking of ourselves as a part of the same organism.[15]

It has been noticed that people partake in pro-environmental (2009, 73) behaviors often for reasons unrelated to the environment (Whitmarsh, 2009). Some recycling behaviors are predicted by concern for the environment (i.e., reusing and reducing), but others (i.e., using a recycling bin) may not be (Barr, 2007). Indeed, a cognitive and unemotional approach to predict an individual's connection to and care for the environment cannot satisfy the goal; it is necessary, in fact, to consider also the positive and negative effects that interventions would produce on an individual's morals, values, social norms, emotions, habits, and other contextual factors (Steg and Vlek, 2009). Other emotionally charged factors may also influence one's behavior toward or against the environment which consists of wanting to follow the pro-environmental examples of others (Sussman and Gifford, 2013), feelings of personal responsibility or guilt (Kaiser and Shimoda, 1999; Kaiser et al., 1999), and intimate individual motivation (Pelletier et al., 1999), especially when it is self-determined motivation (Green-Demers, Pelletier, and Ménard 1997; Seguin et al., 1998; Osbaldiston and Sheldon, 2003).

Emotional, ethical, and axiological dispositions are as important as normative cognitively based dispositions in caring for the environment. For example, Manni et al. (2017) conducted a study on 12-year-old students and how they cared for the environment. During six weeks of thematic group work focusing on environmental and sustainability issues related to food,[16] some students were observed and interviewed in their daily school practice (2016). The scholars wanted to investigate the role of emotions in students' experiences and learning processes as they pertain to environmental and sustainability issues (2016, 451). Wals (2011) argued that if we want environmental and sustainability education to be transdisciplinary, value-laden, and socially transformative, education needs to reconsider the traditional dualistic view that separates cognition from emotion. In support of this, Lundegård (2008) affirmed that one's understanding of the environment passes through one's own values and emotional experiences. I also believe that once we reduce the space between our professional work and the space that this work impacts, we can finally realize that we *are* the environment; only then can real care for the environment begin and inform a holistic sense of life that cannot exclude emotions but rather integrate them as a vehicle to produce meaning in what we do. In fact, in this study, Manni and colleagues (2017) discovered that emotions were the means through which these young students could initiate the elaboration of their experiences and transform them into values (2016, 455). They noticed how powerful and upsetting emotional experiences can increase students' engagement in environmental issues (Nussbaum, 2003; Ojala, 2015). In the above mentioned study conducted by Manni et al. (2016), students spontaneously chose which topic they wanted to focus on based on the emotions that they experienced in connection with certain discussions or activities. For example, one group chose to focus on diabetes because one of the students felt for her friend as she was affected by that disease, or another group decided to talk about sustainable food because they watched a film with a plot about a teenager that tried to convince his whole family to become vegan. At the end of the movie, one upset student stated loudly "Meat is tasty," and another student in support of him continued "Meat rules." This emotional reaction sparked the class discussion about sustainable food. The latter group conducted their IT-based work to understand food according to its property of taste, environmental sustainability, and personal health. The emotional reactions that students had to the film

> resulted in a change in the students' values towards food production, both for their own health and for the sake of the environment. However, the students' opinions on the tastiness and consumption of meat were unchanged. Instead, the meaning-making process increased the value dimensions associated with the question about sustainable food and its production. (2016, 460)

In conclusion, I do believe that emotions play an important role in the development of those core values that can support the growth of a healthy society and environment. Since I believe that education regarding emotions plays an important role for integrating them into our personal and professional lives without becoming their slaves, I will dedicate the rest of this chapter to a short excursus on the philosophical and psychological understanding of emotions.

III. How Do We Know Emotions?

"How do we know emotions?" would be a more productive question than "What are emotions?" as it allows us to assume a subjective point of view toward a psychophysical phenomenon that seems to be regulated by laws of its own. As I will show, emotions seem to be, in fact, the main bridge that connects our human life to the organism of life itself insofar as they translate into bodily sensations and feelings the answers of our body to the environment. Philosophy and psychology are the two main disciplines that focus on the study of emotions; as I will show, their inquiries ran together until the publication of James' work (1845–1910); after that, they took different paths reflecting somehow the dualism introduced by the Galilean scientific revolution and the consequent Cartesian substance dualism. Psychology privileged the bodily aspect of emotions, while philosophy the cognitive one. I hope it will emerge from this short overview that a dialogue between the two is still possible and even more necessary in order to educate ourselves to this essential part of our being.

III.1 A Philosophical Outlook on Emotions

Some psychology textbooks (e.g., Oatley and Jenkins, 1996; Myers, 1998; Gleitman et al., 1999; Niedenthal et al., 2006; Wade and Tavris, 2006; Baumeister and Bushman, 2008) set the beginning of the study of emotions with Darwin. I would consider this timeline inexact. Plato, in fact, was one of the first to reflect on emotions and describe them as a physiological expression of the appetites and desires of the body. Based on the dichotomic opposition of mind and body, he followed Pythagoras' archaic teaching and stated that the body is the *sema*, sepulcher, of the *psyche*, soul;[17] as long as we are trapped in a carnal body, emotions will confuse us and will not allow the pure rationality of our soul to contemplate the truth "because the body confuses the soul and does not allow it to acquire truth and wisdom whenever it is associated with it" (Phaedo, 66b). After having experienced the death of his teacher, Socrates, in his *Republic* and *Phaedrus,* had Plato present a refined description of the human soul which would be of valuable importance for Freud's future theory (Georgiades, 1934; Ricoeur, 1970; Santas, 1955; Bennett, 1973). Plato divided the human soul into three parts—reason, spirit, and appetite—and treated them as three different subjects. Reason was the arbiter between spirit, which pursues knowledge (spirit), and appetite, which needs immediate sensual satisfaction. According to Knuuttila (2004, 8), for Plato the desires that move the sensuous satisfaction are not irrational per se. Emotions are cognitive responses to the awareness of certain needs. Yet, differently from the regulative role of reason, emotions can become irrational when they overstimulate our senses. If that occurs, it would be the sign of an unbalanced soul whose reason failed its regulative job.

Similarly to his teacher Plato, Aristotle also considered the human soul as a tripartite essence organized in rational, sensuous, and vegetative strata. While the rational part is responsible for rational cognition (φρόνησῐς, *phronesis*, meant as reason in practice, a rational guidance for cognition and wisdom), emotions and imagination were considered as attached to the sensuous part of the soul and for this they should have been subjected to the regulation of rationality. In his *Nicomachean Ethics*, Aristotle affirmed that the highest purpose of a human being is eudaimonia (εὐδαιμονία), loosely translated as happiness or human flourishing; that state can be achieved only if there is the teleological obedience of the parts to its whole. Emotions shape every part of human life; they inform ethical, social, and political choices, and humans long for happiness. For a human being to be happy, it means that one's emotions need to obey reason and avoid excesses. The problem is that the passions (πάθος) that move emotional states are conceived in Greek as passive events similar to rain; emotions, too, are seen as physiological events that we happen to passively experience and to even suffer from, as expressed in the word's etymology (πάσχειν, paschein means to suffer).[18] Yet, each emotion involves a minimal level of agency, an ἔργον (ergon), an active reaction that is based on one's beliefs and assessments. This means that even though emotions are passive conditions of our physiology, they involve a reactive movement (κῑνησῖς) hopefully aimed at reaching balance and control. In that sense, emotions are interpreted as a means to transform nature (φύσις), or at least our understanding (λόγος) of it (physiology as φύσις+λόγος), into meaning: what is passively experienced from nature (πάσχειν) is reactively (ἔργον) translated into meanings. Through emotions, one can passively gather information about a given situation and act (hopefully) wisely upon it. If I receive a warm hug in a moment of need, I will feel warm toward the person who hugged me because I interpret that warmth around my body as a sign of affection toward me. In that sense, emotions are the connecting bridge between nature and the meaning that we assign to them. If a person repeatedly treats us well and each time he/she does so we feel good, then we learn that it is a good thing to treat people well. A habitual emotional experience becomes a core value through time. As Oatley (2002, 137–41) remarked:

> Aristotle's notion of habituation: the idea that "it is possible to develop various emotional capacities by engaging in actions which are characteristically associated with particular emotions (…) and, after some time and effort, the emotions themselves may come more naturally" was the map of our values. In that sense, the environment plays an important role in the constitution of our character.

If we live in a good environment, surrounded by good people, we have a better chance to live experiences that will direct our character toward good values and, accordingly, a flourishing happy life. In that sense, for Aristotle, emotions have nothing intentional and to a certain extent we cannot be held responsible for them.[19] Yet, if we consciously contribute to the well-being of the environment through our virtuous habits, we intentionally train our emotions toward positive outcomes.

In his *Metaphysics,* Aristotle wrote:

> "Affection" means: (a) In one sense, a quality in virtue of which alteration is possible, e.g., whiteness and blackness, sweetness and bitterness, heaviness and lightness, etc. (b) The actualizations of these qualities, i.e., the alterations already realized, (c) More particularly, hurtful alterations and motions, and hurts which cause suffering, (d) Extreme cases of misfortune and suffering are called "affections."
>
> *Metaphysics* (1022bbff)

According to this text, "affections" are the lower level of the emotional state where passions develop. The word *affection* comes from Latin *facere* (to do) *ad* (to); literally affection happens to us like a footprint on the sand. We are the sand, and the footprint is the effect of natural events on us. In that sense, an affection always involves an alteration. Using a nonmetaphorical language, the experiences we have, the life we live involves an alteration of our status quo. Etymologically speaking, an emotion is what is moved by (*motus e* from Latin) this event (affection) and is presented to us in the form of a physiological change that we need to interpret. Passive affective qualities do not modify the substance of but only the quality of our experience: feeling warm does not modify the heat of the water but modifies the sense that we have of something warm when we touch it (Aristotle, categories, 9a36–9ba). The change does not arise in the natural substance to which the natural element belongs but in us; for this reason, our lifestyle (δίαιτα) is considered a disposition (διάθεσις), that is, a passive affective quality. Our character is the sum of the changes produced by affections and emotions, that is, the molding of organic matter on our specific nature. A person who has grown up in a green and peaceful setting would be more likely to become an adult respectful of the environment as opposed to someone who has been exposed to violence at a young age who might have acquired a natural susceptibility to the pathos of violence, and he/she might be more easily inclined to it when experiencing the same pathos. A pathos is not a permanent quality and is susceptible to change, though it takes an active effort, ἔργον (Categories, 9b20, 10a–11). A person who grew up in a violent environment can change his/her disposition toward that violent pathos into something more loving, similarly to how a person who has been sunburnt can protect his/her skin from the sun with a soothing cream. The natural event does not permanently inform who we are even when the event is particularly traumatic, yet it generates a disposition that we can decide to accept or change. In fact, transforming the passivity of that event (from Latin, *e-venire* something that befalls us) into an active positive meaning requires active efforts. Hence, a pathos is not necessarily a misfortune, but it is an observable change of the natural behavioral pattern. Nature has, in fact, a recursive structure that continuously affects itself (animals, humans, plants) in an observable and measurable way. The pathos of a certain emotion can be seen as the bodily way in which nature thinks of or speaks to itself. If we want to understand nature, we need to understand emotions as they are the key to accessing an important aspect of nature's language. Emotions are the way in which the intersubjective and interaffective character of nature reveals itself through variations. The agent (nature as a whole-part structure) and the patient (natureas a part-whole structure) communicate to each other through the movement (e-motion) generated (κίνησις) by the affection.[20] This correlation, though, according to Aristotle does not need to be immediate. "The human being who grieves us 'touches' us, but we do not necessarily thereby touch him, and the poet's tragedies affect us without our affecting him or them" (De Generatione et Corruptione, 323a28–34).

In Stoicism, too, the reflection on emotions was a central component for achieving happiness and understanding the human relationship to nature. According to Gill (2017, 143–165), early Stoics considered emotions as a way to relate to the world. Zeno of Citium, for example, considered emotions as an inaccurate knowledge of reality; even more radically, Chrysippus defined emotions as disturbances of the soul, and he thought we should eliminate them in order to achieve happiness (see also, Nussbaum, 1994, 390–401; Price, 1995, 167–170). In Stoic language, happiness[21] can be achieved through α-πάθεια (a-patheia), the absence of these irrational movements that disturb the placidity of (our) nature. If we live free from these disturbances and according to nature, then we would reach calm and stable serenity free from desires, fears, or anxiety. Yet, what is Nature for the Stoics?

Living in agreement with nature comes to be the end, which is in accordance with the nature of oneself and that of the whole, engaging in no activity wont to be forbidden by the universal law, which is the right reason pervading everything, and identical to Zeus, who is the director of the administration of existing things (Diogenes Laertius, 7: 88).

Stoics see Nature as a universal reason; being in harmony and at home with this reason is what gives human beings a solid rational ground on which to gain trust and calmness toward life. For example, Cicero stressed how the development of emotional patterns begins during the first contacts with the environment, long before the child grasps propositional judgments (Nussbaum, 1994, 389–390). So, although emotions are cognitively based, they are first informed by our contact with nature. Living according to nature for Stoics meant living according to the sequence of the events, accepting the lawfulness of the whole, and recognizing being part of this intelligent whole. Desires arise when this acceptance is not complete and we want more. To be happy, we need to learn how to be nature, that is, resisting the qualitative changes Aristotle described by not letting the irrational movements affect us. Oikeiosis (οἰκείωσις), which means to be at home, is the key value conducive to a happy life because it means to familiarize with our nature and our destiny and accept it as a superior intelligence. In that sense, thinking ecologically is a redundant expression; becoming familiar with our οἶκος (home) means to learn how to connect with each other as an organism aware of its constitution. Being respectful and accepting of this interconnection is the key to happiness. Thus, Stoic *apatheia* does not encourage us to disregard emotions but to eliminate the irrational ones so that we can reach more easily our inner solid equilibrium.[22]

During the Middle Ages, we find important theories of emotions being discussed by a relevant line of thinkers such as Avicenna, Albertus Magnus, Duns Scotus, Bonaventure, and William of Ockham (Knuuttila, 2004), but it is with Augustine and Thomas d'Aquinas that the dichotomy between mind and body, rationality and passions, God and Nature becomes stronger. While Stoicism proposed a rationalist psychology according to which emotions are mistaken value judgments, in the Middle Ages it was more common to adopt a Platonic and Aristotelian view on the argument. Augustine reintroduced the Platonic distinction between rationality (the symbol of the spirit) and the passions of the body which were to be condemned because they prevented the spirit from reaching eternal peace. This way of interpreting emotions was the general prevailing voice before the Franciscans introduced the idea of passions as the intellectual faculty of the will to connect spirit and body (Knuuttila, 2004); that is, the soul can be moved by bodily will exerted from control of emotions.[23] Similarly to this, in *The City of God*, Augustine proposed an interpretation according to which emotions are irrational movements of the soul driven by the bodily part of our being and the dominating part of the soul should impose laws on them. Similarly to the Franciscan point of view, for Augustine, there is a certain intentionality at the basis of human emotions. He often calls them, in fact, "voluntates" (acts of will),[24] here for example he wrote:

> For what is appetite or joy but will (voluntas) which consents to what we will (volumus)? And what is fear or distress but will which dissents from what we do not will (nolumus)? When this consent to what we will takes the form of pursuit, it is appetite, and when it takes the form of enjoyment of what we will, it is joy. In the same way, when we dissent from something that we do not want to happen, that will is fear, but when we dissent from something which happens and we do not want it to happen, that will is distress.
>
> (*City of God* 14.6)

An emotion is that to which we give our consent. Joy, fear, and distress are all *voluntates* (i.e., appetites that we decide to accept or refuse according to the circumstances). For him, all schools—Platonic, Aristotelian, and Stoic—seemed to arrive at the same conclusion that even though emotions bring a certain evaluative suggestion, they should be kept under control of the higher soul (*City of God* 9.4; 14.19):

> For what does it matter whether things are more properly called "goods" or "advantageous," when a Stoic and a Peripatetic alike get the jitters and grow pale at the thought of losing them? They do not call them by the same names, but put the same value on them.
>
> (*City of God* 9.4)

Emotions, which he called perturbations or sometimes more neutrally *affectiones* or passiones, are similar in animals and human beings, but, differently from animals, human beings have a higher soul which has the power of intellect (*intellectus*) and will (*voluntas*) (*City of God*, 5.11). Once again, according to Augustine, what makes a human being human is its being different from nature, more precisely its being higher than nature. Human beings are better than animals when they exert their emotions according to a *voluntas* inspired by divine reason. Stoic divine rationality which served to show human beings their interconnectedness to the whole of Nature becomes now an ontological principle, a higher force to which our flesh is subjected. Our nature is good insofar as we control it through our will as it expresses itself through those perturbations and desires that often prevent us from being good human beings.

Thomas Aquinas seemed to reach the same conclusions, although, having been influenced by his master Albertus Magnus, he followed a different trajectory. The *Summa Theologiae* is the most extensive treatise on emotions we have from the Middle Ages (II-1.22–48). Being strongly influenced by Aristotle, Thomas Aquinas connected emotions to the appetitive part of our soul and described them as sensitive motive powers caused by external changes and expressed by the evaluations of the soul's cogitative component. The cogitative or rational part of the soul elaborates judgments about these changes and connects them to specific value judgments of the intellect. This theory would explain Augustine's voluntarism because the cognitive part of the soul, the intellect, has the "willing" quality to control the appetitive and concupiscible part by evaluative judgments. Similarly to his predecessors, Thomas Aquinas also considered *passiones animi* (passions of the soul) a quality in common between humans and animals (II-1.22–48). As he wrote:

> It should be noted that there is no difference as regards sensible forms between human beings and other animals, for they are similarly transmuted by exterior sense objects. But there is a difference as regards the aforementioned intentions, for other animals perceive intentions of this sort only by a kind of natural instinct, whereas human beings do so through a kind of consideration. And so the power that is called the natural estimative in other animals is called the cogitative (*cogitativa*) in human beings. It discloses intentions of this sort through a kind of consideration. Accordingly, it is also called particular reason (ratio particularis). Physicians assign a determinate organ for this, namely, the middle part of the head, for it considers individual intentions just as intellective reason considers universal intentions.
>
> (ST I.78.4)

According to this passage, humans and animals are equally guided by appetitive functions (both need to eat, sleep, and fornicate at times), but while animals are guided by instincts, humans are guided by a cognitive intention. That is, a *ratio particularis* (particular reason) that allows them to estimate the consequences of their affections. This cognitive function has the power to guide human beings toward their well-being. As Peter King notices:

> Aquinas's theory of the emotions (*passiones animae*) is cognitivist, somatic, and taxonomical: cognitivist because he holds that cognition is essential to emotion; somatic because he holds that their physiological manifestations are partially constitutive of emotions; taxonomical because he holds that emotions fall into distinct natural kinds which are hierarchically ordered.
>
> *(King, 1999)*

In medieval philosophy, the study of emotions often took into consideration internal spiritual experiences as they were interpreted through the lens of Christianity, while modern philosophy produced theories on emotions that connected several areas of philosophy, such as epistemology, ethics, and axiology. A rich list of philosophers—Descartes, Pascal, Hobbes, Spinoza, Shaftesbury, Hutcheson, Hume, and Kant—questioned the role that emotions played in our knowledge, in the decisions we make, and the system of values we construct to guide our lives (Deonna and Teroni, 2012).

In order to show how disregarding our emotions has affected modern life, I will focus on only a few of these thinkers. To begin with, Descartes and Spinoza held a cognitivist and rationalist view about emotions although in different ways. Descartes gave equal importance both to the embodied and cognitive aspects of emotions. He maintained that emotions were bodily appearances connected to the soul. Although emotions reside in the brain, they arise as affections caused by movements of our lower spirit which, as it was in the previous theories, make humans similar to animals (*spiritus animales*). Anticipating modern neuro-physiological theories, Descartes believed that these affections were generated in the brain but traveled throughout the body by nerves: "the perceptions, sensations, or commotions of the soul which we relate particularly to the soul and are caused, maintained, and strengthened by some movement of the spirits" (Descartes, 1984, 328). While passions arise because of a bodily movement, what makes this movement a human emotion is our awareness of the movement and the interpretation we give it. For this reason, Descartes held the idea that passions are perceptions, that is, a mental state based on human cognition. It is difficult to place their origin in one specific of the two poles of his dualism, *res cogitans* and *res extensa*: scholars, such as Prinz (2004), considered emotions as belonging to the brain, the res cogitans, while Harre' (2002, 68) stated that: "Descartes has attempted to create a hybrid psychology, giving space both to immaterial and to material aspects of the 'mechanism' of cognition and emotion." According to Harre's interpretation, it seems that despite Descartes being the father of the dualism responsible for separating the body from the spirit, nature from life, and being from meaning, he sought, in fact, to find a way to explain the degrees of separation between the two poles. From this perspective, Descartes' theory of passions presented a much less dichotomic distinction between spirit and body because his intention would be to prove that the human body was a fully functional machine and emotions were not a shortcoming but another functional tool belonging to this complex human machine. His focus, in fact, was still framed within a theodicy aimed at proving the goodness of God who has granted us a body well equipped to survive. Accordingly, emotions are not defects of the spirit but have the functional role to prepare the body for actions: fight if threatened, run if scared, hug if in love, and so on. Descartes presented emotions as having "a mixed ontological status that cannot be referred either to the mind alone or to the body alone" (*Principles*, AT VIII 23, CSM I 209, see also

Brown and Schäfer, 1888; Hoffman, 1990). For Descartes, there are mainly six emotions (wonder, love, hatred, desire, joy, and sadness) that, combining with each other, generate good and bad actions whose positive and negative value is based on the benefit they had for the functioning of the body. In his *Meditations on First Philosophy* (1641) (and the corresponding sections of the 1644 *Principles of Philosophy*), the goal of his theory was to prove the goodness of a God that equipped us with sufficient means to cope with the outside world. It was Descartes, one of the first after Galen[25] and Hippocrates (460 B.C.E. 470 B.C.E.), who emphasized the connection between bodily health and emotional well-being. That was the topic of the epistolary exchange between Descartes and Princess Elisabeth of Bohemia between 1643 and 1645. Their exchange began when, on May 6, 1643 (AT III 660, Shapiro, 2007, 61–62), Elisabeth questioned Descartes' dichotomic system and asked how it was possible that two different substances (res) such as the body (extensa) and mind (cogitans) could influence each other. To Elisabeth, Descartes replied by showing us that they actually form a unit and when negative emotions prevail negative health follows. Elisabeth was suffering from "low grade fever" which he considered as being caused by melancholy and sadness for which he recommended the Stoic cure of mastery of the mind over the body and trust in the rationality of the cosmos by reading Seneca (Descartes to Elisabeth, September 1, 1645, AT IV 281-2, modified from CSMK 262). Yet, Elisabeth was still not convinced and, as a usual fierce interlocutor of Descartes, objected to this and asked if there was a way to tend to emotions without the power of our will and to achieve involuntary happiness. This question was pivotal for many modern theorists of emotions, Spinoza included, who seemed to hold a position closer to Elisabeth's than to Descartes'. According to Spinoza, emotions belong completely to mental states and he criticized Descartes' theory for being inexact and of no use to the science of affections:

> I know, of course, that the famous Descartes, although he too believed that the mind has absolute power over its own actions, nevertheless sought to explain human affects through their first causes, while also showing how a mind can have absolute dominion over its affects. But in my opinion, he showed nothing but the cleverness of his intellect, as I shall show in the proper place.
>
> *(Spinoza, 2001, Preface to Part III)*

Spinoza rejected Descartes' dualism according to which the body and the soul belong to two different substances. He dismissed the role that Descartes had attributed to the pineal gland because it was anatomically incorrect and non-explanatory of the supposedly connecting function between *res cogitans* and *res extensa*. Spinoza maintained that it was impossible for human beings to gain control over their emotions and be autonomous from them because they *are* our emotions. In fact, for Spinoza, there is only one living nature called Substance or God to which both body and soul belong. This substance is full of movements (accidentes); there is no movement that happens to the body that does not happen to the mind as well. The mind shapes the body as much as the body shapes the mind (Spinoza, 2001, 217). "On the other hand, the ideas in the mind can double up on each other, something that bodies cannot do" (2014, 217). For Spinoza, emotions were affections which meant forces generating movement in the body (in that sense similar to Aristotle's theory).

By "affect," I understand states of a body by which its power of acting is increased or lessened, helped or hindered, and also the ideas of these states. Thus, if we can be the adequate cause of any of these states, the effect in question is what I call an "action;" otherwise, it is a "passion" (2014, III, 3).

Consequently, we exert control over our emotions only to the extent of its affects because some of them arise passively, like the previously mentioned footprint in the sand. Active affections trigger subjective decisions to act in a wide variety of ways: "Different human beings can be affected differently by one object; and one person can be affected differently at different times by one object" (2014, III, 51, 70). In the realm of affections, there were no simple and easy mechanisms to predict effects or reactions.[26] Differently from some of his predecessors, Spinoza did not encourage any form of objectification or subjection of humans to nature (and vice versa) by adducing the cause of a higher rationality (as in Stoicism),[27] or a pineal gland (as in Descartes), or the Idea (as in Plato). Spinoza proposed a system of parts and whole in which each part is at the same time the whole and vice versa. We are the environment and the environment is us—something close to what is today called entangled humanism (Ignatov et al., 2019); emotions are the cognitive way with which we become aware of our participation to the whole as a part and as a whole. The human mind is its affects and the more these affections become active the more the human mind can become aware of being a whole and accordingly being a power to act (*conatus*). Bodies (humans, mineral, vegetal, etc.) are continuous with and dependent on other organisms in everything similar to them. The human body can individuate itself because in this net whenever it transforms passive affects into active ones, meaning through awareness is produced. In this transformation lies the subjective identity of the human being in respect to the whole, nature, the universe: the human being is aware of being interconnected to the whole. The active affections contribute to keep the identity of the individual within what he called a "systems-environment boundary." From this point of view, Spinoza talked about all humans as an interconnected body that on the one hand sought to preserve its own boundaries and on the other acquired the knowledge of being the whole and found its physical ground in the whole as a sole organism (2014, Part V).

As we can see with Spinoza, the study of emotions starts intersecting more and more with the psychological study of identity. It is with Hume, and later on with James, that the official encounter between psychological and philosophical studies of emotions would take place.

Hume's studies of emotions were a part of his investigations of human nature. Although his theory of emotions has been judged as "a complete muddle" and has been "thoroughly discredited" (Alston, 1968; Solomon, 2008), I believe analyzing it helps to prepare our discussion of the relationship between philosophy and psychology on the problem of emotions and health sciences. According to his critics, in identifying emotions with feelings, Hume failed to see the cognitive component of emotions. As we will see during the description of his argumentative strategy, it seems that was exactly the point of his argument, reducing the space that cognitive reason holds in every form of knowledge; since his radical approach directly attacked the limits of reason, it is not through logical consistency that his theory can be judged. In his work, Hume explained knowledge as the combination of impressions and ideas. He wrote, "impressions and ideas are 'like players' in a theater who successively make their appearance, pass, repass, glide away, and mingle in an infinite variety of postures and situations" (2000, 253). Emotions are for Hume "reflective impressions" that include unlocalized feelings of pleasure and pain (2000, 2.1.1.1, T 1.1.2.1; SBN 275, 7–8), and he often used the two terms, "reflective impressions"[28] and "emotions," interchangeably (2000, 2.1.5.4, T 2.1.9.5, T 2.2.9.20; SBN 286, 305, 380).[29] Reflective impressions are forms of perceptions that distinguished themselves from sensations because they are less vivid; while sensual or reflexive perceptions are without any previous perceptions, reflective impressions are byproducts of the former ones:

> Original impressions or impressions of sensation are such as without any antecedent perception arise in the soul from the constitution of the body, from the animal spirits, or from the application of objects to the external organs. Secondary, or reflective impressions are such as proceed from some of these original ones, either immediately or by the interposition of its idea. (2000, 275)

What we feel generates, according to Hume, a gentle and violent movement. The gentle movement produces beauty and ugliness in actions, external objects, and art; the violence creates love, hate, sadness, joy, pride, and humility. This is where some of Hume's detractors raise their objections; Hume, in fact, equated feelings to emotions and failed to see the cognitive component (and hence the intentionality) involved in emotions (Solomon, 1984), except, I would add, for indirect feelings. In fact, Hume explained experiences of pleasure and pain as originating from direct feelings; such feelings as hunger, thirst, desire, disgust, sadness, hope, fear, and despair are all considered direct feelings. Indirect feelings, instead, are generated by a composition of impressions and ideas. In this group, we can find feelings like pride, humility, ambition, vanity, love, hate, jealousy, mercy, malice, nobility, and others connected to those. Hume wrote: "Reason is, and ought only to be the slave of the passions, and can never pretend to any other office than to serve and obey them" (2000, 38, 415).

Differently from rationalism, Hume focused his theory on subjective experience. Accordingly, for him, it was not our reason that sets goals and controls our action through will, but instead emotions and desires that are the driving force of human nature. Since reason is only a formal power that can organize the chaotic material provided by impressions, reason is only a slave to impressions. "Impulse arises not from reason, but is only directed by it ... nothing can oppose or retard the impulse of passion, but a contrary impulse" (2000, 413). Hume's theory prepared us for an experimental view of science whose foundations are always open to questioning and in which feelings and emotions represent the main drive and the strongest bias. As Shouse nicely put it, Hume's skepticism told us that "we cannot prove through reason." But with it he also said that "since we cannot know, cannot prove in the strict sense, we must believe" (Shouse, 1952, 514). Nature brings itself to knowledge through life and our will to believe is the starting point to moving us forward.[30]

According to Hume's theory, feelings are the actual driver of human life and knowledge, they are the limits that constrain our science and the strength that accompanies each step of our quest.

> It seems then that Nature has pointed out a mixed kind of life as most suitable to the human race, ... Indulge your passions for science, says she, but let your science be human, and such as may have a direct reference to action and society.... Be a philosopher, but, amidst all of your philosophy, be still a human being.
>
> *(Hume, 1777)*

His work paved the way for a fruitful dialogue between philosophy and psychology. Written by philosopher and psychologist William James, the book Will *to* Believe (1896), which discussed skepticism and the idea of accepting beliefs without evidence, would be the point where psychological and philosophical theories of emotions converged under the sign of a radical empiricism. In the *Spirit of William James* (1938), Perry even wrote that "James's empirical forerunners of the British school were not good enough empiricists to suit James" (85). In the ninth chapter of the *Principles of Psychology* (1890), James attacked Hume's empiricism because he considered the three suppositions untenable. According to Hume, "sensations came to us pure and single" (1950, Vol. 1, 233), at different times in our minds while we are experiencing life, and that the ever-changing flow of thought in our minds was due to the combination of these simple sensations and their corresponding ideas. According to James, sensory experience appears to us as "sensibly continuous" like a stream (1950, 1, 237); it is impossible to distinguish its unit as much as the drops of a river make the river itself. Moreover, knowledge cannot come from the combination of these sensible units because this stream is Heraclitean. It is physiologically impossible (1950, 1, 232–233) that the same occurrence happens twice; accordingly, human thought cannot be described according to elementary units of impressions and ideas. Our habit of identifying a similar sound, taste, or sight led us to think that our sensory experience is the same; the fact is that the object of our physiological experience is the same, but the nature of our physiological reaction to it is not so. The same type of food can taste different for us in different ways each time we eat it and so will the emotions we feel when we listen to the same sonata.

"The trouble with the emotions in psychology," he wrote,

> is that they are regarded too much as absolutely individual things. So long as they are set down as so many eternal and sacred psychic entities, like the old immutable species in natural history, so long all that can be done with them is reverently to catalogue their separate characters, points, and effects. (1950, 2, 449)

In order to overcome this problem, James stressed the attention on the physiological component of the emotion, or, better yet, on the feeling that triggered it. For James, in fact, emotions generate from feelings that stem from physiological and neurological changes. These changes can occur when relevant information is perceived. Aristotle's theory of emotion as a material change recurred in James' theory again but with a more solid physiological knowledge of the human body. As James put it, "My theory … is that the bodily changes follow directly the perception of the exciting fact, and that our feeling of the same changes as they occur is the emotion" (1950, 2, 449). The emotion does not cause the behavior; rather, such behavior might induce the bodily changes that are at the basis of a given emotion. Emotions, according to James (1997, 21), result from bodily changes without themselves causing any action.

> "The trouble with the emotions in psychology," he wrote, is that they are regarded too much as absolutely individual things. So long as they are set down as so many eternal and sacred psychic entities, like the old immutable species in natural history, so long all that can be done with them is reverently to catalogue their separate characters, points, and effects. (1950, vol. 2, 449)

According to James, identifying each type of emotion as an isolated fixed unit is a mistake because it misses the flow of interconnected changes that emotions are in fact registering from the outside environment. Accordingly, emotions can be defined as those feelings emerging from the effects that the environment exerts on us. Feeling the bodily feeling is the emotion which generates the physiological change that we can observe through behaviors. Understanding that the bodily feeling is the cause of a certain physiological change leads to seeing behaviors as a way to psychological analyses of emotions. Until then, the empiricist tradition considered the physiological change as the trigger of an emotional state, but as James put it:

> If we fancy some strong emotion, and then try to abstract from our consciousness of it all the feelings of its characteristic bodily symptoms, we find we have nothing left behind, no "mind-stuff" out of which the emotion can be constituted, and that a cold and neutral state of intellectual perception is all that remains. ... What kind of an emotion of fear would be left, if the feelings neither of quickened heart-beats nor of shallow breathing, neither of trembling lips nor of weakened limbs, neither of goose-flesh nor of visceral stirrings, were present, it is quite impossible to think. Can one fancy the state of rage and picture no ebullition of it in the chest, no flushing of the face, no dilatation of the nostrils, no clenching of the teeth, no impulse to vigorous action, but in their stead limp muscles, calm breathing, and a placid face? The present writer, for one, certainly cannot. The rage is as completely evaporated as the sensation of its so-called manifestations.
>
> *(James, 1997, 173–174)*

III.2 Transition to a Psychology of Emotions

It was with the development of psychological studies on emotions that the connection between emotions and environment became more and more evident. The physician Carl Lange arrived at a similar theory through an independent path (1885) and made James' theory more applicable to real life examples; similarly to James, he explained emotions through this sequence of events: Emotion Stimulus → Physiological Response Pattern → Affective Experience[31]

Emotions are a recognizable physiological response to a certain external stimulus. They express themselves into a form of experience rather than into a visible single-emotion event. The James-Lange model was later questioned by Cannon (1927). He argued that the body cannot be the sole cause of emotions since some of the visceral changes are too difficult or ambiguous to feel and they can occur in both emotional and nonemotional states. The body as the entire environment is responsible for the arousal of emotions. This understanding pushed psychology and philosophy to map with more exactness the physiology of emotions in response to the connection with the environment in order to see if there was actually a part of the brain from which emotional states stem and can be explained.[32] Papez (1937) and later MacLean (1949) presented an actual physiological model that would explain how the limbic system,[33] a group of interconnected cortical and subcortical structures dedicated to linking visceral states and emotion to cognition and behavior (Mesulam, 2012), works in relation to perception and emotions.

The word *limbic* was first used by Broca (1824–1888) to name the area close to the pineal gland situated at the limb or edge of other structures that seemed to be responsible for the functioning of our emotional intelligence; it is here that we locate our emotional brain. Giving reason both to James-Lange and Cannon, Papez[34] understood that "emotion may arise in two ways: as a result of psychic activity and as a consequence of hypothalamic activity."[35] The limbic system can be defined as "a complex arrangement of transitional structures situated between a visceral 'primitive' subcortical brain and a more evolved cortical one"[36] (Yakovlev, 1948; MacLean, 1952). The anatomy of the limbic system, as we know it today, is very close to the model presented by MacLean.

The physiological and neurological information gathered by these studies allowed the flourishing of a systematic study of emotions. In her *Emotion and Personality* (1960), Arnold presented emotions as states that are not only triggered by objects in a reflexive or habitual way but also as meaningful interpretations of the effects that the environment exerts upon us.[37] This theory is important because it raised the problem of the intentionality of emotions from both a physiological and epistemological point of view, which I will discuss in length in the next chapter. Emotions are in fact states that *refer to* the environment as it presents itself through objects or mundane situations, and it is its interpretation that makes an emotion the kind of emotion that it is for us. As Frijda (1986, 1988) noticed, following the appraisal model, there are laws of situational meaning that explain emotions as results of particular meanings. "Input some event with its particular meaning; out comes an emotion of a particular kind" (Frijda, 1988,

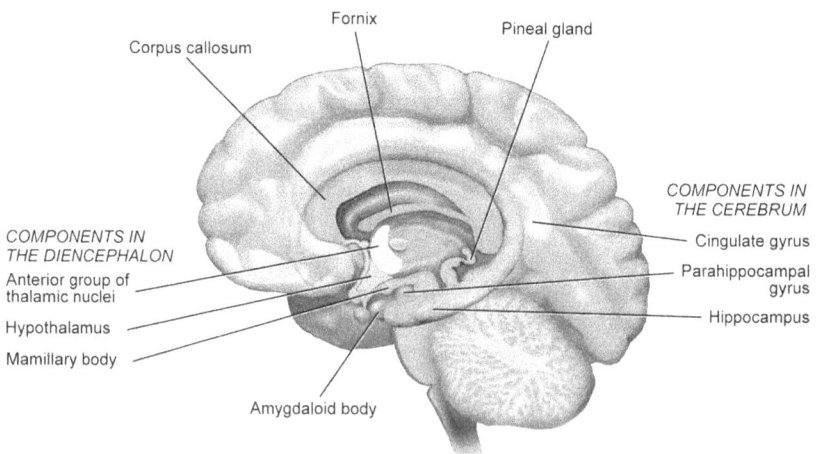

The Limbic System

FIGURE 2.1   Blausen.com staff (2014). "Medical gallery of Blausen Medical 2014." *WikiJournal of* Medicine 1(2). doi:10.15347/wjm/2014.010. ISSN 2002-4436.

349). According to this model, including Arnold's, when we praise something a special cognitive mechanism associated to the given emotion is triggered, such as a readiness to perform a particular diagnostic action, for example, to strike out in fear (Dewey, 1985). Emotions are assumed to be appraisals not immediately available to conscious awareness.

Arnold's work was followed by an appraisal approach method which led to the construction of basic emotion models that boosted the recognition of the basic patterns of emotions.[38] For instance, Tomkins' *Affect, Imagery, Consciousness* (1962, 1963) explained emotions as triggered by objects and events in the world. According to this model, emotions triggered by the environment produce similar instances that share something biological in common with the environment; they are biologically analogous and/or homologous in the sense that they look like each other and share similar origin. For example, the emotion of pleasure shows the same bodily pattern (bodily activation, facial actions, experience) that is activated in the feeling of pleasure so that every time this emotion arises in different parts of the world it is easy to recognize it as always the same and humans can understand each other on that basis. This seems to go against James' intuition of the fluidity of emotions because, in a way, it is possible to indicate emotions in their individuality.[39] Biologically, emotions originate from instincts; in modern approaches, it is believed that neural programs or circuits are hardwired into the brain at birth according to specific sources of emotions.

Although a few basic emotion models place the experience of emotion at the heart of an emotional episode which is interpreted within the limits of its evolutionary context (e.g., Panksepp, 1998), other models consider the individual emotion as the trigger of a specific experience as the emotion itself is bearer of its own psychophysiological pattern. According to Panksepp, in fact, every emotion can be distinguished into three levels according to the biological structures of the brain in which it arises.[40] Panksepp focused more on this first level, the raw emotional experience, while the second and third levels are composed of memory mechanisms and learning and all the cognitive complexities of reasoning.

For example, we can connect the first level, which relates to the immobilizing terror we might experience after a car crash, to the secondary level, which refers to the memory of signs, places, and smells of the crash, and to the tertiary level, which represents the moment in which we discuss and describe the accident. These three levels represent three different systems of reaction to stimuli through which we can learn how to activate our being in relation to the stimuli found in the environment. The more stimuli these systems can recognize at the same time, the more intelligent that system becomes. This answer is not necessarily immediate or fixed; it can vary in time and according to the relationship between the subject and its environment. There are, for example, models that argue that it is possible to induce the emotion by assuming a certain posture; if you smile, for instance, you would have a higher chance to induce a positive emotional experience (Tomkins 1962, 1963; Strack et al., 1988; Niedenthal, 2007), but this changes according to the subject and their lived experience.

The Schachter and Singer (1962) model developed the two main cognitive and physiological components on which psychological and philosophical studies of emotions seem to be based. This two-layered model explained emotions as cognitive interpretations of a general unexplained arousal. Hence, each emotion is explained as having a cognitive appraisal character (e.g., Myers, 1998; Niedenthal et al., 2006; Wade and Tavris, 2006) and, as in James' intuition, a neuro-physiological aspect, as well (e.g., Cornelius, 1996; Gleitman et al., 1999; Mandler, 2003; Kappas, 2011). This opposed the psychoanalytic models that argued how emotions stem solely from repressed instinctual drives as they cannot be expressed (e.g., Freud, 1920) or fail to interact with the external world (e.g., Lazarus, 1966). In this case, emotions are tightly related to society and the way in which society imposes itself on the biological body. This view opens the doors to a social constructionist approach to emotions (e.g., Dewey, 1894, 1895; Mead, 1895) that see them as a neuro-functional answer to the environment (Averill published his landmark article in 1980) whose essence can be explained as a layered construction of the responses between social environment and individual.

III.3 A Short Reflection

What makes bioethics compelling is the participation of emotions in the decisions we make about each other and the environment in which we live. "It is these people and their problems, and the often conflicting wishes of the people who love and care for them, that capture students' imagination and make bioethics such a compelling field of study" (Davis, 1997, 240). This account of the philosophical and psychological studies of emotions as well as the analysis of cases related to emotions prove how difficult it is to separate individual, intersubjective, and environmental life from the way in which we feel about it. For this reason, it is important to study emotions, educate people to understand emotions, and train people on how to best live with them.

Conclusion

In this chapter, I have presented four reasons why emotions are important in bioethics; I can reiterate these four points with the following titles:

1. Unhealthy people generate an unhealthy environment.
2. We need to care if we want to receive good care. Empty empathy might be harmful.
3. We need emotionally intelligent AI to avoid corrupting in new ways our daily lives.
4. Emotions are engaging and make us human.

In the second part of the chapter, I discussed the philosophical and psychological sources that led to a disparaging attitude toward emotions. Emotions, in fact, were often read as that biological component of our body that clouded our reasoning from functioning correctly. It was interesting to see how two recurrent themes of the theory of emotions emerged both in philosophy and psychology: on the one hand, emotions are considered as the language that nature uses to speak to us; on the other, there has always been the strong belief that we need to control emotions in order to be fully human. What makes us better than animals, and accordingly above nature, is our will to say No to certain emotions. Yet, given the knowledge we have today about the limbic system and the understanding of its interaction with the environment, we have no reason to encourage an inhuman split between reason and emotions since emotions are reasons as well. Negating that system means negating our right to be.

Notes

1 Here is a map with "the latest estimates of mental health disorder prevalence, disease burden rates, and mortality impacts across a number of disorders." Retrieved from https://ourworldindata.org/mental-health.

2 Costello, E. J., Egger, H., and Angold, A. (2005). "10-year research update review: the epidemiology of child and adolescent psychiatric disorders: I. Methods and public health burden." *Journal of the American Academy of Child and Adolescent Psychiatry*, 44: 972–986; Fletcher (2008). "Adolescent depression and educational attainment: results using sibling fixed effects," *Health Econonocs*, 17: 1215–1235; Thapar Collishaw Potter and Thapar (2012). "Depression in adolescence," *Seminar,* 379(9820): 1056–1067. Costing US \$1 trillion annually on global economy. Yet interventions to foster one's emotional well-being are mostly post-hoc rather than preventive ones, and decisions are often left to the private competence and wealth of individuals and families.

3 Campos Mumme Kermoian and Campos (1994). "A functionalist perspective on the nature of emotion," *Monographs of the Society for Research in Child Development,* 59(2/3): 284–303. Studies proved that investing in treatment for anxiety and depression leads to a fourfold return (Brunier, A. "Investing in treatment for depression and anxiety leads to a fourfold return," WHO. Retrieved from http://www.who.int/en/news-room/detail/13-04-2016-investing-in-treatment-for-depression-and-anxiety-leads-to-a-fourfold-return).

4 According to Cairns' guide (1973), Husserl's use of *Gemüt* points to the wide domain of human emotional life. More precisely, it indicates the sphere of emotion and volition, including feelings, affections, desires, and sentiments. Hereafter, I will use the word *Gemüt* in this latter sense. In addition, in Hua XLII, 241, Husserl writes about *Gemüts-* and *Willens-Sinn* in order to indicate the essential "meaning" or "sense" proper to this sphere. Us, we should not conflate *Gemüt* with feelings, as feelings might indicate any personal way of feeling in that sense. The same can be said in logic. Husserl proved in his discussion of Frege's terminology in *Logical Investigations* (LI I, §15) that the *Sinn* expressed by *Bedeutung* is not the same as *Gedanken* (thoughts). Meaning in the sense of giving a meaning to something (*Sinnsgebung*) is not the same as expressing a thought that can be grasped by many people. In both cases, what we want to avoid is to conflate personal affective or linguistic meaning with the essential one. Depending upon context, I will sometimes follow Hart's translation of *Gemüt* as "heart."

5 Retrieved from https://hms.harvard.edu/magazine/mental-health/safety-net.

6 On this point, one can also read: Rotenstein et al. (2016).

7 I do support those who define empathy as a disposition. Whether you refer to affective, cognitive, or somatic empathy its definition as an emotion, feeling, or bodily disposition would change. For more on the definition of *empathy* and its variation according to its affective, cultural, and cognitive implications in culture, see Atkins, D. (2014). *The Role of Culture in Empathy: The Consequences and Explanations of Cultural Differences in Empathy at the Affective and Cognitive Levels.*

8 More on this point can be found in Mehrabian and Epstein (1972); Layton (1979); LaMonica, Carew, Winder, Haase, and Blanchard (1976); Englander (2014).

9 Retrieved from https://www.ourbodiesourselves.org/stories/bad-news/

10 Our bodies, our selves project retrieved from https://www.ourbodiesourselves.org/book-excerpts/health-article/pregnancy-after-infertility-or-previous-pregnancy-loss.

11 Retrieved from https://www.ourbodiesourselves.org/book-excerpts/health-article/pregnancy-after-infertility-or-previous-pregnancy-loss.

12 Here is an example of data collected in relation to the coming back. None of them includes the emotional component of the coming back: *Discharge destination.* Discharge destination is the location where the patient is residing immediately post-hospital discharge and can include home, other hospital, rehabilitation facility, other supported residential facility (including retirement villages, supported residential services, respite and transitional care), low-level care (hostel), high-level care (nursing home), or death. (Zhan and Miller, 2003, 58–63).

13 See Gill (2017): "This is an argument to move out of the 'black box' notion of the algorithm, and promote the idea of 'networked information algorithms' (NIAs); assemblages of institutionally situated code, practices, and norms with the power to create, sustain, and signify relationships among people and data through minimally observable, semi-autonomous action."

14 See Clayton (2012): "Frameworks more sympathetic to ecological thinking had been simmering among psychology's early writings, notably in William James's radical empiricism and Kurt Lewin's field theory, but became realized only in the 1960s through the works of James J. Gibson, Roger G. Barker, and others."

15 See, for example, this list of qualities for functioning organisms: "The distinctive qualities of an ecosystem include the following: (1) its constituents function as participants in a dynamic network of interdependent processes (within system relations); (2) the system operates dynamically to maintain the existing quasi-stable patterns of relationships, or failing that, either collapsing or giving rise to a new quasi-stable pattern; (3) systems are nested hierarchically such that between-level influences are operative; and (4) the system grows out of a history of relationships among its constituents that is continually taking shape in the face of ongoing, contingent events that often originate in comparatively more macro- and microlevel systems" (Clayton, 2012).

16 This is one of the immediate reactions of a student to the issue: "Well, if you look at the polar bears that live at the North Pole, so, yeah, if you travel by car a lot, then a lot of fumes are released, right, and clouds form, right, and there's this thing around Earth and you just get more of it and then when the Sun's rays shine in, like, on Earth, like they stay then, well they bounce on Earth, right, and then they can't get out again, because of that thing that's around Earth, the gas, and then the Sun's rays stay in there and it gets so warm that the ice melts and then the polar bears can't live anywhere, yeah like that" (Manni et al., 2016).

17 See "… being permitted as initiates to the sight of perfect and simple and calm and happy apparitions, which we saw in the pure light, being ourselves pure and not entombed in this which we carry about with us and call the body, in which we are imprisoned like an oyster in its shell" (Plato, *Phaedrus* 250c).

18 Cf. the entry under pathos in Liddell and Scott, *Greek-English Lexicon* (New York, 1883).

19 See also on this point, Rorty (1984, 524).

20 See "Perception consists in kinesthai and paschein, in being moved and acted upon" (416b32-5).

21 As Plutarch writes: "There is no other or more appropriate way of approaching the theory of good and bad things or the virtues or happiness than from universal nature and from the administration of the world. ... For the theory of good and bad things must be attached to these, since there is no other starting-point or reference to them that is better, and physical speculation is to be adopted for no other purpose than for the differentiation of good and bad things" [Plutarch, On the Contradictions of the Stoics 1035c-d (SVF 3.68, trans. LS 60A)].

22 For example, Zeno maintained that there are four kinds of emotions: sorrow, fear, desire, and delight, *epithumia, phobos, hêdonê, lupê/ἐπιθυμία, φόβος, ἡδονή, λύπη* (Diogene Laertius, 1925, VII, 111). He presented a proper taxonomy according to which desire and pleasure are good emotions, the former directed to the future, the latter to the present. Fear and sorrow are bad emotions, the former directed to the future and the latter to the present. Pseudo Andronicus will follow a similar table and explain these basic four emotions in these terms: "Distress is an irrational contraction, or a fresh opinion that something bad is present, at which people think it right to be contracted. Fear is an irrational leaning away, or escape from an expected danger. Appetite is an irrational reaching out, or pursuit of an expected good. Pleasure is an irrational elation, or a fresh opinion that something good is present, at which people think it is right to be elated" [On Emotions 1.1 (SVF 3.391, LS 65B)]. In his De Placitis Hippocratis et Platonis, Galen showed the interconnection between Zeno and Chrysippus with these words: "In the first book of his On Emotions Chrysippus tries to prove that emotions are certain judgements of reason while Zeno did not regard them as the judgements themselves but contractions, expansions, elations and dejections of the soul which supervene on judgements. Posidonius, disagreeing with both, praises and accepts Plato's view. He disputes the view of the followers of Chrysippus arguing that emotions are neither judgements nor supervenient upon them, but certain movements of other irrational powers, which Plato called appetitive and spirited" [PHP 5.1.4-6 [(92.17-25)].

23 See Duns Scoto, William Occam, and their followers, for example.

24 See also, "Love, then, striving to have what is loved, is appetite; and having and enjoying it, is joy; and love fleeing what is opposed to it, is fear, and experiencing this when it happens is distress. Now these are bad if the love is bad, and good if it is good" (Augustine, *The City of God,* 14.7).

25 See, for example, Mattern, S. on Galen and his patients, 2011. 2: "Anger and anxiety could cause or exacerbate epilepsy; along with diet, temperament, lifestyle, and environmental factors they could contribute to any number of feverish illnesses; anxiety in particular could trigger a sometimes fatal syndrome of insomnia, fever, and wasting, or transform into melancholy." More: "*I came to the conclusion that she was suffering from a melancholy dependence on black bile, or else trouble about something she was unwilling to confess.*" Galen, As quoted in Stanley W. Jackson (1969).

26 Despite the difficult predictability of affections, Spinoza describes in great systematic detail particular emotions in his *Treatise on the Emendation of the Intellect* and the *Short Treatise on God, Man and His Well-Being.*

27 As it concerns his relationship with the Stoics, he seems to disagree with them on two main points: the belongingness of human beings to nature and human freedom. In Stoicism, divine rationality or the power of cosmos seems to have an alternative that is not accepted in Spinoza's system. "Spinoza shares with them an ideal of freedom, in contrast with being hostage to fortune, in a world that unfolds according to its own law. But just as he denies the possibility of complete autonomy, so too

does he reject the notion that a 'good' suicide might express such autonomy, holding instead that any sort of self-destructive behavior is the result of defeat by external causes (IVP18s, see also IVP20). And Spinoza's vilification of the passions does not extend to emotions, or 'affects,' in general: he approves—in almost Epicurean fashion—of moderate joy, the kind of joy associated with activity" (Schmitter, *Stanford Encyclopedia of Philosophy*).

28 Unfortunately, we have omitted here Locke's research on emotions that in many points inspired Hume's. Locke, for example, describes emotions as "internal sensations" (1975, 229–230). On Locke's view, these internal sensations result from ideas of good and evil; for Hume, their immediate causes are impressions of pleasure and pain along with, in some cases, ideas of external things.

29 For more on this point, see Haruko (2003). "The origin of the indirect passions in the *Treatise*: An analogy between books 1 and 2," *Hume Studies*, 29: 205–221, 213; Alanen, "Powers and Mechanisms of the Passions," 187; Cohon (2008). Hume's indirect passions. In Elizabeth Radcliffe (ed.), *A Companion to Hume*. Malden, MA: Blackwell, 161 and 181n8. However, Hume makes it clear that "simple impressions" such as love and hatred are "without mixture or composition" (T 2.2.1.1; SBN 329). These impressions can mix or blend with each other, and thus form new impressions, but in so doing they do not retain their parts (T 2.2.6.1; SBN 366).

30 Hume (2000, 269). "Most fortunately it happens that, since reason is incapable of dispelling these clouds, nature herself suffices to that purpose, cures me of the philosophical melancholy and delirium, either by relaxing this bent of mind, or by some avocation, and lively impression of the senses, which obliterate all these chimeras. I dine, I play a game of backgammon, I converse, and am merry with my friends; and when, after three or four hours' amusement, I would return to these speculations, they appear so cold, and strained and ridiculous, that I cannot find in my heart to enter into them any further. Here, then, I find myself absolutely and necessarily determined to live and talk and act like other people in the common affair."

31 In that sense, it can be interesting to consult Ekman atlas of emotions at http://atlasofemotions.org/.

32 Although the 30 years between 1930 and 1960 were defined by Cornelius as "Dark Ages" because in the study of emotions in Paul Ekman's description it was largely assumed that facial behaviors (or "emotional expressions" as they are usually called) were, for the most part, culturally determined.

33 See Catani, M., and Schotten, M. (2012-03): "The use of the term 'limbic' has changed over time. Initially introduced by Thomas Willis (1664) to designate a cortical border encircling the brainstem (*limbus*, Latin 'border') the term has been used in modern neuroscience to indicate a progressively increasing number of regions dedicated to a wide range of functions (Mega et al., 1997; Marshall and Magoun, 1998). Paul Broca (1878) held the view that 'le grand lobe limbique' was mainly an olfactory structure common to all mammalian brains, although he argued that its functions were not limited to olfaction. After Broca's publication the accumulation of experimental evidence from ablation studies in animals broadened the role of the limbic structures to include other aspects of behaviour such as controlling social interactions, regulating predatory behaviour (Brown and Schäfer, 1888), consolidating memories (Bechterew, 1900), and forming emotions (Cannon, 1927). Anatomical and physiological advancements in the field led Christfield Jakob (1906) and James (1997) to formulate the first unified network model for linking action and perception to emotion."

34 See "A revised limbic system model for memory, emotion and behaviour." "The limbic system according to James Papez (1937) is an exact duplicate of Jakob's original drawing. Papez never quoted the work of Jakob and it is possible that he didn't know about his work, which was published in an Argentinean journal with scarce

international diffusion (La Semana Médica). Nevertheless the similarities between the two models are striking. To give credit to the work of Jakob we suggest the use of the eponym Jakob-Papez circuit. a, anterior nucleus; cc, corpus callosum; cn, caudate nucleus; cp, cingulum posterior; d, gyrus dentatus; f, fornix; gc, gyrus cinguli; gh, gyrus hippocampus; gs, gyrus subcallosal; h, hippocampus; m, mammillary body; mt, mammillo-thalamic tract; p, pars optica hypothalami; pr, piriform area; sb, subcallosal bundle; t, tuber cinereum; td, tractus mammillo-tegmentalis; the tractus hypophyseal."

35 See Papez (1937): "Incitations of cortical origin would pass first to the hippocampal formation and then down by way of the fornix to the mammillary body. From this they would pass upward through the mammillo-thalamic tract, or the fasciculus of Vicq d'Azyr, to the anterior nuclei of the thalamus and thence by the medial thalamocortical radiation (or anterior thalamic projections] to the cortex of the gyrus cinguli (…) The cortex of the cingulate gyrus may be looked on as the receptive region for the experiencing of emotion as the result of impulses coming from the hypothalamic region (…) Radiation of the emotive process from the gyrus cinguli to other regions in the cerebral cortex would add emotional coloring to psychic processes occurring elsewhere."

36 See Dell'Acqua (2013): "The cortical components of the limbic system include areas of increasing complexity separated into limbic and paralimbic zones (Mesulam, 2000). At the lower level the cortical areas of the amygdaloid complex, substantia innominata, together with septal and olfactory nuclei display an anatomical organisation that lacks consistent lamination and dendritic orientation. These structures are in part subcortical and in part situated on the ventral and medial surfaces of the cerebral hemispheres. The next level of organisation is the allocortex of the olfactory regions and hippocampal complex, where the neurons are well differentiated into layers and their dendrites show an orderly pattern of orientation. The corticoid and allocortical regions are grouped together into the limbic zone of the cerebral cortex as distinct from the paralimbic zone. The latter is mainly composed of 'mesocortex', whose progressive level of structural complexity ranges from a simplified arrangement similar to the allocortex, to the most complex six-layered isocortex."

37 See also Barrett et al. (2007).

38 This period also saw the publication of Stanley Schachter and Jerome Singer's (1962) article entitled "Cognitive, Social, and Physiological Determinants of an Emotional State," which is classified as an appraisal approach by some psychologists.

39 Yet, emotional responses are rarely uniform, however, and basic emotion models deal with the variability in emotional responding by positing the existence of display rules (cultural norms influence the expression of emotion, e.g., Matsumoto et al., 2008) or some other kind of cognitive processing after the fact (Izard et al., 2000).

40 See Roediger (2004): This is what unfortunately happened with the school of thought of behaviourism, which rules the field of academic psychological studies up till the sixties of the last century, and which means to study only the observable behaviour, forbidding the use of introspective reports. For such reasons, Panksepp identifies behaviorism as one of the factors hindering the study of emotions. Starting from the middle of the twentieth century, the practice of using calculating machines allows us to see man as a machine equipped with software, establishing a metaphor with which one can conceive the invisible thought inside the head in a scientifically acceptable way. Software is actually an implementation of that part of philosophy called *formal logic*, which deals with rules of reasoning equivalent to exact operations upon symbols. Using the metaphor of thought as software is a typical trait of the school of thought that in psychology is called *cognitivism*, which replaces behaviorism as the dominant trend starting from the seventies. Therefore, in psychology we have first a behavioral tradition which bans referring to personal experience, and then a cognitivism which allows speaking of invisible subjective worlds, but only to pick

out the rational aspects more akin to logical thought. According to Panksepp, the influence of behaviorism and cognitivism delayed till today a systematic scientific study of emotions, and this influence is still working in many scholars in the field of neuroscience.

Bibliography

Alanen, L. (2000). "Powers and mechanisms of the passion," In Traiger, S. (ed.). *The Blackwell Guide to Hume's Treatise*. London: Blackwell, 187–201.

Alston, William (1968). "Moral attitudes and moral judgments", *Noûs*, 2 (14): 1–23.

Andrews, B. K., Karcz, S., and Rosenberg B. (2008). Hooked on a feeling: emotional labor as an occupational hazard of the post-industrial age, *New Solutions*, 18(2): 245–255.

Arnold, M. B. (1960). *Emotion and Personality*. New York: Columbia University Press.

Atkins, D. (2014). *The Role of Culture in Empathy: The Consequences and Explanations of Cultural Differences in Empathy at the Affective and Cognitive Levels*. Doctor of Philosophy (PhD) thesis, University of Kent.

Augustine of Hippo (2012). *The City of God*. Translation by W. Babcock, notes by B. Ramsey. Hyde Park, NY: New City Press.

Banner, N. F. (2013). "Mental disorders are not brain disorders", *Journal of Evaluation in Clinical Practice*, 19, 509–513.

Barr, S. (2007). "Factors influencing environmental attitudes and behaviors: A U.K. case study of household waste management", *Environment and Behavior*, 39(4): 435–473.

Basaglia, F. (2000). *Conferenze Brasiliane*. In Basaglia Franca Ongaro, Giannichedda Maria Grazia (eds.). Milan: Raffaello Cortina Editore.

Baumeister, R. F., Bushman, B. J. (2008). *Social Psychology and Human Nature*. San Francisco, CA: Wadsworth.

Bechterew, W. (1900). "Demonstration eines gehirns mit Zestörung der vorderen und inneren Theile der Hirnrinde beider Schläfenlappen", *Neurological Foundations of Cognitive Neuroscience*, 20, 990–991.

Blackmore, E. R., Côté-Arsenault, D., Tang, W., Glover, V., Evans, J., Golding, J., and O'Connor, T. G. (2011). "Previous prenatal loss as a predictor of perinatal depression and anxiety", *The British Journal of Psychiatry: The Journal of Mental Science*, 198, 373–378. https://doi.org/10.1192/bjp.bp.110.083105.

Blum, R. W. Nelson-Mmari, K. (2004). "The health of young people in a global context", *Journal of Adolescent Health*, 35(5): 402–418.

Bostrom, N., Yudkowsky, E. (2011). "The ethics of artificial intelligence". In *Cambridge Handbook of Artificial Intelligence*, K. Frankish, W. Ramsey (eds.). New York: Cambridge University Press.

Bouquet, Fabrice, Chipeaux, Sébastien, Lang, Christophe, Marilleau, Nicolas, Nicod, Jean-Marc, and Taillandier, PatrickArnaud, Banos, Christophe, Lang, and Nicolas, Marilleau (2015). "1 - Introduction to the Agent Approach". In *Agent-based Spatial Simulation with Netlogo*. Elsevier.

Broca, P. (1878). "Anatomie comparée des circonvolutions cérébrales: le grand lobe limbique", *Review of Anthropology*, 1, 385–498.

Broedner, P. (2019). "Coping with Descartes' error in information system", *AI and Society Journal of Knowledge*, 34(2): 203–213.

Brown, S., Schäfer, E. A. (1888). "An investigation into the functions of the occipital and temporal lobes of the monkey's brain", *Philosophical Transactions of the Royal Society B*, 179B, 303–327.

Campos, J. Mumme, D. Kermoian, R., and Campos, R. (1994). "A functionalist perspective on the nature of emotion". *Monographs of the Society for Research in Child Development*, 59(2/3): 284–303.

Cannon, W. B. (1927). "The James-Lange theory of emotion: A critical examination and an alternate theory", *American Journal of Psychology*, 39, 106–124.

Casacuberta, D. (2015). "Ethical and technical aspects of emotions to create empathy in medical machines". In *Machine in Medical Ethics*, S. P. Van Rysewik M. Pontier (eds.). New York/Dordrecht: Springer.

Catani, M., Schotten, M. (2012-03). "Limbic system". *Atlas of Human Brain Connections*. Oxford, UK: Oxford University Press.

Choudhry, M. (2013). *An Introduction to Value-at-Risk*, Fifth Edition.

Choudhry, S. A., Li, J., Davis, D., Erdmann, C., Sikka, R., and Sutariya, B. (2013). "A public-private partnership develops and externally validates a 30-day hospital readmission risk prediction model", *Online Journal of Public Health Informatics*, 5, 317–325.

Chaudhry, S. I., McAvay, G., Chen, S., Whitson, H., Newman, A. B., Krumholz, H. M., and Gill, T. M. (2013). "Risk factors for hospital admission among older persons with newly diagnosed heart failure: Findings from the Cardiovascular Health Study", *Journal of the American College of Cardiology*, 61(6): 635–642.

Charland, L. C. (1998). "Is Mr. Spock mentally Competent? Competence to consent and emotion", *Philosophy, Psychiatry, & Psychology*, 5(1): 67–81.

Clayton, S. (2012). *The Oxford Handbook of Environmental and Conservation Psychology*. Oxford: Oxford University Press.

Cohon, R. (2008). "Hume's indirect passions,". In *A Companion to Hume*. E. Radcliffe (ed.). Malden, MA: Blackwell, 18, 161–181.

Colaizzi, P. (1978). "Psychological research as the phenomenologist views it". In *Existential Phenomenological Alternatives for Psychology*, R. Vall and M. King, (eds.). New York, NY: Oxford University Press.

Cornelius, R. R. (1996). *The Science of Emotion. Research and Tradition in the Psychology Of Emotion*. Upper Saddle River (NJ): Prentice-Hall.

Costello, E. J., Egger, H., Angold, A. (2005). "10-year research update review: The epidemiology of child and adolescent psychiatric disorders: I. Methods and public health burden", *Journal of the American Academy of Child and Adolescent Psychiatry*, 44, 972–986.

Davidson, R. J., Scherer, K. R., and Goldsmith, H. H. (eds.) (2003). *Handbook of Affective Sciences*. Oxford University Press: New York.

Davis, J. N., Lyman-Hager, M. A. (1997). Computers and L2 Reading: Student Performance, Student Attitudes1, Foreign Language Annals, 30, 58–72.

Dell'Acqua, F., Scifo, P., Rizzo, G., Catani, M., Simmons, A., Scotti, G., Fazio, F., (2010). "A modified damped Richardson-Lucy algorithm to reduce isotropic background effects in spherical deconvolution", *Neuroimage*, 49, 1446–1458.

Deonna, Julien, and Teroni, Fabrice (2012). *The Emotions: A Philosophical Introduction*. London: Routledge.

Descartes, R. (1984–1991). *The Philosophical Writings of Descartes*, In J. Cottingham R. Stoothoff, D. Murdoch, and A. Kenny (eds.). Cambridge, Cambridge University Press, 3 vols.

Dewey, J. (1895). The theory of emotion, *Psychological Review*, 2(1): 13–32.

Dewey, J. (1985}1916). Democracy and education. The Middle Works of John Dewey, 9 Edited by Jo Ann Boydston. Carbondale & Edwardsville: Southern Illinois University Press.

Dreyfus, H. L. (1978) *What Computers Can't Do: The Limits of Artificial Intelligence*. New York: Harper Collins.

Dreyfus, H. L. (1988). "The socratic and platonic basis of cognitivism". *AI & Society*. Springer, Berlin.

Dreyfus H. L., Taylor C. (2015). *Retrieving Realism*. Cambridge, MA: Harvard University Press.

De Castro, L. (2015). "Research ethics, cross-cultural dimensions of", *International Encyclopedia of the Social & Behavioral Sciences*, 508–513.

Englander, M. (2014). "Empathy training from a phenomenological perspective", *Journal of Phenomenological Psychology*, 45(1): 5–26.

Fabian, Freyenhagen, Tom, O'Shea (2013). "Hidden substance: Mental disorder as a challenge to normatively neutral accounts of autonomy", *International Journal of Law in Context*, 9(1): 53–70.

Farny, Steffen, Kibler, Ewald, and Down, Simon (2019). "Collective Emotions in Institutional Creation Work". *The Academy of Management Journal*, 62.

Fletcher, J. M. (2008). "Adolescent depression and educational attainment: Results using sibling fixed effects", *Health Econonics*, 17, 1215–1235.

Foltz, P. W. (2001). "Semantic processing, statistical semantics". In W. Kintsch (ed.). *The International Encyclopedia of the Social and Behavioral Sciences* (online: http://lsa.colorado. edu/papers/dp1.LSAintro.pdf).

Foucault, M. (2016). *History of Madness*. In J. Khalfa, editor, translator and J. Murphy, translator. New York: Routledge.

Fredrickson, B. L. (2000). "Why positive emotions matter in organizations: Lessons from the broaden-and-build theory", *The Psychologist-Manager Journal*, 4, 131–142.

Freud, S. (1955). Beyond the pleasure principle (1920). Standard Edition, 18, 7–64. London: Hogarth Press.

Freyenhagen, Fabian (2009). "Personal autonomy and mental capacity", *Psychiatry*, 8, 465–467.

Frijda, N. H. (1988). "The laws of emotion", *American Psychologist*, 43(5): 349–358.

Futoma, J., Morris, J., Lucas, J. (2015). "A comparison of models for predicting early hospital readmissions", *Journal of Biomedical Informatics*, 56, 229–238.

Gauthier, David (1986). *Morals by Agreement*. Oxford University Press.

Georgiades. P. (1934). *De Feud a Platon*. Paris:Fasquelle.

Gill, K. S. (2017). *Uncommon Voices of AI*. Springer: Berlin.

Gill, K. S. (2019). "From judgment to calculation: The phenomenology of embodied skill", *AI & Society* 34, 165–175.

Giorgi, A. (2009). *The Descriptive Phenomenological Method in Psychology: A Modified Husserlian Approach*. Pittsburg, PA: Duquesne University Press.

Gleitman, H, Fridlund, A. J., and Reisberg, D. (1999). *Psychology*, 6th. New York: Norton.

Gold, K. J., Sen, A., Schwenk, T. L. (2013). "Details on suicide among US physicians: data from the National Violent Death Reporting System", *General Hospital Psychiatry*, 35, 45–49, https://doi.org/10.1016/j.genhosppsych.2012.08.005.

Green, J. M., Kafetsios, K., Statham, H. E., and Snowdon, C. M. (2003). "Factor Structure, Validity and Reliability of the Cambridge Worry Scale in a Pregnant Population", *Journal of Health Psychology*, 8(6): 753–764.

Green-Demers, I., Pelletier, L. G., and Ménard, S. (1997). "The impact of behavioural difficulty on the saliency of the association between self-determined motivation and environmental behaviours", *Canadian Journal of Behavioural Science/Revue canadienne des sciences du comportement*, 29(3): 157–166.

Grisso, T., Appelbaum, P. S. (1995). "The MacArthur Treatment Competence Study. III: Abilities of patients to consent to psychiatric and medical treatments", *Law and Human Behavior*, 19(2): 149–174.

Harre', R. (2002). *Congitive Science: and Introduction*. London: Sage Publication.

Haruko, I. (2003). "The origin of the indirect passions in the *Treatise*: An analogy between books 1 and 2" , *Hume Studies*, 29(205–221): 213.

Hastie, Trevor, Tibshirani, Robert, FriedmanJerome, and Franklin, James (2004). *The Mathematical Intelligencer*, 27, 83–85.

He, D., Matthews, S. C., Kalloo, A. N., and Hutfless, S. (2014). "Mining High-Dimensional Administrative Claims Data to Predict Early Hospital Readmissions", *Journal of the American Medical Informatics Association*, 21(2): 272–279.

Herbart, J. F. (1906). S. Werke, G. Hartenstein (ed.), *Lehrbuch zur Psychologie*. Leipzig: Voss.

Hinton, G. E., Osindero, S., Teh, Y.W. (2006). "A fast learning algorithm for deep belief nets", *Neural Computer* 18(7): 1527–1554.

Hinton G. E., Salakhutdinov, R. R. (2006). "Reducing the dimensionality of data with neural networks", *Science*, 313(5786): 504–507.

Hoffman, P. (1990). "Cartesian Passions and Cartesian Dualism", *Pacific Philosophical Quarterly*, 71, 310–333.

Hollenstein, Tom, Lanteigne, DiannaCole, P., Hollenstein, T. (2018). "Emotion regulation dynamics in adolescence. In , (eds.). *Emotion Regulation*. New York: Routledge.

Hume, D. (1777). An Enquiry Concerninghuman Understanding retrieved online: http://web.mnstate.edu/gracyk/courses/web%20publishing/enquiryI.htm.

Husserl E. (1970). *The Crisis of European Sciences and Transcendental Phenomenology. An Introduction to Phenomenological Philosophy*, D. Carr (trans.). Evanston, IL: Northwestern University Press.

Ignatov, A., Grove, N. S., Livingston, A., and Connolly, W. E. (2019). "Entangled Humanism as a Political Project: William Connolly's Facing the Planetary", *Contemporary Political Theory*, 18, 115–134.

Jackson, S. W. (1969), "Galen—on mental disorders", *Journal of the History of the Behavioral Sciences*, 5, 365–384.

Jaffe, J., Diamond, M. O. (2011). *Reproductive Trauma: Psychotherapy with Infertility and Pregnancy Loss Clients*. American Psychological Association.

Jakob, C., (1906). "Nueva contribución á la fisio-patología de los lóbulos frontales", *La Semana Médica*, 13, 1325–1329.

James, S. (1997). *Passion and Action: The Emotions in Seventeenth-Century Philosophy*. Oxford: Oxford University Press.

Kaiser, F. G., Ranney, M., Hartig, T., and Bowler, P. A. (1999). "Ecological behavior, environmental attitude, and feelings of responsibility for the environment", *European Psychologist*, 4(2): 59–74.

Kaiser, F. G., Shimoda, T. A. (1999). "Responsibility as a predictor of ecological behavior", *Journal of Environmental Psychology*, 19(3): 243–253.

Kansagara, D., Englander, H., Salanitro, A., Kagen, D., Theobald, C., Freeman, M., and Kripalani, S. (2011 October). "Risk prediction models for hospital readmission:

A systematic review [Internet]". Washington (DC): Department of Veterans Affairs (US). Available from: https://www.ncbi.nlm.nih.gov/books/NBK82578/.

Kappas, A. (2011). "Emotion and regulation are one!", *Emotion Review*, 3, 17–25.

King, P., "Aquinas on the Passions". In *MacDonald and Stump* (1999), 101–32.

Knuuttila, S. (2004). *Emotions in Ancient and Medieval Philosophy*. Oxford: Oxford University Press.

Kouchaki, M. (2015). "Professionalism and moral behavior", *Business & Society*, 54(3): 376–385.

LaMonica, E. L., Carew, D. K., Winder, A. E., Haase, A. M. B., and Blanchard, K. H. (1976). "Empathy training as a major thrust of a staff development program", *Nursing Research*, 25(6), 447–451.

Layton, J. M. (1979). "The use of modeling to teach empathy to nursing students", *Research in Nursing and Health*, 2(4): 163–176;

Lazarus, R. S. (1966). *Psychological Stress and the Coping Process*. McGraw-Hill.

La Rochelle, H., Bengio, Y., Louradour, J., Lamblin, P. (2009). "Exploring strategies for training deep neural networks", *Journal of Machine Learning Research* 1, 1–40.

Liddell, H. G., Scott, R. (1883), *Greek-English Lexicon*. New York: Oxford Clarendon Press.

Leis-Newman, E. (2012 June), Miscarriage and loss. *Monitor on Psychology*, 43(6).

MacLean, P. D. (1949). "Psychosomatic disease and the 'visceral brain': recent developments bearing on the Papez theory of emotion", *Psychosomatic Medicine*, 11, 338–353.

MacLean, P. D. (1952). "Some psychiatric implications of physiological studies on frontotemporal portion of limbic system (visceral brain)", *Electroencephalography and Clinical Neurophysiology*, 4, 407–418.

Mandler, J. M. (2003). Conceptual categorization. In D. H. Rakison , L. M. Oakes (eds.). *Early Category and Concept Development: Making Sense of the Blooming, Buzzing Confusion*, Oxford University Press, 103–131.

Manni, A., Sporre, K., and Ottander, C. (2017). "Emotions and values – a case study of meaning-making in ESE", *Environmental Education Research*, 23, 17, 4, 451–464.

Mark, R. M. T., McPherson, R., Miyamoto, I., Kaye, and J. L., (2015). *Information Security Analytics*. Syngress.

Marshall, L. H., Magoun, H. W., (1998). *Discoveries in the Human Brain*. New Jersey: Humana Press.

Mata, D. A., Ramos, M. A., and Bansal, N. (2015). "Prevalence of depression and depressive symptoms among resident physicians: A systematic review and meta-analysis", JAMA, 314(22): 2373–2383.

Mead, George Herbert, (1895). "A theory of emotions from the physiological standpoint", (Abstract of a paper read to the third annual meeting of the American Psychological Association, 1894), *Psychological Review*, 2, 162–164.

Mega, M. S., Cummings, J. L., Salloway, S., Malloy, P., (1997). "The limbic system: An anatomic, phylogenetic, and clinical perspective", *The Journal of Neuropsychiatry and Clinical Neurosciences*, 9, 315–330.

Mehrabian, A., Epstein, N. (1972). "A measure of emotional empathy", *Journal of Personality*, 40, 525–543.

Mesulam M. (2012). "The evolving landscape of human cortical connectivity: facts and inferences", *NeuroImage*, 62(4): 2182–2189. https://doi.org/10.1016/j.neuroimage.2011.12.033.

Miles, S. H. (1998). "A challenge to licensing boards: The stigma of mental illness", *JAMA*, 280(10): 865.

Myers, D. G. (1998). *Psychology*. New York, NY: Worth Publishers.

Niedenthal, P., Krauth-Gruber, S., and Ric, F. (2006). Psychology of emotion: Interpersonal, experiential, and cognitive approaches, *Journal of Educational Psychology*, 432.

Niedenthal, Paula. (2007). "Embodying Emotion", Science (New York, N.Y.)., 316. 1002–1005.

Nussbaum, M. (1994). *The Therapy of Desire: Theory and Practice in Hellenistic Ethics*. Princeton: Princeton University Press.

Nussbaum, M. (2003). "Capabilities as fundamental entitlements: sen and social justice", *Feminist Economics*, 9(2–3): 33–59.

Niedenthal, P. M., Krauth-Gruber, S., and Ric, F (2006). *Psychology of Emotion: Interpersonal, Experiential, and Cognitive Approaches*. New York: Psychology Press.

Oatley, K. (2002). "Emotions and the story worlds of fiction". In M. C. Green, J. J. Strange, and T. C. Brock (eds.). *Narrative Impact: Social And Cognitive Foundations*. Lawrence Erlbaum Associates Publishers, 39–69.

Oatley, K., Jenkins, J. M. (1996). *Understanding Emotions*. Blackwell Publishing.

Obama, M. (2018). *Becoming*. New York: Crown Publishing.

Ojala, M. (2015). "Hope in the face of climate change: associations with Environmental engagement and student perceptions oftTeachers' emotion communication style and future orientation", *Journal of Environmental Education*, 46, 133–148.

Oksenberg Rorty, A. (1984). "Aristotle on the metaphysical status of pathe", *The Review of Metaphysics*, 37(3): 521–546.

Osbaldiston, R., Sheldon, K. M. (2003). "Promoting internalized motivation for environmentally responsible behavior: A prospective study of environmental goals", *Journal of Environmental Psychology*, 23, 348–356.

Panksepp, J. (1998). *Series in Affective Science. Affective Neuroscience: The Foundations of Human and Animal Emotions*. Oxford University Press.

Papez, J. W. (1937). "A proposed mechanism of emotion", *Archives of Neurology & Psychiatry*, 38, 725–743.

Pelletier, L. G., Dion, S., Tuson, K., and Green-Demers, I. (1999). "Why do people fail to adopt environmental behaviors? Towards a taxonomy of environmental amotivation", *Journal of Basic and Applied Social Psychology*, 29, 2481–2504.

Plutarch, (2020) *Moral. On the Stoic Self-Contradiction*. Loeb Edition

Price, A. W. (1995). *Mental Conflict*. London: Routledge.

Swanson, K. M. (1999). "Effects of caring, measurement, and time on miscarriage impact and women's well-being", *Nursing Research*, 48(6): 288–298,10.1097/00006199-199911000-00004.

Stoljar, D. (2000). "Physicalism and the necessary: A Posteriori", *Journal of Philosophy*, 97(1), 33–55.

Retrieved from: https://qz.com/1239762/cambridge-analytica-scandal-all-the-countries-where-scl-elections-claims-to-have-worked/.

Ricoeur, P. (1970). *Freud and Plato*. Yale: Yale University.

Rommes, A. G. L., Avenier, Marie, Denyer, David, Hodgkinson, Gerard, Pandza, Kar, Starkey, Ken, and Worren, Nicolay. (2015). "Toward Common Ground and Trading Zones in Management Research and Practice", *British Journal of Management*. 26.

Rotenstein, L. S. Ramos, M. A. Torre, M., et al. (2016). "Prevalence of depression, depressive symptoms, and suicidal ideation among medical students: A systematic review and meta-analysis", *JAMA*, 316(21): 2214–2236.

Ruckmick, C. A. (1929). "Why we have emotions", *Scientific Monthly*, 28, 252–262.

Ryan, A. M., Krinsky, S., Adler-Milstein J., Damberg, C. L., Maurer, K. A., and Hollingsworth, J. M. (2017). "Association between hospitals' engagement in value-based reforms and readmission reduction in the hospital readmission reduction program", *JAMA Internal Medicine*, 177(6): 862–868.

Santas, G. (1955). *Plato and Freud: Two Thwories of Love*. New Jersey: Wiley Blackwell.

Schachter, S., Singer, J. (1962). "Cognitive, social, and physiological determinants of emotional state", *Psychological Review*, 69(5): 379–399.

Schmitter, A. M. (2013). "17th and 18th century theories of emotions", *The Stanford Encyclopedia of Philosophy*.

Searle, J. R. (2010) *Making the Social World. The Structure of Human Civilization*. Oxford: Oxford University Press.

Seguin, C., Pelletier, Luc, and Hunsley, John. (1998). "Toward a Model of Environmental Activism", *Environment and Behavior*, 30, 628–652.

Seguin, C., Pelletier, L. G., and Hunsley, J. (1999). "Predicting environmental behaviors: The influence of self-determined motivation and information about perceived environmental health risks", *Journal of Applied Social Psychology*, 29, 1582, 1604.

Shapiro, L. (2007). "The embodied cognition research programme", *Philosophy Compass*, 2: 338–346.

Shouse, J. B. (1952). "David Hume and William James: A Comparison", *Journal of the History of Ideas*, 13 (1/4): 514.

Simon, Bennett (1973). "Plato and Freud", *The Psychoanalytic Quarterly*, 42(1): 91–122.

Solomon, R. C. (1984) *What is an Emotion*. Oxford: Oxford University Press.

Solomon, R. C. (2008). "The philosophy of emotions". In M. Lewis, J. M. Haviland-Jones, and L. F. Barrett (eds.). *Handbook of Emotions*, 3–16. The Guilford Press.

Spinoza, B. (2001) *Theological-Political Treatise*, S. Shirley, (trans.). Indianapolis, Hackett.

Steg, Linda, Vlek, Charles (2009). EEncouraging pro-environmental behavior: An integrative review and research agenda", *Journal of Environmental Psychology*, 20, 309–317.

Strack, F., Martin, L. L., and Stepper, S. (1988). Inhibiting and facilitating conditions of the human smile: A nonobtrusive test of the facial feedback hypothesis, *Journal of Personality and Social Psychology*, 54(5): 768–777.

Sussman, R., Gifford, R. (2013). "Be the change you want to see: Modeling food composting in public places." *Environment and Behavior*, 45(3): 323–343.

Thapar, A., Collishaw, S., Potter, R., and Thapar, A. K. (2012). "Depression in adolescence", *Seminar*, 379 (9820): 1056–1067.

Tomkins, S. S. (1962). *Affect, Imagery, Consciousness: Vol. 1. The Positive Affects*. Springer: Tompkins.

Tomkins, S. S. (1963). *Affect, Imagery, Consciousness: II. The Negative Affects*. Springer.

Tulandi, Al-Fozan, Al-Fozan, H. M. (2009). Spontaneous abortion: Risk factors, etiology, clinical manifestations, and diagnostic evaluation. In: Levine, D., and Barbieri, R. L., (eds.). UpToDate clinical reference library. Waltham, MA: Wolters Kluwer. [Retrieved April 9, 2010]. from http://www.uptodate.com/patients/content/topic.do?topicKey=~treIIBdkibqkdbS.

Vlek, C., Steg, L. (2007). "Human behavior and environmental sustainability: Problems, driving forces and research topics", *Journal of Social Issues*, 63(1): 1–19.

Wade, C., Tavris, C. (2006). *Psychology*. 8th. Upper Saddle River; NJ: Pearson Education.

Weizenbaum J (1976). *Computer Power and Human Reason: From Judgment to Calculation*. San Francisco: W. H. Freeman.

Whitmarsh, Lorraine. (2009). "Behavioural responses to climate change: Asymmetry of intentions and impacts", *Journal of Environmental Psychology*, 29, 13–23.

Wolf, A. (1905). *Short Treatise on God, Man & His Well-Being. Studies in Logic*. Cambridge: Cambridge University Press.

Woods-Giscombé, C. L., Lobel, M., and Crandell, J. L. (2010). "The impact of miscarriage and parity on patterns of maternal distress in pregnancy", *Research in Nursing & Health*, 33(4): 316–328. https://doi.org/10.1002/nur.20389.

Yakovlev, P. J., 1948. "Motility, behavior and the brain; stereodynamic organizationand neural coordinates of behavior", *The Journal of Nervous and Mental Disease*, 107, 313–335.

Zeanah C. H., Danis B., Hirshberg L., Benoit D., Miller D., Heller S. S. (1999). "Disorganized attachment associated with partner violence: A research note", *Infant Mental Health Journal*, 20, 77–86.

Zhan, C. Miller, M. R. (2003a). "Administrative data based patient safety research: A critical review", *Quality & Safety in Health Care*, 12, 58–63.

Zhan, C., Miller, M. R. (2003b). "Excess length of stay, charges, and mortality attributable to medical injuries during hospitalization", *JAMA*, 290(14): 1868–1874.

3

INTENTIONALITY OF EMOTIONS

Introduction

In the previous chapters, we saw how important it is for bioethics to acknowledge emotions, especially for a bioethics meant as a conscientious ethics of life (βίος). Most of the difficult choices that we have to make in relation to our health, environment, and use of technologies are animated and moved by emotions. Yet, emotions are still too often interpreted as a nuisance that needs to be silenced to make space for a more objective answer. As I will show in this chapter, objectivity might often be a pretense behind which an irresponsible use of the intentionality of emotions hides while constituting a distorted, sometimes harmful, reality. Examples of this can be seen in the cases that I have examined in Chapters 2, such as the effects of emotional imbalance on doctors' professional and personal lives (II.1), the engagement of young students in environmental issues (II.4), and the use of emotional manipulation for political gain (II.3). These cases showed how the emotional grip is often the *via regia* to constituting and shaping the complexity of our reality; if this grip is hidden behind the illusion of an emotionless objectivity, we risk constructing most of our reality out of external influences without ever taking responsibility for the meanings that this new reality produces. Hence, in this chapter, I will address the following questions: Can we be responsible for our emotions and the reality attached to them? Or, are emotions just a physiological reaction? Are they rational? If so, what kind of rationality can be ascribed to them?

One of the most important layers of our motivational and decisional lives is constituted by emotions. Instead of discarding emotions as an annoying nuisance, I believe that understanding their intentional and motivational structure is a necessary step toward awareness in the choices we make in every moment of our lives, especially when it comes to bioethical matters. Thus, in what follows, I will describe what I mean by intentionality of emotions and investigate if it makes sense to speak of emotional responsibility; then I will examine cases of emotional oversight in medical health care and architecture in order to show what kind of tangible reality the intentionality of emotions can generate.

I. Intentionality in This Study

Intentionality[1] is a complex term whose roots come from the Greek *enteinein* which translates into Latin as *intendere* and into Arabic as *Ma qul* or *Ma na*. The etymology refers to the "tension" of "aiming at" something; this tension joins our inner sense of reality to the outer world. In Plato's *Cratylus*, the intentional directedness of consciousness toward its object is described through the metaphor of an archer drawing a bow to aim an arrow at a target. Hence, first intentionality refers to this tension that invisibly connects humans to an "external something." In his *On Ideas*, as well as in book IX of his *Metaphysics*, Aristotle also reflected on the problem of intentionality where he argued against Plato's theory of the forms. He believed, in fact, that intentionality has not only an epistemological but also a practical, sensitive side. He explained intentionality as the change that it effects in the act of aiming at. Even though intentionality is a riddle more than an answer to a problem, in Chapters 2–4 and 12 of *On the Soul*, he explained both sensations and understanding as intentional states. He gave the example of a signet ring in wax. He says that the intentional object is the form received without matter, a form that changes our way to see that form. Basically, he used this example to say that intentionality has nothing to do with existence, as Parmenides and Plato affirmed; instead, it does not have a matter but it has a form that changes our way of intending that substance. Intentionality points out how the bodies change in giving themselves to us. In the example of the signet ring in the wax, the ring is a body that changes itself in its way of being perceived by us without a real change happening to its matter. Intentionality is this change–the signet ring–it is the *phantasmata*, the representations that come to us as the outcome of our experience. In this sense, intentionality as a change is explained by the representation or ability to reduce our thoughts to an abstract content that we can use as a symbol or a token of what the object is; although it has no ontological relevance, its property is mediated by this representation and is conceivable by reflecting on the changes that inform the act.

On a similar note, Stoics, for example Zeno and Cleantes, conceived intentionality as *ennoemata*, that is, thoughts that replace the concreteness of what was meant through representations dwelling in our soul. Similar to this, an interesting way to explain the intentional act is the expression παρών-απών (*paron apon*), present absence (Aristotle, *On Memory and Recollection* 1, 450a25 ff.). Reflecting upon my own acts entails that I set aside the object that is outside of me in order to attend to the object as held in my consciousness, an object that is now present in me as a token of the tension that connects me to the outside world, a "presence in absence."

Brentano, and later on his disciple Husserl, revived the studies around intentionality by emphasizing its reflective quality. For Brentano, intentionality is the mark of mental phenomena[2] as it refers to the "objectual in-existence" (Brentano, 1874/2008) of the content of one's lived experience in a renewed form, while for Husserl it indicates the way in which consciousness aims at the object. Both cases point to intentionality as a reflective experience in which the subject transforms what was present in front of him/herself into a "present absence" that continuously connects him/her to the world while constituting meanings and values that give a regulative sense to this interconnection. To this extent, the intentional content becomes the means one uses to constitute one's own reality while establishing meaningful bonds with the life-world; yet, it is not easy to describe this structure. Is this intentional content a mental representation, a perception, or a bodily feeling? How can we define the essence of what constitutes our sense of reality?

I.1 Intentional Objects

The biologist W. Freeman wrote, "All actions are emotional, and at the same time they have their reasons and explanations. This is the nature of intentional behavior."[3] Deep down, intentionality is the reason, or tension, that moves all our actions from their emotional roots. This is because intentionality expresses the continuous flow of our lived experiences. "It is of the very nature of consciousness to be intentional" said Jean-Paul Sartre, "and a consciousness that ceases to be a consciousness of something would *ipso facto* cease to exist" (1940, 211). Therefore, the human world and its reality are intentionally constituted. The way in which human beings exist is referential, that is, by relating to what is outside of them: looking at a flower, holding hands, drinking coffee. This simple tension that connects us to the external world through reference (*Beziehung auf*) can be described as an intentional lived experience which transforms the objects as they exist outside of us into content that is there for us. In every simple act, this intentional lived experience builds a personal and intersubjective reality (Ferrarello, 2016, 2102) that can be investigated by looking back at the intentionality structure peculiar to the content of that experience.

The current debate concerning the content of intentional acts takes inspiration mostly from the works of Brentano and Husserl. According to McDonald (2015), Brentano is the one who mediated and resurrected the tradition of the ancient medieval philosophy by reintroducing the distinction between *esse intentionale* and *esse objectivum*; the object as it stands outside and independently of us (*esse objectivum*) has a structural difference from the object as it is meant by us (*esse intentionale*). Some of the interpreters mitigate Brentano's notion of inexistence of the *esse intentionale* by assigning a locative meaning to the "in." The object as it is meant by us does not "exist" in the same way as real objective things do, but, instead, it takes some space in our mind as a conceptual content. Jacquette (2004, 102), for example, described the existence of the intentional object as a psychological space. Others, for example, Chrudzimski and Smith (2004, 205), questioned the extent of the ontological commitment implied in the inexistence of the intentional object by emphasizing Brentano's change of heart in later years (Grossmann, 1969, 18). It is certain that the extent of Brentano's ontological commitment to the ontological reality of the "*esse intentionale*" gave rise to a major division between analytic and continental interpretations. The apple of discord verges on whether intentional objects exist according to a proper ontological category or if they exist as inten*s*ions (with an *s*) (i.e., as instantiations of meaning).[4] The majority of thinkers are ascribed to this latter solution (Frege, Russel),[5] while "the intentional-object theorists" (Meinong[6]) defend the ontological status of the intentional objects by separating existence from their being. In fact, according to Meinong, for example, for an object to be it does not need to exist. Existence (being-there) and beingness (being) belong to two different categories; intentional objects do not exist, but they are, for example, a round square is without the necessity to exist.[7]

Therefore, *according to the current debate, the intentional contents of one's experience, that is, the way in which reality appears to and around one's environment, can be either a meaning or a potentially existent being.*[8] Moreover, this intentional content is not an entity that comes out of nothing but is inextricably interconnected with one's emotions. Emotions, as their etymology shows, set in motion our actions and concretely inform each moment of our life; yet, their reality is invisible to the eyes. In the following sections, I will show what role emotions play in the constitution of intentional contents as meanings (inten*s*ions) or as potentially existing beings. In particular, if we relate to intentional content whose structure is mainly intentional, such as friendship, what kind of status would be possible to attribute to that qualitative constitution of intersubjective[9] reality.[10] Understanding the extent of the ontological status one can assign to emotional reality and how responsible one is in relation to the constitutive agency of emotions can affect, for example, the way in which we are going to conceive the clinical encounter, the planning of a neighborhood, or the political administration of wealth.

I.2 The Problem of Intentionality of Emotions

It does not seem problematic to claim that emotions point to an object and therefore hold an intentionality of their own. We are scared by one event or we are happy because of another. In both cases, emotions refer to objects that go beyond themselves; in that it is not problematic to affirm that emotions can be intentional. The question is what kind of intentionality is that? Are emotions intentional through and through, or do they find their ultimate intentional root in primordial self-referential nonintentional instincts? If emotional intentionality is through and through, then the contents of emotions are intentional, too. This means that they can be understood (and accordingly to a certain extent we are responsible for them), and their onto-logical status can be described. On the other hand, if the intentionality of emotions is at the very essence instinctive and self-referential, there is not much we can do to educate our emotions toward well-being.

There are two basic interpretations of this problem which go under the categories of weak and strong intentionalism: either emotions do not fully entail a reflection on the content-experience, and hence are not fully intentional, or they do. According to proponents of weak intentionalism such as Crane (1998), certain properties of emotions are not fully intentional; for example, a sudden pang of anxiety is a reaction to a concrete event that does not entail any mental activity but mostly an instinctive reaction to the environment. For this reason, for him, emotions are not thoroughly intentional.

I.2.1 Strong Intentionalism of Emotions

Strong intentionalism states that emotions have an axiological (Husserl, 1901/ 1984) and hedonic (Colombetti, 2005) valence (positive, negative, or neutral[11]) which is, in a way, a reflective representation of the content of the experience; yet, it is still not clear in what terms we can explain this reflective quality.

Strong intentionalism of emotions has deployed two different theoretical strategies to explain this point, one focused on the emotions themselves and the other on the theory already developed for perception (Harman, 1990; Dretske, 1995; Tye, 1995; Lycan, 1996; Byrne, 2001) and bodily sensations (Block, 1983; Tye, 2000; Dokic, 2003; Bain, 2003, 2007; Hall, 2008). This latter theory identifies the intentionality of emotions with the perceptual experience of values that are accompanied by the expression of bodily sensations (Pitcher, 1971) or, as in James, with perceptions of bodily changes.[12] Pain, for example, has been explained as the experience of a negative value which purports a negative hedonic quality.

If so, though, this strategy would silence the motivational power intrinsic to emotional states. If emotions are explained as a perceptive experience of a positive or negative quality situation, how do they motivate us to persist in a negative experience, as in the case of a tormented relationship? Literally, emotions (e-movere) are motivating (motus) movements. If we equate emotions to perceptions, their motivational strength disappears (Smith, 1994). Perceptions, in fact, might have no emotional impact on us. Moreover, a second problem of this strategy is determined by the fact that perceptions seem to have a transparency that emotions do not possess. As De Sousa wrote, emotions are two-faced since they have a double function: they refer to an object but at the same time they affect us, while perceptions are always focused on the object without triggering in us any affective response. A third problem is connected to the reality of the perceptual object versus the reality of a value[13]: seeing a beautiful painting is different from the value we attribute to the sight of the painting. Both acts are actual and real, but their qualities differ from each other.

The former strategy, instead, focuses on emotions themselves; philosophers such as Nussbaum (2001), Solomon (1980, 1988), and Neu (2000) have defended the idea of emotions as evaluative beliefs or judgments or experiences of values (De Sousa, 1987 and other versions of it in Tappolet, 2000; Goldie, 2000, 2004; Prinz, 2004; Deonna, 2006; Döring, 2007). Joy, for example, is the judgment that something is joyful or that we experience the value of joy. Yet, the problem of this position is the probable contrast that might arise between the doxic judgment and the value experience. I might judge that this party is a joyful event, but I am not able to genuinely value it as such. So, even if my emotions are rational and legitimate for me, the unhappiness I feel would be considered unacceptable according to its doxic presupposition. This is true especially in phobias; it is possible that one fears lizards even though the same person is aware of the fact that they are absolutely inoffensive.

For this reason, Deonna and Teroni[14] proposed a third solution according to which the intentionality of emotions is through and through because emotions are attitudes that we take in relation to objects provided by a cognitive base. "Each emotion consists in a specific felt bodily stance towards objects or situations, which is correct or incorrect as a function of whether or not these objects and situations exemplify the relevant evaluative property" (2014, 89). This solution seems to be very close to the one I would propose to adopt by using Husserlian phenomenology.

I.3 Intentionality of Emotions versus Sensations and Feelings[15]

Section 15 of Husserl's fifth *Logical Investigation* is almost entirely dedicated to this problem of the intentional essence of sentiments and feelings. In this section, Husserl addressed the positions of his teachers, Brentano and Stumpf. According to Brentano, the intentional essence describes what the act does when consciousness tends toward something. In the act of love something is loved, in the act of knowing there is something that is known, in the act of desire something is desired, and so on (Hua XIX, LI V, Section 10). This leads Husserl, like Brentano, to state that the conceptual component of representations (as in strong intentionalism) is a necessary character for the aboutness of the intentional essence to be possible. Husserl, quoting Brentano at the end of Section 10, wrote, "Nothing can be judged about, nothing can likewise be desired, nothing can be hoped or feared, if it is not presented" (Hua XIX, 370; En. tr. 97).

Yet, differently from Brentano, Husserl stated that "we take intentional relation, understood in purely descriptive fashion, as an inward peculiarity of certain experiences, to be an essential feature of 'psychical phenomena' or 'acts' (…). That not all experiences are intentional is proved by sensations and sensational complexes" (Hua XIX, 368–369; En. tr. 96–97).

From this passage, it is clear that both Husserl and Brentano agree that re-presentation is a fundamental feature of intentionality and sentiments and feelings do not share this feature because their reference to their contents "are neither referred to, not intentionally objective, in the whole" (Hua XIX, 369; En. tr. 97). Yet, according to Husserl, the intentionality or the intentional reference is not determined by representation in itself, but by the ability of the object to self-represent itself as a whole and accordingly to be a self-giving object. "Intentional experiences have the peculiarity of directing themselves in varying fashion to presented objects, but they do so in an intentional sense. An object is referred to or aimed at in them, and in presentative or judging or other fashion" (Hua XIX, 372; En. tr. 98). The core sense of intentional acts is based on a more alive and embodied sense of representation.

For this reason, Husserl criticized Brentano's sense of intuitive representation. If the object were given as a whole to the subject, we would fall into some form of psychologism according to which the thing as we think it equates completely to the concreteness of the thing itself. For example, if I think that this person is detestable, then the reality of that person would coincide with its being detestable with no chance to redeem its own concreteness. As Husserl writes: "It is always quite questionable to say that perceived, imagined, asserted or desired objects (etc.) enter consciousness (…) or to say conversely that 'consciousness' or 'the ego' enters into this or that sort of relation to them" (Hua XIX, LI V, 372; En. tr. 98).[16]

Intentionality is not determined by a form of directionality that goes from the subject to the object or vice versa (*concreta* to *abstracta*), because both directions are copresent. Intentionality accompanies the act; it is that with which the act constitutes itself in a particular form of time.

As Husserl wrote, there is no "ego as a relational center" (Hua XIX, LI V, 376; En. tr. 100) (12b), but there is the "I that lives in the act. (…) The idea of the ego may be specially ready to come to the fore, or rather to be recreated anew, but only when it is really so recreated, and built into our act, do we refer to the object in a manner to which something descriptively ostensible corresponds" (Hua XIX, LI V, 376, En. tr. 100). Emotional reality results from the ongoing copresence and coparticipation of subject and object, where the object can be simply its environment or another being.

In the act, we discover the correlation of whole-I and whole-act: "we have here in the actual experience described, a correspondingly complex act which presents the ego, on the one hand, and the presentation, judgment, wish etc. of the moment, with its relevant subject matter" (Hua XIX, LI V, 376, En. tr. 100). "The peculiarity of intending, of referring to what is objective, in a presentative or other analogous fashion" (Hua XIX, LI V, 378; En. tr. 101) means that the intention is what is self-given or meant; that is, an intuitive representation in which the object is given to the subject as a whole (a universal instantiation) and as a part of the stream of lived experience of the consciousness. The object is given as a conceptual presentation determined as a whole in an ideal or logical concept.

> The term intention hits off the peculiarity of acts by imaging them to "aim" at something (...). In talking of "acts" on the other hand, we must steer clear of the word's original meaning: *all thought of activity must be rigidly excluded.*
>
> *(Husserl's emphasis, Hua XIX, LI V, 379; En. tr. 103)*

Intentionality is the act, but the act is not meant in a traditional way as the act of the I that imparts a directionality to the object or vice versa; both the embodied attitude and the conceptual reference to the object are equal components of the intentional act-content.

The sense of the intentional act here is deeply intertwined with the notion of representation we described above. Representation is the ideal whole that determines itself while giving itself sensuously to us; it is the whole that we determine as a meaning. Therefore, when Husserl wrote that "we cannot avoid distinguishing a narrower and wider concept of intention" (Hua XIX, LI V, 379; En. tr. 103) and that sentiments are paradoxically not intentional, but are intentional at the same time, he is restating his theory of intentionality as simultaneously practical and reflexive. Intentionality is what is in the flow of data and what determines this flow; the difference between these two aspects is only temporal and not epistemological or ontological.

I.4 The Intentionality of Pain and Pleasure

As Fisette (2018) remarked, Husserl's theory of the intentionality of emotions is strongly influenced by the long-standing debate on this same topic between his teachers, Stumpf and Brentano, that began in 1899 and ended with Brentano's death in 1916. The main terms of this debate can be summarized in the following way: according to Brentano there are three categories of acts: representations, judgments, and sentiments. Brentano considered emotions as acts that are different from sensory feelings. In fact, according to Brentano, sensory-feelings can trigger emotions but are not themselves emotions. Emotions are, like sentiments of hate and love, high-level acts that are based on representation and affect the representation with a *Mitempfindung* (i.e., a feeling of pleasure or pain).

Stumpf did not agree with this position. He divided phenomena into two main groups: intellectual functions (perceptions, representations, and judgments) and affective functions (emotions, desires, and will). Under the affective functions, he groups sense-feelings and, in particular, anhedonic feelings. There are people who can no longer feel pleasure while doing things that used to give them pleasure. Stumpf gives the example of musicians: it occurred that certain professional musicians lost their *sense of* pleasure, although no specific event caused that change. For Stumpf, this clinical example proves that emotions, taken as *Gefuelsempfindungen* (i.e., pain or pleasure), have no intentional object, but rather are like sensory qualities (like colors or sounds). For this reason, sensations do not involve judgment or representations (differently from other emotions) because they are entirely rooted in sensory life.

Husserl, being a disciple of both Brentano and Stumpf, seems to have taken an intermediate position in this debate. Indeed, in his fifth *Logical Investigation*, he stated that, differently from what Brentano had claimed, pain and pleasure are not intentional because, as stated by Stumpf, they are sensory qualities. Yet, emotions are intentional because, as Brentano remarked, some emotions can be animated by sensory feelings. This would put Husserl in the group of those defending weak intentionalism because the intentional roots of emotions would be sensorial and not intentional. Yet, as we will see in the following sections, the introduction of the genetic approach and passive intentionality led him to espouse a strong intentionalist position in relation to emotions.

According to Husserl, in fact, we can refer to objects that appear to us through the representations[17] that are interwoven with those objects. Sentiments are not intentional because they are self-referential since they arise as an organic reaction to change. Sentiments are not given as a whole but contribute to create a whole by eliciting emotional states. "They [sentiments] are not acts [intentional acts], but are constituted through them" (Hua XIX, 390; En. tr. 109).

On the one hand, this means that Husserl presented sentiments as interwoven with representations even when they are given as nonindependent moments. The intentional objects are entangled with or are comprised of representations, even the feelings with which we feel objects are made of representations. On the other hand, "feeling considered in itself, involves nothing intentional, that it does not point beyond itself to a felt object" (Hua XIX, 388 En. tr. 107). An intentional act of feeling refers to itself as its own object; namely, the sentiment itself given in the form of a represented unity. "We can only direct ourselves feelingly to objects that are presented to us by interwoven presentations (…) only its union with a representation gives it a certain relation to an object" (Hua XIX, 388 En. tr. 107). "The special essence of pleasure demands a relation to something pleasing (…). They all owe their intentional relation to certain underlying presentations" (Hua XIX, 390 En. tr. 109).

In this passage, Husserl showed how *abstracta* (the object as meant) and *concreta* (the object itself) are interrelated, but we name them differently because they imply two different temporal viewpoints. Emotions as sensory feelings and emotions as reflective emotions are given at once as a phenomenon, although when we analyze them it seems that these two steps are connected to each other from a causal-spatio-temporal relationship. We need friends in order to define and feel what friendship is; vice versa, friends need friendship in order to be felt or recognized as friends. If we express this sentence in logical terms, we need to introduce a causal connection, but, in reality, the two instances occur at once.

I.5 Strong Intentionalism of Emotions in Husserl

For Husserl, emotions are intentional through and through because their intentional reference owes something to certain underlying representations. At the same time, these representations are not independent of emotions; rather, they are interwoven with emotions in their peculiar temporal manner. In the description of intentional acts, we need to set aside causal or temporal relationships as they are traditionally meant and accept a viewpoint of temporal dualism (Chapter 1; Waller, 2014). In emotional data, there is no before and after or cause and effect—unless we logically reconstruct these data in a predicative representational manner. Instead, there is a co-foundation that complies to two different forms of time, the living present of emotions and the linear time of logic, in which the parts appear as a systematic unit; that is, a unit that is at once epistemologically and ontologically determined (more on this point in Chapter 4).

To use an example, a club needs members in order to be a club; similarly, my friendship needs friends in order to be considered friendship. Also, from the other direction, members need a club in order to be considered members; similarly, friends need friendship in order to be friends. Therefore, "the relation between founding (underlying) presentation and founded act cannot be correctly described by saying that the former *produces* the latter" (Hua XIX, 390; En. tr. 108). The intentionality of emotions is not weakened, as Crane (1998) seems to have affirmed, because of their proximity to sensory-feelings, as if emotions were an effect or an aftermath produced by sensory feelings. Rather, emotions are intentional through and through because they are interwoven with sensory feelings and these sensory feelings bring about the instantiations of a referential feeling (friends, to use the example above) that allows us to name a content and to recognize in it the whole of its sensory parts (more on parts and whole in the next chapter). *The role of emotions cannot be discarded at any step of the constitution of the reality of our intentional content.* Emotions and sensory-feelings relate to each other in the same way as parts relate to the whole "these relations are purely presentational: we first have an essentially new type of intention (…). Instead of representing a pleasant property of the object, it [the stimulus of pleasure] is referred merely to the feeling subject, or is itself presented and pleases" (Hua XIX, LI V, 395; En. tr. 111). The wholeness of our lived experience is given to us through the interplay of sensory feelings and emotions with our referential skills to make contents present. "Joy concerning some happy event is certainly an act. But this act which is not merely an intentional character, but a concrete and therefore a complex experience does not merely hold in its unity an idea of the happy event and an act-character of liking that relates to it; a sensation of pleasure attaches to the idea" (Hua XIX, LI V, 394 En. tr. 110). Here we have two kinds of representations present: the representation with which feeling joy is given and the representation to which this feeling of joy is attached. The sensuous and the conceptual, the natural, subjective and the phenomenological (or scientific) ones are given simultaneously. "The formation and use of our expressions will at times therefore point to sensory contents, at time to act-intentions, so giving rise to the equivocations in question" (Hua XIX, LI V, 396 En. tr. 111).

I.5.1 Risks of Reductionism

In order to avoid any reductionist and scientistic approach that would equate the two forms of representations, sensuous and cognitive, we need to resist the temptation to choose in favor of the truthfulness of just one of them. Our mind needs to entertain the idea that there are two radically different forms of time which allow the coexistence of sensory animating intention in sentiments and the representational cognitive intentions of meanings; the former is a living present form of time and the second is the causal time. The causal time explains through the linearity of our conventional time how the co-occurrence of sensory data unfolds to us according to a before and after; yet this explanation does not co-incide with the nature of their sensory meaning. This sensuous layer of intention coexists, in fact, with the theoretical or conceptual intention without one being before the other or being its cause. As the sensuous layer determines the parts of the concreteness of the object into a whole, the conceptual layer of the intention determines the meaning of the object by reflecting on its conceptual re-presentation. The reference is intentional where it extends to something that goes beyond the act itself, that is, when there is a relatable whole or entity; this integrity is given through coexistent perceptual and conceptual steps.

In order to avoid reductionism, we need to avoid assimilating reference to content, perceptual to conceptual instantiations, and real to ideal (potentially existing) being since their temporal structure is radically different. If I say I do not like Amy, it does not mean that Amy is not a likeable person; similarly, if I think of certain whales, it does not mean that whales are the whales I think of. Reductionism, and consequently scientism, would tend to reduce the diversity of the two into an equation with the result that reality would be reduced to what appears in the linear conventional time to the observer, in this case the scientist. Following this, the number with which the scientist measures reality would re-duce the being to the number, the content to its reference, the percepts to their concept, the ideal to the real. Instead, the coexistence of this binomial (reference/content, conceptual/perceptual, ideal/real, living present/causal time) is a com-plexity that needs to be entertained and respected when trying to explain life and its reality; if one of the parts is reduced to the other, the complexity of life risks being overly simplified and its sanctity desecrated by the point of view of the strongest one as it happened to be in Tuskegee and Willow. An idea cannot obscure the real, in the same way as my reference is not the only way to explain this content. In the first edition of *Logical Investigations*, Husserl did not yet possess the tools to keep these boundaries clear; we had to wait until 1908, with the introduction of the epoché and reduction, to have an instrument to enhance a clear distinction between these two realms.

I.6 Epoché and Reduction: Toward a Responsible Use of the Intentionality of Emotions

Husserl introduced the epoché and reduction as a way to solve the problem of the correspondence between the intentional object and the object in itself. How can one be sure what we know, that the reality as we experience it is the reality as it is. Similarly to Aristotle, Husserl affirmed that the alterity or transcendence of the object presents itself in the form of a riddle that unfortunately, both for Husserl and Aristotle, can never be solved (Hua III, 38; En. tr. 30). Indeed, this riddle is unsolvable, because to answer the question would require possessing the answer before posing the question. How do we know what we know if we rely upon our already existing knowledge?

A way to get closer to the solution of the riddle would be if we adopted a disinterested, impersonal and almost egoless view; in other words, if we got rid of or at least temporarily suspended the sovereignty of the personal subject implied in the activity of knowing. We can know what we know if to know it we use "knowing" and not our personal act of knowing (i.e., if we parenthesize our own nature[18] in the actual act of knowing). In this case, knowing would be different from I know. We need to *become* an external or transcendent object in order to answer the riddle about the appearance of it to us. Being committed to truth, as a scientist or as any professional, means committing yourself to developing a capacity to set aside your personal character in order to embrace the crisis of meaning that any transcendence involves. The acts through which we create our reality can be biased by our own personality, beliefs, and presuppositions; being a good doctor, nurse, or scientist means to recognize and drop the natural, naive attitude with which we live in the world and assume a theoretical and reflective one that questions all the beliefs we have assumed as real in order to interpret real life as it appears to us in that moment. In order to get the essence of what we call reality, we need to reflect on it from an impersonal perspective, where "impersonal" signifies a standpoint freed from the natural attitude that characterizes everyday egoic life. We need to parenthesize all of our previous assumptions about the object that transcends our capacity to grasp it and try to look at it with new impersonal eyes.

This implies that "every transcendency that is involved must be bracketed, or be assigned the indifference, of epistemological nullity, an index that indicates: the existence of all these transcendences, whether I believe in them or not, is not my concern here; this is not the place to make judgments about them; they are entirely irrelevant" (Hua III, 39; En. tr. 31).

Therefore, in the modes of givenness, every transcendency, even that of our bodies as transcendent objects, can be known only if we bracket the facticity of its existence. This operation is known as *epoché*. The epoché is for Husserl "a methodological device that suspends one's participation in the belief characteristic of the natural attitude, the belief, that the world and its objects exist" (Drummond, 2007, 68). The epoché facilitates our change of attitude from a natural to a theoretical one, which enables us to grasp and reflect upon our previously unrecognized limiting assumptions. It is thanks to the epoché that we assume a critical scientific attitude, both cognitively and emotionally; in fact, by means of the epoché, we recognize that we are already living a crisis of meaning and commit ourselves to the search for truer meanings (Hua, VI, first part).

I.6.1 Ethical Epoché

Husserl specifically mentioned the researcher's enacting of an *ethical epoché* to emphasize the emotional responsibility involved in the act of suspension (Hua VI, 485 ff and 349 ff). It is thanks to this suspension that we are able to scrutinize ourselves through reflection (*Besinnung*) and make ourselves available to the open-ended determination of what our real life is. Enacting the epoché means disengaging ourselves from the expectations of anticipated future egoic willing and even from our heart's desire (Hua XIV, 485) in order to tend to what is given outside of us.

Through this device, we neutralize and suspend our personal belief in what we know or feel in our natural attitude in order to focus, instead, on the directness of what is given to us, that is, on the "force" or "tension" through which we established a contact with that which transcends us. In this way, intentional acts are the *via regia* to begin the exploration of the riddle of the transcendent (Hua III/1, 191) and the epoché is the means to keep separated the conceptual anticipation around the intentional object from its sensuous presentation. The celebrated call, "Back to the things themselves" (Hua XIX/1, 22) expresses exactly this kind of anti-intuitive commitment in which scientists, whether practical or theoretical, suspend their natural attitude in life in order to reflect in a more awake manner upon the things themselves as they are given to us. In this case, their referential assumptions on reality are suspended in order to make space for the givenness of reality itself to speak to them.

I.7 An Epistemological and Emotional Riddle

As stated before, the transcendency of reality and the immanence of the intentional object are not only cognitively problematic, but emotionally as well. How can we be sure that we are not alone and that all that we feel and know is not just a projection of ourselves? How can we prove that what we feel and what we know is not just a figment of our imagination? "Reaching its object has become enigmatic and dubious as far as its meaning and possibility are concerned" (Hua II, 24, 27). Whenever I inquire into the facticity of an object, its wholeness dissolves. When I investigate a factual object, the trees outside of my window, for example, I cannot be sure that what I see is really there as I see it or is the trick of my eyes. In short: how do we avoid solipsism? This is the problem that dominates Husserl's *Cartesian Meditations*.

> Whatever exists for a man like me and is accepted by him, exists for him and is accepted in his own conscious life, which, in all consciousness of a world and in all scientific doing, keeps to itself. All my distinguishing between genuine and deceptive experience and between being and illusion in experience goes on within the sphere itself of my consciousness (…) Every grounding, every showing of the truth and being, goes on wholly within myself.
>
> *(Hua I, 115)*

As this passage states, our being a person is by itself the same as being an external object for others. As far as we remain natural objects, that is, as far as we remain a person in a natural attitude who does not reflect or commit to epoché, there is no way to discern between deception and reality. This is true both for what pertains to the sphere of cognition and the sphere of heart (*Gemüt*). To the extent that we live our lives as natural things, there is no way to thematize our lives and know or feel what this life itself really means and feels like. If we remain in a natural attitude, we cannot reflect on ourselves and grasp the actual meaning we are embodying in our lives. Coming to know the truth and becoming ever freer is the outcome of an ongoing commitment to a transcendental attitude, that is, to that shift in which we decide to set aside our natural personal attitude in order to engage in scientific inquiry. If we are unable to set aside our natural attitude and its unexamined assumptions, all that we know or decide to do could be a deceptive, harmful game. As we will see in the last two sections, being able to entertain this point of view would avoid harmful behaviors in the way in which care professionals approach their clients or even how architects conceive social space. Being able to thematize our experience, analyze our intentions, and see how their emotional and cognitive components constitute reality would allow for the constitution of a more harmonious reality.

According to Landgrebe, we have a "sensing ego, and this is in a fashion such that the ego is conscious of itself not only as a thinking ego but also as one which is sensuously determined" (Landgrebe, 1981, 173–174). Therefore, the riddle of transcendence, how do we know something that goes beyond our own limits, dominates the whole sphere of being, in its cognitive and sensuous essence; both ego's intention and ego's conscious determination need to be thematized in order to resolve the riddle. Being aware of the biases of our ego and its intentions in the way it constitutes its sense of reality is important for leaving enough space to other beings to appear in the horizon of our reality and to contribute to the constitution of its meanings and emotions.

For Husserl, every natural being obeys natural laws, and so does the functioning of intentionality. Even "the numerous cases that are naturally and understandably ranked as cases of theoretical or practical aiming" (Hua XIX/1, 392; LI, 563) can be seen as functional responses to our surrounding world. The job of the phenomenologist is to explain the essence, or *Washeit*, of this being by bracketing as much as possible all the natural theoretical and practical attitudes that can interfere with the essence.[19] The phenomenological bioethicist should be able to commit him/herself to becoming as impersonal as impossible, parenthesize all his/her assumptions in order to look into the essence of the lived experience. For example, although we know what anxiety is, and there is a manual that describes this phenomenon and tells psychotherapists what to do, the phenomenological attitude would encourage them to put aside what is written in the manual in order to grasp a description of the phenomenon as it presents itself in from of them, in a way that is as loyal as possible to the phenomenon itself. This seems to be the most scientific way to learn from the things themselves: let them speak through their own voice.

> Pure phenomenology (…) does not build upon the ground given by transcendent apperception, of physical and animal, and so of psychophysical nature, it makes no empirical assertions, it propounds no judgments that relate to objects transcending consciousness: it establishes no truths concerning natural realities.
>
> *(Hua XIX, 765, 862)*

As a science striving for presuppositionlessness, phenomenology accepts that it will be lived as an ongoing crisis (Hua, VI, first part) and indeed seeks to use that crisis as its method and foundation. Phenomenology is the science that takes the insolubility of the riddle as foundational and calls for its own ongoing renewal as a science (Hua XXVII, 3–13; 43–57). In this sense, a bioethics that participates upon this ground of instability can benefit from an ongoing research and openness to the matter of the phenomenon so that no topic is taken for granted but is the starting point of new scientific research and investigation.

In the following sections, I will describe the essential matter on which epoché and reduction apply and how important these two theoretical devices are in bioethics, especially when discussing the responsibility we hold toward the intentionality of our emotions and their constitutional power in relation to reality.

II. Practical Intentionality or Intentionality of Matter

In Manuscript E III 5 (Hua XV, 593–597), Husserl introduced the expression *impulsive intentionality* (*Triebintentionalitaet*) as a pre-direct, non-volitive, and essentially egoless form of intention. "I have introduced it not as an egoic [intentionality] (characterized in the widest sense intentionality of willing) [but] as founded in a *Ichlose* passivity" (*Universale Teleologie*) impulse that moves everyone from the inside. "The pure hyle is somehow without I" (Manuscript C IV, 18) because the vegetative state of our brain does not require an active presence from us. Most of our bodily decisions are made without us being aware of them: swallowing, digesting, sleeping at night, and so on.

This primal hyle (*Ur-hyle*) is the matter of our nature that is at the basis of instincts which corresponds to undifferentiated material. For example, a person appears to me in a manifold of appearances that gather chaotic hyletic matter into an intelligible form (Hua XVI, 49–50). "The proper appearance and the improper appearance are not separate things; they are united in the appearance in the broader sense" (Hua XVI, 49). Real and ideal, the intuitive and the conceptual are given all at once. "This [the real] appearance is not presentational, although it does indeed make its object known in a certain way" (Hua XVI, 50); the real is not presentational because its appearance is given to us in a first perceptually instinctive manner. "Only what is presented is perceived, given intuitively" (Hua XVI, 50).

What Husserl called "hidden intentionality" (Hua XVI, 21) is a part of that practical intention that comes into being as the primal hyle presents itself and gives itself intuitively. This form of intentionality, properly speaking, is not yet fully reflective because it prepares the ground for reflection (Hua XL, 366; En tr. 21). Yet, we cannot conclude that it is not intentional at all or does not relate to what is phenomenologically intentional because it conveys the content of an object that is beyond or in proximity of something. For example, I instinctively do not trust that person, I turn my head if I see something disgusting, and so on. We would not be able to reflect on any meaning or intentional essence if the matter did not present itself. This is the form of intentionality through which we can see the dynamic pre-reflective dialogue between ourselves as subject and the matter of which we are done (body) and which surrounds us (environment). "Purely through their (pre-hyletic data) own essence and in passing from one mode to the other, *they [subject/matter] found* the consciousness of the unity and of the sameness of what is given to consciousness in them" (Hua XL, 366; En tr. 21). There is "a background lived-experience" that "finds" a way to become "sameness" or "unit" or "present" (Hua XL, 366; En tr. 21). The passivity of our vegetative state holds an intentionality whose responsibility we rarely claim and whose motivations and contents we rarely question; yet this intentionality is equally responsible to the constitution of reality that surrounds us.

"Primordiality is a system of impulses. This intentionality has its transcendent 'goal' in the primordiality as proper goal" (E III 5, cit. in Paci 260–262). This passive and egoless intentionality comes to Being as a *Triebsystem* (system of instincts). It strikes the I—first as a biological body and then as a volitional one—in the form of impulses that animate the matter and stimulate its interpretive side. In this way, the hyletic matter becomes given (F I 24, 41 b). There is continuously a prima hyle there and it adheres in all developed hyle; therefore, conscious I-ness transforms itself continuously into dying [i.e. everything is deposited into a form of possibility (loss of memory)]. This is the form of directness that is at the very basis of ethical acts; being responsible during a medical encounter, for example, involves being able to check also where our biological body (Koerper) is at the moment of the encounter. When the ego—still dormant and egoless—is struck by the movement of hyletic matter, it has the choice to become an I and accordingly act toward a specific chosen direction, or not. Making this direction meaningful is a responsibility of any care-giving professional.

II.1 Intentional Essence

In the first section of the fifth *Logical Investigation*, Husserl defined consciousness as "a comprehensive designation for 'mental acts' or 'intentional experiences' of all sorts" (Hua XIX, 346; En. tr. 81). He dedicated the following sections of the book to explaining what intentional acts are and what makes them intentional. From Sections 20 to 22, he described the essence of intentional acts meant not as acts in which "we live" (Hua XIX, 411; En. tr. 119) but as the phenomena, which appear to us when we reflect on them. An intentional essence is that which makes an act an objectifying one—that is, an act in which the object is presented to us.

The primary structure of an intentional essence is comprised of a correlation of matter and quality. They are unthinkable separately (Hua XIX, 416; En. tr. 122) because quality is the way in which matter presents itself, while matter is that which the quality presents; the former stands for the representational component of the intention, the latter for its sensory component. The two, though, cannot be thought of separately.

"Act quality is undoubtedly an abstract aspect of the act" (Hua XIX, 43; En. tr. 212), and the matter is to a certain extent its concretum. Using the example given by Husserl in the assertion "Ibsen is the principal founder of modern dramatic realism" (Hua XIX, 411; En. tr. 119), the content matter relates to Ibsen and the quality is the assertion in which this content is presented. Or, in the case of a red patch, the matter would be the concreteness that makes the color red and its quality "red" (where the quotes would stand for "representation of").

"The quality can be combined with every objective reference (…) and only determines whether what is already presented in definite fashion is intentionally present as wished, asked, posited in judgment etc. The Matter must be that element in an act which first gives it reference to an object (…) but also the precise way in which it is meant" (Hua XIX, 415; En. tr. 121). The matter is that side of the intentional essence that determines "that it grasps the object but also as what it grasps it." The matter corresponds to Stumpf's sensory qualities and the quality to Brentano's representation—this is the brilliant synthesis Husserl operated from using the teachings of his two masters.

Husserl continued, "the intentional essence does not exhaust the act phenomenologically" (Hua XIX, 416; En. tr. 123). We could not speak about intentional essences if "the fullness or vividness of the sensuous contents" (Hua XIX, 415; En. tr. 121) did not help to "build" the act. Besides quality and matter, the intentional essence needs the concreteness of life in order to operate. The fullness is what exceeds and animates the intentional essence; it is fullness that causes the act of apprehension (*Auffassung*) and therefore the intentional act to grasp the content of the life-world. The intentional act can be directed to an object if there is a fullness, a concrete object, that stimulates that directness.

When we examine the intentional essence, it seems that there is an emotional sensuousness and a material concreteness toward which the quality of our intentional act reacts in determining it according to a specific quality. As we will see in the following sections, it is in fact due to this concrete sensuousness that we are stimulated to our intentional reaction, which is first of all emotional and then epistemological. We want to pull out the data of what appears to us and determine the meaning that their presence has for us.

II.2 Active, Passive, and Practical Intentionality

Husserl attributed intentional essence to a wide variety of acts: cognitive, emotional, and instinctive acts can be intentional, but even sexual, affective, and impulsive acts possess that referential and reflective quality that is the mark of intentional acts. This means that our range of ethical reflection and personal responsibility is quite wide, as well. In my research (2015, 2016, 2018), I have organized all these different forms of intentionality into three main groups: active, passive, and practical intentionality. While active intentionality entails a position-taking (Stellungnahme) and a meaning-giving (Sinngebung) activity in cognitive and axiological direction (Hua III, 207), passive intentionality is a synthetic process that takes place mainly on two egoless organic layers: those of spontaneous (i.e., sensory affections) and non-spontaneous syntheses (i.e., emotions) (Hua XXXIII). The spontaneous syntheses bring together the percepta of our experience according to a principle of homogeneity, while the non-spontaneous ones group around a meaning to assign to these organic data. Through the layers formed by these syntheses, we constitute the material core around which the meaning- and value-giving activity of active intentionality revolves. The transition from egoless synthetic processes to egoic meaning-giving (Sinngebung) activity is characterized by practical intention. In fact, the sphere of irritability (Hua XXXIII, text 1), the layer of affections and reactions, represents the lowest level of affections from which the ego emerges and reacts to the irritating affecting matter by deciding what position it is going to take (Hua XXXIII, text 1, 5, 6, 9, 10). This reactive emergence is rooted in the volitional body (Hua-Mat IV, 186) which bridges nature (passive syntheses) and reflection (active intention). The ego reacts to matter by deciding whether to accept and validate that matter as its own. Some of the material content provided to the ego will remain in the form of passive syntheses; other content will be organized through values and meanings. While the realm of passivity provides heretofore formless matter with a logical or graspable form, the realm of activity is the constitutive pole through which a given number of synthetic layers are comprised in a graspable meaning. The practical intention is that phronetic act through which the subject decides to move toward a self-constituting act in recognizing the interconnection between passive syntheses and its own activity as a self-reflecting subject. *Practical intentionality is a form of practical reflection and "aiming at" that is not naïve, and hence does not equate to action* (Hua XIX, 358). Similarly to thinking, practical intentionality is a form of reasoning that aims at matter in a constitutive way while keeping the distinction between perceptual and conceptual, real and ideal. In *Logical Investigations* (1901), Husserl wrote: "The term intention hits off the peculiarity of acts by imagining them to aim at something and so fits the numerous cases that are naturally and understandably ranked as cases of theoretical and *practical aiming*. In talking of acts, on the other hand, we must steer clear of the word's original meaning: all thought of activity must be rigidly excluded."[20] *Practisches Abzielen* (practical reference) does not refer to a natural action; instead, it refers to a practical and reflexive aiming at—a being consciousness of—that Husserl explains as intentionality in the mode of wakefulness (Hua XLII, 51).

II.3 Examples of Practical Intentionality and Emotions

To give an example (Figure 3.1, Example A) of the arc described by practical intentionality, we might refer to a very common lived experience: it might happen that while in line at the post office a person is hungry (lower passive layers, sensory affections), feels low on energy, and is in a low mood (higher passive level, feelings). This person finds him/herself becoming angrier and angrier (emotions) at the employer because he/she is slow (practical intention). An individual who is used to dealing with his/her emotions would invalidate that anger and attribute that emotion to something personal (active intentionality); *vice versa*, somebody who is not used to this education will act upon it and attribute a meaning or even a value (active intentionality) to that moment of distress [e.g., I feel angry at that employer (meaning) because people at work should give their best (value)].

As shown in Figure 3.1, the reactive emergence of passive physiological matter reaches the volitional body bridging together nature (passive syntheses) and mind (active intention); the volitional body decides whether to accept and validate that matter as its own or to reject it as inappropriate on a meaning level. The volitional body does not know yet what decision it made because reflections, hence the assignation of meanings and values, arise on active levels and are recognized *post hoc* once the subject is awake and takes ownership and responsibility for their own body.

The directionality of the intentional arc could spin in the opposite way; let us assume (Figure 3.1, Example B) that two persons who are in a romantic relationship engage in an uncomfortable conversation. One of the two begins to feel uneasy. While still talking, the hand of this latter starts rummaging in her pocket to

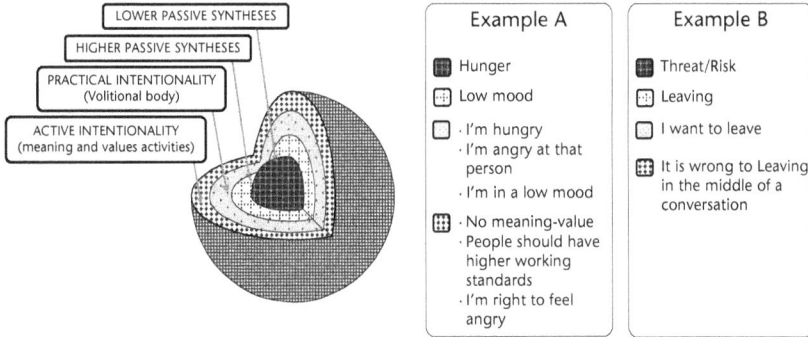

	Example A	Example B
	▦ Hunger	▦ Threat/Risk
	▣ Low mood	▣ Leaving
	▢ · I'm hungry · I'm angry at that person · I'm in a low mood	▢ I want to leave
	▦ · No meaning-value · People should have higher working standards · I'm right to feel angry	▦ It is wrong to Leaving in the middle of a conversation

FIGURE 3.1   Dynamic layers of the intentional arc: Starting with the passive intentionality comprising the lower and the higher passive syntheses, which builds the core, the corona is layered in practical intentionality and active intentionality. Example A: Hunger. Hunger is expressing itself in a living being black. This results in low mood blue. Low mood irritates the volitional body, which awakes to a decision expressed by a practical intentional act. I'm hungry/I'm in a low mood yellow. The interpretation of this organic state and the connected feeling can lead to different outcomes: Either I'm angry at my surrounding or I dismiss my anger because I realize that it is caused by lack of food intake green. Example B: Threat/Risk. Unease triggered by confrontation black. Desire to leave blue. Looking for the keys of the car yellow. This act requires an interpersonal meaning that the subject ignores for lack of awareness green.

look for the key to the car. The partner notices this and accuses her of always running from arguments. She is startled and does not understand what he's talking about until he points out that she is looking for the key to her car. At that point, she can choose whether or not to acknowledge the decision that her body made, or to take responsibility for that small action which might increase the connection with her partner and more importantly with herself. In this case, the intentional arc shows that something from the outside is exerting a force that results in two opposite directions. In fact, on the level of active intentionality, she knows that according to her scale of meanings and values it is not acceptable to abandon an important conversation, but on a passive level the two layers of egoless intentionality push her volitional body toward a flight mode. She is ignoring her emotions although her body cannot, which might result in a worse fight that leads to disconnection and loneliness. Even if her subjectivity is fully engaged in the confrontation, and committed to her partner, something more complex is happening on the intentional level. In fact, the practical intentionality of her volitional body validates the demands of passive intentionality and this hurts the feelings of her partner. To him, the act of preparing to leave has meaning; while to her, there is no meaning because she has not yet made a conscious decision to act. Even a well-educated person, whose awareness and sense of responsibility are higher than normal, may not have the tools to interpret what happens on a passive and practical intentional level and yet many of the most meaningful exchanges happen on that level. One's personality is built upon many of these moments that have the power to reduce or increase distance with the people we love. Practical intention is that phronetic act through which the subject decides to move toward a self-constituting act in recognizing the interconnection between passive syntheses and its own act. The bridge between active intention and passive synthesis is represented by the practical "Ich will und ich tue" (I want and I act) which operates through the means of the emotions that awake the volitional body to a specific action. Being unaware of what's occurring during these moments results in a high level of emotional instability which tremendously impacts our feelings of well-being.

Accordingly, on average, people are not equipped to express themselves during the times when it counts the most. My forthcoming book *The Role of* Bio-*Ethics in Emotional Problems* is dedicated to a description of this distance. Practical intention is that phronetic act through which the subject decides to move toward a self-constituting act in recognizing the interconnection between passive syntheses and its own act. The bridge between active intention and passive synthesis is represented by the practical intention, the "Ich will und ich tue" which operates through the means of the emotions that awaken the volitional body to a specific action. Despite the long-standing debate between Stumpf and Brentano, I do not believe that emotions can be reduced solely either to bodily reactions as a tickle or itch as Stumpf stated or to two basic sentiments such as love and hate, as Brentano claimed. It is important to maintain intact the different nature of the sensuous as well as doxic components of their intention. Practical intentionality is a *Seinsmeinung*, being's self-expression that connects the different temporal nature of mind and body as intention of the being in a knowing act. This form of intention brings together the physiological matter of the body and the spiritual meanings and values of the mind represent a new frontier to the study of the emotional life to increase societal well-being.

III. Cases

In what follows, I am going to examine two practical cases in which neglecting the intentionality of emotions and their constitutional power toward reality has had a damaging effect on society. The first case refers to pain management and emotions; the second case concerns architecture and the unemotional pretense with which common spaces have been organized.

III.1 The Case of Medical Bias in Pain Management

One example of irresponsible use of emotional intentionality in bioethics is the administration of pain treatment. From what has emerged in the literature, it is clear that a biased way of looking at the human body in clinical trials and scientific studies has made its way to wider society. A prevailing view according to which the male body is the fittest one for studies (Bierman, 2007; Kiesel, 2017; Franks, 2019) has led to the consideration that male bodies are the better proxy for research than female bodies, even if the object of research regards the female body. The reason why male bodies are considered better is because they are not subjected to emotional interference. Among those[21] who denounced this problem, Cahill (2017) was the one to dedicate the first ever published neuroscientific journal issue on the topic of sex differences in medical neurological studies. In his work, Cahill (2017) explained that the male body has been seen over the decades as more adequate to medical and anatomical investigations because it is free from the emotional "nuisances" caused by the hormonal cycle. Hence, for years, the best way to study women has been through men because they do not suffer from "the nuisance of emotions" (2017). This reductionist attitude, which flattened one's scientific reference to normative guidelines and eventually to normality, saw the female body as an imprecise variation of the male body.

This assumption led, of course, to very biased trials and studies. One of the most startling examples came from a study on the impact of diets on estrogen's metabolism as a leading cause of breast and uterine cancer conducted by the Journal of National Cancer Institute (Longcope, 1990). Even if the study was clearly targeted at female subjects, all the experiments were conducted on men. Moreover, other studies showed how women who go through coronary bypass surgery are less likely to be prescribed painkillers than men who received the same surgery; or, in an emergency room in the United States, women wait 65 minutes before receiving an analgesic for acute abdominal pain while men wait 49 minutes (Kiesel, 2017); or, still, women are less likely to receive CPR from bystanders (39% versus 45% of men) because of the fear of touching a woman's chest (American Heart Association, 2018). The study "Brave Men and Emotional Women" (2018) summarized in an excellent way these and more gender biases relating to gendered formal and informal norms in health care.

This unquestioned emotional assumption that still impacts the patient-provider encounter and doctors' diagnostic capacity is a good example of an irresponsible way of treating the intentionality of emotions. Instead of applying the epoché on personal assumptions in relation to one's own emotions and reducing the givenness of the human body to the appearance of that specific human body that is in pain, a normative routine which has been predefined as normality prevails. Most of the meanings and values assigned to new medical cases depend on societal pre-given meanings. Let us consider, for example, how it would unfold during a typical medical encounter between a male doctor and a female patient who complains of fatigue and chest pain. It might happen that the passive intentionality of the doctor is programmed on a number of biases that implicitly inform the doctor's behavior at school (gender-biased literature) and in his private life (the "brave man" type). Hence, when the practical intentionality calls for the moment of awakeness in responding to the lived experience of the woman, instead of looking attentively to the symptoms that the woman in his office is lamenting, he only sees a woman, the one he interiorized in his studies and personal life. Therefore, the awakening of practical intention does not elicit a new meaning that fits into the specific case the doctor is handling at the moment because it is not accompanied by any epoché and reduction exercise, that is, his assumptions are not questioned and his attention is not focused on the present lived experience. The meanings and values produced from that encounter are almost egoless units emerging from the passive syntheses of intentionality. The volitional body of the doctor as well as the volitional body of the patient did not allow for a change of attitude but, instead, accepted the pre-given script formed by previous societal lived experiences. Objective treatment passes through a sense of normality that is completely oblivious of the phenomenon as it stands in front of them during that clinical encounter.

The dormant way of treating emotions in general, as if they are the reason why objectivity is lost and of which one should feel ashamed, is producing a growing number of imprecise studies, misdiagnoses, and dismissing behaviors that certainly do not contribute to the well-being of society. Being aware of our passive, active, and practical intentionalities as they pertain to the constitution of our sense of reality and our being open to other ways in which the real comes to us is necessary for us to assume a responsible scientific attitude.

Society has passively built a script around the role of genders, but this script does not serve anymore to our well-being. The "brave man" and the "emotional woman" are on average mis- or underdiagnosed human beings, the former for depression and emotional disorders, the latter for physical pain (2018); men are not allowed to be emotionally unstable or depressed, women should complain less. We need to become ourselves awake and present to our lived experiences in order to care adequately for each other. The educational movie, *Men and Medicine* (1936), for example, showed how males were considered as fitter for the medical profession because of their emotionless approach to medicine, while the movie *Molly Grows Up* (1953) showed how the female hormonal cycle was an unfortunate happenstance with which women had to cope in their daily life while keeping them regularly away from the rest of the society. Referring to the menstrual cycle as the curse, or the haunted mountains for breasts, the valley of doom for buttocks, or the happening for pregnancy shows clearly how awkwardly the intentional layer of meaning and values was already excluding women from the strangeness of their body and accordingly from an equal participation in society. This could happen because of a lack of emotional awakeness in relation to one's own intentional life.

Therefore, as mentioned above, this general disparity led to treating women's pain and medical needs with less scrutiny than men until today (Chen et al., 2008). Magliato (Heart Matters, 2010), one of the few female heart surgeons in the United States, explained how heart disease kills 8 million women per year and is the leading cause of death for women in the world because of an implied bias connected to the way in which the emotional life of women is commonly perceived. The reason why such a preventable disease still causes so many deaths is because women's pain is dismissed or, at best, underdiagnosed as an emotional pain—something that is only in your head. A heart attack's symptoms are different in women than in men: extreme fatigue, shortness of breath, jaw pain, upper abdominal pain; they are not as known as male symptoms because the female body is often excluded from medical trials and so there is less information about them. Since women are considered overly emotional in the way in which they express their pain, when they complain about a symptom they are not listened to as much as others. The case of Katherine Leo, today co-founder of the SCAD Alliance, an association that helps people to prevent SCAD (Spontaneous Coronary Artery Dissection) heart problems, is a case in point. She is a survivor of this form of malpractice; one day she went to the doctor with the suspicion that she was having a heart attack but was dismissed by the doctor because her worry was considered overly sensitive. Katherine began her journey with SCAD in 2003, soon after the birth of her second son. After several weeks of misdiagnoses, she survived a heart attack and an emergency double bypass surgery. Determined to find the cause of SCAD and prevent it from happening to others, she connected with fellow survivors through social media and used their collective voice to launch research at the Mayo Clinic. Women are seven times more likely than men to be misdiagnosed and sent home from the hospital (*Wall Street Journal*, April 24, 2012).

The situation becomes even worse in cases of African-American women. The Institute of Medicine (IOM) showed that 3–6% of black Americans are more likely to be denied treatment or receive less care even if in possession of equal insurance coverage and patient income as the white population (Smedley et al., 2003). "As a result, African Americans are 40% more likely to die from breast cancer, 20% less likely to receive treatment for depression, and 2 times more likely to receive a less desirable treatment for diabetes, such as limb-amputation, than their white compeers" (Families USA 2014). Compounding this problem is the fact that there are not enough black men working within the medical field; only about 2% of the graduating medical class of 2015[22] in the United States were black men (Ansell and McDonald, 2015), so racial differences make it even more difficult to relate, especially when startling assumptions are in place. A study (Hoffman, 2016) revealed that a substantial number of white lay people, medical students, and residents hold false beliefs about biological differences between blacks and whites and demonstrated that these beliefs predict racial bias in pain perception and treatment recommendation accuracy (Hoffman, 2016). It also provided the first evidence that racial bias in pain perception is associated with racial bias in pain treatment recommendations. This study showed that 14% of interns believed that African-American nerve endings are less sensitive, while 17% of interns believed that their blood coagulates more quickly than whites. For this reason, and several others, the mortality gap between African-Americans and whites, as noticed by Dr. Adewale Troutman, increased by a number of 83,000 deaths per year. The belief that

African-Americans feel less pain or that their pain is inevitable prevents adequate care for their medical problems and increases their level of mortality.

If an African-American woman gives birth to a child, she is more likely to die due to complications. From a 2015 study, it emerged that the United States had the highest rate of maternal mortality in the developed world. Every year, about 50,000 U.S. women are severely injured and 700 die during childbirth. The United States has a rate of 26 deaths per 100,000 live births. The United States is one of just five high-income countries to have a rate above 15 deaths per 100,000 live births (Kassebaum et al., 2016).

Exercising a responsible and awake intentionality of our emotions through the practice of epoché and reduction—becoming aware of the role that our volitional body exerts in relation to passive, active, and practical intentionality—can be a way to produce more favorable meanings and values for the dynamism of our professional life.

III.1.1 Pain Treatment: The Invisible Sickness

Another problem that arises from the missed encounter between the lived ex-perience of the patient and that of the provider is the growth of invisible illnesses that are "just in the head." Since the Cartesian substance dualism informs a worldview that separates body from mind, whenever a problem arises that has no immediate biological explanation, it belongs immediately to the mind; hence, exclusion from society and forced isolation seems to be required.

This is the case with myalgic encephalomyelitis (ME) or chronic fatigue syndrome (CFS). CFS is an excruciating medical condition that manifests itself in long-term fatigue, chronic illness, and other persistent problems that prevent the individual from carrying on with their ordinary life. This condition is a devas-tating multisystem disease that causes dysfunction of the neurological, immune, endocrine, and energy metabolism systems. It often follows an infection and leaves 75% of those affected unable to work and of these 25% are homebound and bedridden. An estimated 15–30 million people worldwide have ME (2007, 2017).

Apparently, this condition has been present for decades (it was first recorded in 1934, 2017) under different names: "epidemic fever," "mass-hysteria" (1978, 1973), "mononucleosis," and "Epstein-Barr Syndrome" (1988, 2015). In 2015, the Institute of Medicine proposed calling it "systemic exertion intolerance disease" (2015). To date, it is not yet clear what causes it; those in favor of a psychological explanation interpret it as a conversion or functional disorder and propose a treatment based on cognitive behavioral therapy or psychoanalysis. Moreover, since 85% of those affected by this syndrome are women, those in favor of a psychological explanation have also proposed treating it as a form of hysteria (McEvedy, 1970).

Today, in Denmark, health authorities have the ability to force people affected with this disorder out of their home and to intern them in a hospital because they consider the family in some way involved in the worsening condition of the individuals. Danish physician Per Fink (2012, 2017) maintained that the government was allowed to treat people affected from this condition without their consent because of their mental instability. Karina Hansen is one of the cases that Per Fink has treated without consent. The health authorities tried to remove Karina from her home in 2012. After that attempt, she arranged for her parents to have an attorney to defend their status as guardians (2016) but it did not work. When she was 24 years old, she was removed from her home and taken to Hammel Neurocenter (2013, 2015). They treated her with CBT and graded exercise therapy (GET). Her parents were denied the ability to see her; months later her sister was granted a visit and found her condition had severely deteriorated from the time she had been at home, where she had been capable of occasionally standing up and communicating with others. Recently, her parents have been allowed limited contact with her because they are still considered part of her problem.

The fact that this disease has not received yet a clear diagnostic description triggers a vicious circle for which the researchers who want to study this disorder do not receive enough funds since the disease is considered mental—that is, inexistent since invisible.[23] Even though 15–30 million people are affected by this problem, there is no FDA approval for treatment and a growing lack of education and awareness in relation to this problem.

ME seems to belong only to the *res cogitans*, hence people suffering from it disappear in the solitude of their minds; they truly become "the ghost in the machine" without any machine, though, because their bodies are often incapable of moving. Jennifer Brea explained her fears in these words:

> Sickness does not terrify me. Death does not terrify me. What terrifies me is that you can disappear because somebody tells the wrong story about you.
> *(Brea, J. Unrest, film documentary)*

We have not built any adequate narrative about this and other problems that medicine seems to attribute to emotional disorders. The biased view for which emotions are a disturbing nuisance mutes any attempt to give emotions a dignifying narrative outlet. The lack of a diagnostic is not a sufficient reason to prevent care providers from relating with the lived experience of their patients and listening to their stories. Pre-given labels generate expectations that shut the doors to any serious scientific research and to any possibility of assigning meaning to the lived experience of the suffering people:

> I remained in the hospital for four years. I was in a semi-coma. (…) I was a lost cause. The nurses were getting frustrated at me for not getting better.
> *(Jessica, England, the world of one room)*

A big campaign called #millionmissing was launched to sensitize people to this disorder. "Things can change if people see us," Brea said in her documentary. Squares all over the world have been filled with empty shoes to indicate the presence of these invisible human beings whose condition is "just in their head" and whose space left in society remains "just in their head." Jennifer's husband said:

> There are moments in which I see us through other people's eyes and somehow that's much sadder than when I'm just kind of living our life together. This is normal for us. It's only when other people observe how not normal it is. I'm forced to recalibrate. (…) You know what it is about being observed? It's that people feel sorry for me. ⟨his eyes well up⟩ And I don't know why ⟨reflecting pause⟩ It hits a nerve.
>
> *(Unrest, film documentary, min. 34)*

Being able to observe. Being able to stay in the lived experience that is given in that specific encounter can often be the biggest gift we can offer to people who are in pain. Taking time to stay in that lived experience before our active intentionality starts assigning meanings and values that are not truly connected with the practical and passive intentions that unfold in front of us in that given situation. Being with the story would allow us to be connected in the moment and to truly see the other person. The encounter offers passive data that can elicit moments of wisdom, attention, and care (practical intention) from which we can produce meanings and values (active intention) that are actually congruous to that lived experience, that singular encounter. Being afraid of one's own inadequacy might lead to assigning meanings and values out of habituation and personal projection which are often disconnected from the experience in which we are living. The pain of being observed not for who you are and what you are living but for the projection and cliché that the observer has in mind amplifies a sense of disconnection and pain. "What terrifies me is not death (…) is that I can disappear because one tells the wrong story." Learning how to observe and gather true meanings to tell the true story out of that observation is the first step that we can take in case of unclear medical conditions.

III.2 Emotional Bias in Architecture

Another example of the way in which our society pays the toll for emotional irresponsibility is reflected in the urban design of common spaces. The way in which cities have been organized has contributed to increasing loneliness (Kelly, 2012): half a million of Japanese, for example, are suffering from social isolation; *hikikomori* are those people who lack the basic energy to even get off their sofa. They cannot leave their home for weeks and suffer from chronic depression (Teo, 2013).

In 2018, the minister of the United Kingdom appointed the Minister for Loneliness to fight off the physical consequences of isolation. Loneliness has been estimated to impact a person's physical health as much as smoking 15 cigarettes per day, thus reducing life expectancy significantly. Urban design is responsible for this epidemic. Churchill was not wrong in saying that "we shape our buildings and afterwards our buildings shape us."[24]

The famous architect, Daniel Libeskind explained (2004) how emotions have been exiled from architecture for decades. With time, architecture became a form of attraction that had nothing to do with emotions. A neutralized space and not an emotionally charged one is that which is required from the architect to plan. He cited, as an example, the new national gallery in Berlin as the perfect expression of emotionless architecture: its big glasses and gray colors and the neutrality that the building expresses is, he affirmed, a statement of oppression. Emotion, for Libeskind, is self-reflection in the space; it is what makes the space human. Despite the neutrality of feelings that a building has to express, symbols are emotions themselves and any shape can become a symbol stating the ego of the architect instead of evoking the emotions of the people who are going to use the space. Proust, for example, described how standing in San Marco Cathedral in Venice brought to him a sense of nostalgia evoked by the unevenness of the pavement. It would be more favorable if architects became responsible for their own emotions when planning the space rather than imposing their emotions unconsciously on their users.

On a similar note, Adrian Bica claimed that architecture seems to have forgotten its users and the sense of intimacy, safety, and belongingness that a space should create. He said that on the wave of the Cartesian grid at the end of the seventeenth century buildings were conceived as unmeasurable entities, as if no human being should have lived there, but God only. Later on, the technological criterion—the other face of Cartesian res extensa—of optimization, functionality, became the benchmark for effective architecture: buildings looking in all alike the products they sell (i.e., McDonalds, Wendy's etc.). In line with the body/mind dualism, this form of architecture sees the users as commodities among other commodities, their body-object belongs to place-objects. For example, fast-food chains resemble more and more the products they sell and their spaces are the same everywhere because their space is the commodity they are selling and has a key role in adding meaning and value to the experience of their users. No emotional response is possible in this space; the sense of belongingness and participation is all left to the brand behind which people disappear. Our identity is reduced to the products we consume so that the reductionist process of reification is complete.

Today, cubicle offices, for example, are the byproduct of an efficient way of organizing space even if they clearly do not work. For example, they create stress and lower performances: low ceilings seem to induce lower cognitive processes (Meyers-Levy and Zhu, 2007). Architectural design can solve—or make—problems. Shapes, materials, and plants are just a few of the design elements that make a workspace truly work and keep the neighborhood in mind. The development of an urban culture rooted in privatization and individualism moved the center of life from the public ground to private individual habitative spaces. While in the nineteenth century being together was seen as a form of relaxation, with the dawning of the twentieth century public spaces became an area of transition where eyes do not meet and no conversation or interactions are allowed. Benches disappear or are made more uncomfortable, squares are replaced by streets with shops selling products; the public space becomes a hostile space especially for the poor people who witness the growth of defensive and hostile architecture. An example of this defensive and hostile architecture is "crime prevention through environmental design" (CPTED) which has been developed in several cities and incorporates measures such as anti-homeless and skateboarding spikes, blue lights in public bathrooms to prevent drug users from finding their veins, uncomfortable benches to avoid loitering, and so on.[25]

Libeskind thought that architecture had to tell a story in what it produces: we are introduced to the building through a hallway that prepares the visitors to the kind of space they are going to use, the doors to the various rooms generate a different narrative related to the function that each room has, and so on. Stripping emotions away from a story transforms that story into a report, so it does for architecture as well. Transforming the space into an emotionless product, transforming human beings into products, amplifies our loneliness, anxiety, depression, and all the emotional problems that are plaguing our society. A world built around an emotionless architecture lacks meaning and, as a result, we are living in a space with which we are unable to establish any connection and in which we cannot connect with each other. The buildings we enter every day are unable to evoke the emotions they once did. The contrast expressed by Libeskind between the ought of neutrality and Proust's experience of unevenness in the San Marco Cathedral is an example of this. Losing touch with the place where we work every day, being unable to connect with others when spending time outside, and being unable to go outside at all reduces tangibly the space we have to be whole human beings. Clearly, this is not conducive to a healthy society.

To give one last example, according to some scholars (Richards, 2007; Serenyi, 1974), the celebrated architecture of Le Corbusier lacked, on purpose, this emotional quality. Richard remarks how most of his famous work, such as Villa Savoye (1928) and the pilgrimage chapel at Ronchamp (1955) might consider as an exception to his "mentally disturbed city planning". Below Richards continues:

> The prospect of German cities bombed flat by the Allies during World War II made him envious—the Germans were able to rebuild from ground zero. He made plans that would mean (as he put it himself) the "Death of the Street." In proposing the elimination of side alleys and shops, in granting limited space for cafés, community centers, and theaters, in

dispersing them over great distances, and constructing them of uninviting concrete, glass, and steel (…) He forgot cities exist to facilitate socializing.

(2007, 52 passim)

For this reason, Serenyi compared his work to Fourier's *The Social Destiny of Man* (1808)[26] in that both imagined an ideal society as built around the antisocial drive that regulated, according to both, the inner nature of each human being.

The exemplarity of LeCorbusier's work had important social repercussions; for example, the architect Francesco di Salvo followed LeCorbusier's model with Le Vele di Scampia in Naples. In a particularly poor neighborhood of this Italian city, he created a complex of seven large buildings (three were pulled down between 1997 and 2003 and the last four in 2019) inspired by Le Corbusier's Unité d'habitation in Marseilles. The goal was to create a self-sufficient neighborhood with shops and cafés to reinforce the sense of community and sociality among its inhabitants. Unfortunately, the result was the creation of a big ghetto where small spaces, alleys, and tunnels favored the proliferation of criminality in the already poor neighborhood.[27] The thoughtlessness in relation to that particular neighborhood clashed with the ego of the architect. In this case as well, his active intentionality proposed a meaning based on the passivity of his own studies more than on the awakeness and presence to that specific lived experience and its emotional charge. Erroneously, the architect imposed emotional neutrality instead of accommodating the emotional richness of the neighborhood in which he was working.

To counterbalance this top-down form of urbanization, a movement of cohousing started in Denmark in 1968. The project of building neighborhoods according to a demand from the bottom has now spread all over the world: Italy, Switzerland, Germany, France, Great Britain, Australia, and the United States. The motto of cohousing is marked by a very emotional statement: happiness is given from the sense of community and belongingness. The way to put this emotional guideline in practice has been through participated projects, building community, choosing the people and families who are going to share the habitative units, accepting people with difficult past experiences and integrating them in a healthy environment, and creating common spaces that can be used by their inhabitants as relaxing or actively socializing areas. The Danish cohousing community started in 1960 in Saettedamen in response to an article titled "Children Should Have One Hundred Parents," by Bodil Graae. After 30 years, this architectural project still proves to have successfully improved the quality of life of more than 50 families by preventing isolation and maximizing the quality and contribution that each person can give to and receive from the community (elders, young parents, professionals). A second group that formed was inspired by an article *"The Missing Link between Utopia and the Dated Single Family House"* written in 1968 by Jan Gudman Hoyer who had studied architecture at Harvard. The Danish term *bofællesskab* (living community) was introduced to North

America as *cohousing* by two American architects, Kathryn McCamant and Charles Durrett. Natasha Reid, for example, responded to the housing crisis in London with intimate infrastructures that elicit social integration while coping with the problem of resources. This form of intimate designing questions the idea of towers as a better way to exploit land and density of population by transforming the space into intimate chosen coexistence between individuals through the use of common areas like kitchens, living rooms, and gardens. Cohousing and other forms of architecture, I would say, are rapidly expanding and questioning the way in which the space has been conceived and organized to date.

Conclusion

This chapter is an investigation of the theoretical and practical implications of emotions in our intentional life. In the first part of the chapter, I discussed the meaning of intentionality and argued that emotions are intentional through and through. After having discussed weak (Crane, 1998) and strong (De Sousa, 1987) intentionalism in relation to emotions and the two strategies proposed by strong intentionalism, the perceptual and the evaluative one, I laid out a third alternative (Husserl, 1901/01; Deonna and Teroni, 2012) to present emotions as fully intentional. In his *Logical Investigations*, V, Section 15 (1900/01) Husserl took a position in relation to his masters, Stumpf and Brentano, concerning the problem of the intentionality of sentiments like pleasure or pain. According to Husserl, especially in his later works (1926), emotions can be intentional because their sensory qualities animate the directedness expressed by the way in which the emotion appears to the observer. The way in which Husserl explained the intentional essence of emotions invites us to avoid any reductionist and psychologistic approach in that he kept the sensuousness and the meaning, the real and ideal, as two different temporal substances which instantiate themselves in the appearance of the phenomenon. The fact that emotions can be considered intentional through and through means that we can track the direction of our emotional life and tend to it in a responsible and aware manner. To facilitate the understanding of the complex intricacy of the intentional web, I have organized the different forms of intentionality mentioned by Husserl in three groups: passive, active, and practical intentions. While the passive intentions belong to sensory affections and lower feelings (instincts, pulsions), practical intentions (wisdom, care) define that moment of awakening in which the given-content is considered in an attentive way by the volitional body which decides whether to accept that content as an object and assign a meaning or value to it or to reject it and push it back to the passive layer. Active intentionality, instead, indicates a meaning- and value-assigning act which operates on the content of that lived experience that has been approved by the volitional body. Epoché and reduction are two theoretical devices introduced by Husserl to facilitate the eidetic process of looking at the essential structure of the intentional content and eliciting an ethically balanced way of looking at the multifaceted reality that unfolds from the intentional contents.

In the second part of the chapter, I examined practical cases in which an implied refusal to tend to the intentional power of emotions and a lack of aware participation in one's intentional life can severely impact the well-being of individuals and society. In medicine, the examples of pain treatment management and misdiagnosis in women show how strongly implied personal biases against emotions can harm the life of individuals. Similarly, the examples of neutral emotionless architecture serve as a showcase to prove how impoverishing an emotionless planning can be for the quality of our daily life at home and at work.

Notes

1 For the origins of the concept of intentionality, see Knudsen, C. (1982). Intentions and impositions. In Kenny, A. et al. (eds.) *The Cambridge History of Later Medieval Philosophy*. Cambridge: Cambridge University Press; Caston (1998). "Aristotle and the problem of intentionality." *Philosophical and Phenomenological Research*, 58(2), 249–298. For a general survey, and further bibliography, see Tim Crane 'Intentionality,' forthcoming in the Routledge Encyclopedia of Philosophy, E. J. Craig (ed.) London: Routledge, 1998.

2 "Every mental phenomenon is characterized by what the Scholastics of the Middle Ages called the intentional (or mental) inexistence of an object, and what we might call, though not wholly unambiguously, reference to a content, direction towards an object (which is not to be understood here as meaning a thing), or immanent objectivity. Every mental phenomenon includes something as an object within itself, although they do not all do so in the same way. In presentation something is presented, in judgement something is affirmed or denied, in love loved, in hate hated, in desire desired and so on. This intentional in-existence is characteristic exclusively of mental phenomena. No physical phenomenon exhibits anything like it. We could, therefore, define mental phenomena by saying that they are those phenomena which contain an object intentionally within themselves" (Brentano, 1874/2008, 88).

3 See Freeman W. (2000). "Emotion is essential to all intentional behaviors."

4 To mention also is the difference between intentionality (intention) and intensionality (word reference). For example, a person with a heart and a person with a kidney might have two same intentions, but they have two different intensions because the intensions refer to the meaning presentation (i.e., "heart," "kidney") and to the same content phenomenon, person. The puzzles of intentional inexistence have tried to explain the ontological difficulties of higher semantic levels that can, as Willard Van Orman Quine (1960, 272) says, "carry the discussion into a domain where both parties are better agreed on the objects (viz., words)." In contemporary analytic philosophy, Roderick Chisholm (1957, 298) was the first to contemplate the formulation of "a working criterion by means of which we can distinguish sentences that are intentional, or are used intentionally, in a certain language from sentences that are not." The idea is to examine sentences that report intentionality rather than intentionality itself.

5 In particular, the dispute between the theory of direct reference and either the Fregean distinction between sense and reference or the Russellian assumption that ordinary proper names are disguised definite descriptions can be seen as internal to the orthodox paradigm according to which there are only existing objects (i.e., concrete particulars in space and time).

6 Meinong's theory was openly rejected by Brentano, though.

7 As Jacob (2010) explains: "Meinong (1904) supposed that objects like Zeus, the fountain of youth, Sherlock Holmes, etc., are non-existent objects which exemplify the properties attributed to them. In his view, the fountain of youth is an object that instantiates both the property of being a fountain and that of having waters which confer everlasting life. But it fails to instantiate the property of existence. Meinong seemed to suppose that for any group of properties, there is an object which instantiates those properties. Some of the resulting objects exist and others do not. Russell (1905) found this view of intentional objects ontologically unacceptable since it involves the acceptance of entities such as golden mountains (which are inconsistent with physical and chemical laws) and round squares (which are inconsistent with the laws of geometry). His theory of definite descriptions was precisely designed to avoid these ontological consequences (see section 5). However, by clarifying distinctions proposed by both Meinong and his student Ernst Mally, Parsons (1980) has recently offered a theory of non-existent objects, which is based on the assumption that existence is a special kind of property. This theory uses a quantifier '∃', which does not imply existence. To assert existence, he uses the predicate '$E!$'. Thus, the assertion that there are non-existent objects can be represented in Parsons' theory without contradiction by the logical formula '$\exists x(\sim E!x)$.' Furthermore, Parsons distinguishes between 'nuclear' and 'extranuclear' properties. Only the former, which are ordinary, non-intentional kinds of properties, contribute to individuating objects. The set of extranuclear properties involve intentional properties, modal properties and existence. Armed with this distinction among properties, Parsons (1980) has been able to avoid Russell's objections to Meinong's naive theory of intentional objects. (For further details, see Parsons, 1980.) An original account of the possibility of entertaining true thoughts about non-existent objects, based on the contrast between pleonastic (or representation-dependent) and non-pleonastic (natural or substantial) properties, has been developed by Crane (1998)."

8 Chisholm has defended the theory according to which Brentano's theory involves a psychological and ontological aspect. Existence independence, referential opacity, and truth-value indifference are the distinctive criteria for the intentional use of a sentence. Searle, on the other hand, argues that no syntactic operation performed by the subject would result in a full-rounded semantic content considering the role played by human psychological ability in meaning-making. Intentionality is the mark of a human self-organizing network.

9 Srzednicki (1965, 70, 108), for example, remarks against Brentano's reism that these two statements are not (logically) equivalent: "The statement A is good is different from someone who approves of A does something proper."

10 Similarly to what was stated in the previous two chapters, this debate did not start in the last centuries. See Galilei: "Hence I think that tastes, odors, colors, and so on are no more than mere names so far as the object in which we place them is concerned, and that they reside only in the consciousness. Hence if the living creature were removed, all these qualities would be wiped away and annihilated" (Galilei, 1623, 66) and similar arguments are used in Descartes, *Principles,* vol. I, 254–255.

11 Although Teroni and Deonna do not seem to consider the neutral valence of emotions (Routledge, 2014), I agree with Husserl (1901/1984) in thinking that the adiaphoron is a third possible valence.

12 Ratcliffe (2005) and Ellsworth (1994) provide reasons for thinking that William James gives more attention to the world directedness of the emotions than is usually claimed. Damasio (2000) does for psychology what Prinz (2004) does for philosophy (i.e., he reconciles cognitive and feeling theories of the emotions within a Jamesian framework). The perceptual analogy is nicely drawn in de Sousa (1987, 149–158). Aside from Goldie (2000, Chapter 3) and Tappolet (2000), recent sympathizers of a perceptual approach to the emotions are Deonna (2006), Döring (2007), Johnston (2001),

and Tye (2008). Goldie (2009) persuasively stresses the role of feeling in accounting for the emotions' world directedness. While Deonna (2006) attempts to downplay some of the dissimilarities between emotions and perceptions, Brady (2010), Salmela (2011), Wedgwood (2001), and Whiting (2012) adopt for various reasons a resolutely skeptical attitude toward the approach.

13 Berkeley put the problem in these terms: "It may perhaps be objected that if extension and figure exist only in the mind, it follows that the mind is extended and figured, since extension is a mode or attribute which (to speak with the Schools) is predicated of the subject in which it exists. I answer, those qualities are in the mind only as they are perceived by it? that is not by way of mode or attribute, but only by way of idea." (*A Treatise Concerning the Principles of Human Knowledge.* New York: The Liberal Arts Press, 1957, 46).

14 This problem is part of a long-standing debate concerning nonexistent objects and the problem of representation. Sparked by Brentano's theory, this problem invested thinkers such as Twardoski, Marty, Meinong, Frege, and Husserl who approached a solution that tried to fill the gap between a definition of nonexistent objects as ideals and percepta. If you want to read more of my take on this debate, please see Ferrarello (2016).

15 This and the following sections are a rephrasing of parts of my Husserl's E*thics and Practical Intentionality.* Bloomsbury, 2015, 103–105; 123–128).

16 As Hickerson (2007) noted, James' theory of fringe might be useful to better understand Husserl.

17 As I showed in Chapter 2, the word *Vorstellung* in Husserl is highly problematic. It can point to the *act-matter* through which an object is given to me in a specific manner; it can stand for a *presentation*, meaning the qualitative modification of belief; it can signify a nominal act by virtue of which an object is assigned to a specific name; it can coincide with the objectifying act; or it can be an intuition of a presented object. Here I am using the word in the first sense that blurs the distinction between object-matter and representative.

18 In this section, I am going to use the word *nature* to refer to the natural attitude.

19 It is vital to "dismantle everything that already pre-exists in the sedimentations of sense in the world of our present experience (…), to interrogate these sedimentations relative to the subjective source out of which they have developed and, consequently, relative to an effective subjectivity (…) not the subjectivity of psychological reflection (…), but as a subjectivity bearing within itself, and achieving, all of the possible operations to which this world owes its becoming. In other words, we understand ourselves in this revelation of intentional implications, in the interrogation of the origin of the sedimentation of sense from intentional operations, as transcendental subjectivity" (Husserl, 1901/1984, 47–49 passim).

20 Emphasis mine, Hua XIX, 358: "Der Ausdruck Intention stellt die Eigenheit der Acte unter dem. Bilde des Abzielens vor und passt daher sehr gut auf die mannigfaltigen Acte, die sich ungezwungen und allgemein.verständlich *als theoretisches oder praktisches Abzielen* bezeichnen lassen. (…) Was andererseits die Rede von Acten anbelangt, so darf man hier an den ursprünglichen Wortsinn von actus natürlich nicht mehr denken, der Gedanke der Betätigung mufs schlechterdings ausgeschlossen bleiben."

21 Liu (2016): "In the 1990s, women's advocates teamed up with Congress to draw attention to women's exclusion from clinical research. Even some very large foundational studies only included half of the population. The National Institutes of Health had a policy urging researchers to include women, however, it was loosely implemented, if at all. The FDA also explicitly excluded women of childbearing age from participating in early phase drug trials, in case they accidentally became pregnant. And some researchers argued that women's varying hormonal states and cycles would complicate their results; it was just easier and cheaper to study men, who were

considered a more homogeneous group. The FDA has since dropped their policy. In 1993, Congress passed the NIH Revitalization Act, which requires federally-funded Phase 3 research to include women, and to include enough of them to analyze results by gender. However, Dusenbery said that women still tend to be underrepresented in particular research areas, including heart disease, cancer and HIV/AIDS. Experts have described it to me as sort of an 'add women and stir' approach."

22 After the IOM discovered the presence of health care disparities, it offered one solution to this complex problem: raise awareness (Smedley et al., 2003). Shortly thereafter, many new programs emerged in order to spread the news of the presence of health disparities. In theory, raising awareness among physicians and other health care providers of health disparities was thought to reduce such differences in care by making clinicians more observant in how they treat their patients.

23 On this point, I want once again to remind that it is very important to enforce the Mental Health Parity Act (1996) and treat mental problems with the same dignity and funds as physical problems.

24 Retrieved from https://www.parliament.uk/about/living-heritage/building/palace/architecture/palacestructure/churchill/.

25 Fortunately, we realized the predicament of this form of conceiving the space and initiatives like happy or listening benches started developing in the United Kingdom in order to face the growing problem of solitude.

26 See Richards (2007): "Fourier's basic argument was that human beings are driven by antisocial 'passions' and that their natural tendency is to drift apart or, if forced to live together, become hostile to one another. Fourier's 'ideal' society was shaped to manage this situation. In *The Social Destiny of Man* (1808), he proposed to divide society into units of about sixteen hundred inhabitants apiece—live-in workshops (for want of a better description), each occupying a large building that he termed a 'phalanstery.' The productivity of each unit was to be managed by a professional executive, the 'areopagus,' which would also try managing the social relations of inmates. And just before they started killing each other, as inevitably they would, the inmates would be dispersed to new phalansteries. Serenyi argues that this plan of Fourier's and the urban designs of Le Corbusier are similarly deranged."

27 The movie *Gomorra* (2008) is a useful visual aid to appreciate the magnitude of this problem.

Bibliography

Alan R. T. (2012). "Social isolation associated with depression: A case report of hikikomori", *International Journal of Social Psychiatry*, 59(4): 339–341.

American Heart Association. (2018). "Why women receive less CPR from bystanders", *ScienceDaily*, 5 November 2018. Retrieved 31 August 2020 from www.sciencedaily.com/releases/2018/11/181105105453.htm.

Ansell, D. A., McDonald, E. K. (2015). "Bias, black lives, and academic medicine", *New England Journal of Medicine*, 372, 1087–1089.

Aristotle, Metaphysics, *classics.mit.edu*. The Internet Classics Archive. Retrieved 30 January 2019.

Aristotle, On Ideas, *classics.mit.edu*. The Internet Classics Archive. Retrieved 30 January 2019.

Aristotle, On the Soul, *classics.mit.edu*. The Internet Classics Archive. Retrieved 30 January 2019.

Bain, D. (2003). "Intentionalism and pain", *The Philosophical Quarterly*, 53(213): 502–523.

Bain, D. (2011). "The imperative view of pain", *Journal of Consciousness Studies*, 18(9–10): 164–185.

Berkeley, A. (1957). *Treatise Concerning the Principles of Human Knowledge*. New York: The Liberal Arts Press.

Bierman, A. S. (2007). "Sex matters: Gender disparities in quality and outcomes of care", *Canadian Medical Association Journal*, 17(12): 1520–1521.

Block, N. (1983). "Mental pictures and cognitive science", *Philosophical Review*, 92, 499–541.

Brady, M. (2010). "Virtue, emotion, and attention", *Metaphilosophy*, 41.1–41.2, 115–131.

Brentano, F. (1874/2008). *Psychologie vom empirischen Standpunkt. Von der Klassifikation psychischer Phänomene*, In A Chrudzimski (ed.). Frankfurt: Ontos Verlag.

Byrne, A. (2001). "Intentionalism defended", *Philosophical Review*, 110, 199–240.

Cahill, L. (2010) "Sex influences on brain and emotional memory: The burden of proof has shifted". In I. Savic, (ed.). *Sex Differences in the Human Brain, Their Underpinnings and Implications*, Progress in Brain Research 186, 29–40.

Cahill, L. (2017), "An issue whose time has come", *Journal of Neuroscience Research*, 95, 12–13.

Caston, V. (1998). "Aristotle and the problem of intentionality", *Philosophical and Phenomenological Research*, 58(2): 249–298.

Chen, E. H., Shofer, F. S., Dean, A. J., Hollander, J. E., Baxt, W. G., Robey, J. L., Sease, K. L., and Mills, A. M. (2008). "Gender disparity in analgesic treatment of emergency department patients with acute abdominal pain", *Academic Emergency Medicine: Official Journal of the Society for Academic Emergency Medicine*, 15(5): 414–418.

Chrudzimski, Arkadiusz, Smith, Barry (2004). Brentano's ontology: from conceptualism to reism. In Dale Jacquette (ed.). *The Cambridge Companion to Brentano*. Cambridge University Press, 197–220.

Colombetti, Giovanna. (2005). Appraising valence, *Journal of Consciousness Studies*, 12.

Committee on the Diagnostic Criteria for Myalgic Encephalomyelitis/Chronic Fatigue Syndrome on the Diagnostic Criteria for Myalgic Encephalomyelitis/Chronic Fatigue Syndrome (2015). "Board on the Health of Select Populations; Institute of, Medicine", Beyond Myalgic Encephalomyelitis/Chronic Fatigue Syndrome: Redefining an Illness.

Crane, T. (1998). "Intentionality as the mark of the mental", *Royal Institute of Philosophy Supplement*, 43, 229–251.

Crane, T. (1998) "Intentionality." E. J. Craig (ed.). *Routledge Encyclopedia of Philosophy*. London: Routledge.

Damasio, A. (2000). *The Feeling of What Happens: Body and Emotion in the Making of Consciousness*. New York: Harcourt Brace.

De Sousa, R. (1987). *The Rationality of Emotion*. Cambridge, MA: The MIT Press.

Deonna, J. (2006). "Emotion, perception, and perspective", *Dialectica*, 60.1, 29–46.

Deonna, J. Teroni, F. (2012). *The Emotions: A Philosophical Introduction*. London: Routledge.

Deonna, Julien A., Teroni, Fabrice (2012). *The Emotions. A Philosophical Introduction*. London/New York: Routledge.

Descartes, R. (1649/1989). *The Passions of the Soul*, translated by S. H. Voss. Indianapolis: Hackett.

Dewey, J. (1895). "The theory of emotion. The significance of emotions", *Psychological Review* 2, 13–32.

Dokic, J. (2003). "The sense of ownership: An analogy between sensation and action".

In J. Roessler and N. Eilan (eds.). *Agency and Self-Awareness: Issues in Philosophy and Psychology*. Oxford: Oxford University Press.

Döring, S. (2007). "Affective perception and rational motivation", *Dialectica*, 61.3, 363–394.

Dretske, F. (1995). *Naturalizing the Mind*. Cambridge: The MIT Press.

Drummond, J. J. (2007). *Husserlian Intentionality and Non-Foundational Realism*. Holand: Springer.

Ellsworth, P. C. (1994). "William James and emotion: A century of fame worth a century of misunderstanding?", *Psychological Review*, 101.2, 222–229.

Ferrarello, S. (2016). *Husserl's Ethics and Practical Intentionality*. London/New York: Bloomsbury.

Ferrarello, S. (2018). "Husserl's ethics and psychiatry", ed. Englander, M., *Phenomenology and the Social Context of Psychiatry*. London/New York: Bloomsbury.

Ferrarello, S. (2019). *Phenomenology of Sex, Love and Intimate Relationships*. London/New York: Routledge.

Ferrarello, S., Zapien, N. (2018). *Ethical Experience: A Phenomenology*. London/New York: Bloomsbury.

Fillingim, R. B., King, C. D., Ribeiro-Dasilva, M. C., Rahim-Williams, B., Riley, J. (2009). "Sex, gender, and pain: a review of recent clinical and experimental findings", *The Journal of Pain*, 10(5): 447–485.

Fink, P. (2017). "Syndromes of bodily distress or functional somatic syndromes - Where are we heading. Lecture on the occasion of receiving the Alison Creed award 2017", *Journal of Psychosomatic Research*, 97, 127–130.

Fisette, Denis (2018). Phenomenology and descriptive psychology: Brentano, Stumpf, and Husserl. In Dan Zahavi (ed.). *Oxford Handbook of the History of Phenomenology*. Oxford: Oxford University Press, 88–104.

Franks, D. (2019). "Sex differences in the human brain, neurosociology: Fundamentals and current findings", 101–105.

Freeman W. (2000). "Emotion is essential to all intentional behaviors." In M. Lewis, I. Granic (eds.). *Emotion, Development, and Self-Organization: Dynamic Systems Approaches to Emotional Development*. Cambridge: Cambridge University Press.

Galilei, G. (1623) *The Assayer*. Project Gutenber, online.

Goldie, P. (2000). *The Emotions: A Philosophical Exploration*. Oxford: Oxford University Press.

Goldie, P. (2009) "Getting feelings into emotional experience in the right way", *Emotion Review*, 1.3, 232–239.

Greiner, A. C., Knebel, E. (2003). "Health professions education: A bridge to quality". *Institute of Medicine (US) Committee on the Health Professions Education Summit*. Washington, DC: National Academies Press.

Grossmann, Reinhardt (1969). Non-existent objects: recent work on brentano and meinong, *American Philosophical Quarterly*, 6(1): 17–32.

Guideline 53: Chronic Fatigue Syndrome/Myalgic Encephalomyelitis (or Encephalopathy). (2007). London: National Institute for Health and Clinical Excellence.

Hall, R. J. (2008). "If it itches, scratch!", *Australasian Journal of Philosophy*, 86(4): 525–535.

Harman, G. (1990). "The intrinsic quality of experience", *Philosophical Perspectives*, 4, 31–52.

Hickerson, R. (2007). *The History of Intentionality*. London: Routledge.

Hoffman, K. M., Trawalter, S., Axt, J. R., and Oliver, M. N. (2016). "Racial bias in pain assessment and treatment recommendations, and false beliefs about biological differences between blacks and whites", *PNAS Proceedings of the National Academy of Sciences of the USA*, 113(16): 4296–4301.

Holmes G. P., Kaplan J. E., Gantz N. M., Komaroff A. L., Schonberger L. B., Straus S. E., Jones J. F., Dubois R. E., Cunningham-Rundles, C. Pahwa, S. (1988). "Chronic fatigue syndrome: A working case definition", *Annals of Internal Medicine*, 108(3): 387–389.

Hurley, R. W. Adams, M. C. (2008). "Sex, gender, and pain: An overview of a complex field". *Anesthesia & Analgesia*, 107, 1, 309–317.

Husserl, E. (1901/1984). *Logische Untersuchungen.* U. Panzer (ed.). Den Haag: Martinus Nijhoff.

Jacob, P. (2010). "Intentionality", *Stanford Encyclopedia of Philosophy.*

Johnston, M. (2001). "The authority of affect", *Philosophy and Phenomenological Research*, 53, 181–214.

Kassebaum, N. J. (2016). "Global, regional, and national levels of maternal mortality, 2015", *The Lancet*, 388(10053), P1775–1812.

Kelly, J-F., Breadon, P., Davis, C., Hunter, A., Mares, P., Mullerworth, D., and Weidmann, B. (2012). *Social Cities.* Melbourne: Grattan Institute.

Kiesel, L. (2017). "Women and pain: Disparities in experience and treatment", *Harvard Health Online.* https://www.health.harvard.edu/blog/women-and-pain-disparities-in-experience-and-treatment-2017100912562.

Knudsen, C. (1982). "Intentions and impositions" Kenny, A. et al. (eds.), *The Cambridge History of Later Medieval Philosophy.* Cambridge: Cambridge University Press.

Landgrebe L. (1981) Regions of Being And Regional Ontologies in Husserl's Phenomenology. In: W. McKenna, R. M. Harlan, L. E. Winters (eds.). *Apriori and World. Martinus Nijhoff Philosophy Texts*, vol 2. Springer, Dordrecht.

Langer, A., Horton, R., and Chalamilla, G. (2013) "A manifesto for maternal health post-2015". *Lancet*, 381, 601–602.

Libeskind, D. (2004). *Breaking Ground.* New York: Riverhead Books.

Liu, K. A., Dipietro, M. (2016). "Women's involvement in clinical trials: Historical perspective and future implications unequal treatment: Confronting racial and ethnic disparities in health care", *Pharmacy Practice*, 14(1), 708.

Lloyd Waller, Rebecca (2014). *Descartes' Temporal Dualism.* Maryland: Lexington Book

Longcope, C. (1990). "Relationships of estrogen to breast cancer, of diet to breast cancer, and of diet to estradiol metabolism", *Journal of the National Cancer Institute*, 82, 11, 6: 896–898.

Lycan, W. (1996). *Consciousness and Experience.* Cambridge: The MIT Press.

Magliato K. (2010). *Heart Matters*, New York: Three Rivers Press.

McEvedy, C., Beard, A. (1970). "Royal free epidemic of 1955: A reconsideration", *The British Medical Journal*, 1(5687): 7–11.

McEvedy, C. P., Beard A. W. (1970). "Concept of benign myalgic encephalomyelitis", *British Medical Journal*, 1(5687): 11–15.

Meyers-Levy, Joan, Zhu, Rui Juliet (2007). The influence of ceiling height: The effect of priming on the type of processing that people use, *Journal of Consumer Research*, 34, 174–186.

Neu, Jerome (2000). *A Tear is an Intellectual Thing: The Meanings of Emotion.* Oxford, New York: Oxford University Press.

Nussbaum, Martha C. (2001). *Upheavals of Thought: The Intelligence of Emotions.* Cambridge: Cambridge University Press.

Parish, J. G. (1978). "Early outbreaks of 'epidemic neuromyasthenia'", *Postgraduate Medical Journal*, 54(637): 711–717.

Pitcher, G. (1971). *A Theory of Perception. Princeton.* Princeton, NJ: Princeton University Press.

Plato, *Cratylus*, E. N. Fowler (trans.). The Perseus Digital Library. Retrieved 31 August 2020.

Plato, *Parmenides*. The Internet Classics Archive. Retrieved 30 January 2019 classics.mit.edu.

Prinz, Jesse (2004). *Gut Reactions: a Perceptual Theory of Emotion*. Oxford: Oxford University Press.

Ratcliffe, M. (2005). "Willam James on emotion and intentionality", *International Journal of Philosophical Studies*, 13.2, 179–202.

Richards, S. (2007). "The antisocial urbanism of Le Corbusier", *Common Knowledge*, 13(1): 50–66.

Richardson, J., Holdcroft, A. (2009). "Gender differences and pain medication", *Women's Health*, 5(1): 1–12.

Salmela, M. (2006). "True emotions", *Philosophical Quarterly*, 56.224, 382–405.

Salmela, M. (2011). "Can emotions be modelled on perception?", *Dialectica*, 65.1, 1–29.

Samulowitz, A., Gremyr, I., Eriksson, E., Hensing, G., and Gazerani, P. (2018). "Brave men" and "emotional women": "A theory-guided literature review on gender bias in health care and gendered norms towards patients with chronic pain", *PainResMag*. 2018:6358624.

Sartre, J.-P. (1940/1995). *The Psychology of the Imagination*. London: Routledge.

Schröder, A., Rehfeld, E., Ørnbøl, E., Sharpe, M. L., Rasmus W., and Fink, P. (2012). "Cognitive-behavioural group treatment for a range of functional somatic syndromes: Randomised trial", *British Journal of Psychiatry*, 200(6): 499–507.

Serenyi, P. (1974). Le Corbusier in perspective. Englewood Cliffs, N.J: Prentice-Hall.

Smedley, B. D., Stith, A. Y., & Nelson, A. R. (2003). *Unequal Treatment: Confronting Racial and Ethnic Disparities in Health Care*. Washington, DC: The National Academies Press.

Smith, Michael (1994). *The Moral Problem*. London: Blackwell.

Srzednicki (1965). *Franz Brentano's Analysis of Truth*. Hague: Kluwer.

Tappolet, C. (2000). *Emotions et valeurs*. Paris: Presses Universitaires de France.

Teo A. R. (2013). "Social isolation associated with depression: A case report of hikiko-mori". *The International Journal of Social Psychiatry*, 59(4): 339–341. https://doi.org/10.1177/0020764012437128.

Tuller, D. (2015-02-10). "Chronic fatigue syndrome gets a new name". Retrieved from http://scopeblog.stanford.edu/2015/02/11/chronic-fatigue-syndrome-gets-more-respect-and-a-new-name/.

Twardowski, K. (1894). *Zur Lehre vom Inhalt und Gegenstand der Vorstellungen*. Wien: Hoelder.

Tye, M. (1995). *Ten Problems of Consciousness*. Cambridge: The MIT Press.

Tye, M. (2000). *Consciousness, Color, and Content*. Cambridge: The MIT Press.

Tye, M. (2008). "The experience of emotion: An intentionalist theory", *Revue Internationale de Philosophie*, 243, 25–50.

Wedgwood, R. (2001). "Sensing values?", *Philosophy and Phenomenological Research*, 63.1, 215–223.

Whiting, D. (2011). "The feeling theory of emotions and object-directed emotions", *European Journal of Philosophy*, 19.2, 281–303.

Whiting, D. (2012). "Are emotions perceptual experiences of value?", *Ratio*, 25, 93–110.

4

PART AND WHOLE

Introduction

This chapter presents an alternative view for interpreting human life and its environment that emphasizes its relational character while distancing itself from any form of substance dualism and its correlate reductionism. It will provide a mereological description of the way in which individuals dynamically interconnect to each other from a physical perspective, through the notions of space and niche, and from a biological perspective, through the analysis of brain development and bacterial life. To this purpose, I will take into consideration mereological applications of Husserl's theory of parts and whole in biology, psychology, and bioethics; philosophical reflections on basic terms such as place, individual, object, organism, and environment will be conducive to gaining a greater sense of this interconnectedness.

I. Parts and Whole, a Theory

The term *mereology* was coined in 1927 by Leśniewski[1] from Greek μερος, ("part") and λόγος (study); it indicates the study of parthood relations with the goal of describing the relations of parts to whole and the relations of part to part within a whole. Even though the term is fairly new, its roots date back to antiquity.[2] Aristotle, for example, (*De Anima* 411 b 24) wrote: "In each of the bodily parts there are present all the parts of the soul." Similar statements are found in Meister Eckhart: "the soul is one and indivisibly complete in the foot, and complete in the eye, and complete in every limb" (Meister Eckhart, 1958, sermon 10, 161–165, [3] and in Thomas Aquinas: "*Anima hominis est tota in toto corpore et tota in qualibet parte ipsius*" ("the soul of the human being is complete in all the body and in each of its parts" Thomas Aquinas, 1953, I q 93 a 3). Similarly, in modern philosophy, Kant explained the soul as a whole in my whole body, wholly in each part (Kant, 1766/1900, 49); in his *De Mundiis Sensibilis Atque Intelligibilis* (1770), he asked himself: "how is it possible for several substances to coalesce into one thing (*unum*), and upon what conditions it depends that this one thing is not a part of something else?" (Kant, 1902, AK. II, 389). This question and more are addressed by mereology which became a full-fledged theory in contemporary philosophy thanks to the work of Brentano and his student Husserl. This philosophical theory is useful to explain how parts come together to cooperate in the whole and how these wholes become parts within a larger system. In that sense, mereology can be used to describe the relationship of human individuals to the environment from a metaphysical and ontological point of view and to encourage a more holistic and less individualistic view of life.

I.1 Theory of Parts and Whole in Phenomenology

In the third and sixth *Logical Investigation*, Husserl introduced the theory of parts of the whole through a foundational problem: how do the multiplicity of things, spaces, and geometries "coalesce into the unity of one constitution which makes possible the consciousness of something self-same" (Husserl, 1907, 328)? From a practical point of view, this question would become: how do human beings organize themselves and the multiplicity of their goals within their environment into a communitarian good which allows the society to thrive and be recognized as that society and not any other one?

Foundation is the word that he used to explain the relation between non-independent and independent objects ("*selbstständige und unselbstständige Gegenstände*") and concrete and abstract contents ("*konkrete und abstrakte Inhalte*"). Nonindependent objects were also called parts or moments by Husserl, whereas independent objects were named pieces or species. The former can be *concreta* and if separated from the whole, they might become a whole on their own: the leg of a table, for example. The latter are relative to the whole of which they are part. They are abstract and can be further characterized as a genus or a species (i.e., the green of the grass).

> The foundness of an act does not mean that it is built upon other acts in any manner whatsoever, but that a founded act by its very nature of kind, is only possible as built upon acts of the sort which underlie it, and that, as a result, the objective correlate of the founded act has a universal element of form which can only be intuitively displayed by an object in a founded act of this kind.
>
> *(Hua XIX, II 107—En. tr. 235)*

As this quote says, the founding relationship between founding and founded is such that the founding act is always copresent to the latter, as the universal is present to the particular or, with an example, the human being (abstractum) to its body (concretum).

Therefore, Husserl mentioned two forms of foundation. In the first one, the categorial act founds sensuous data ontologically (Hua XIX, II, 107—En. tr. 235). For example, in order for us to call the students of a school "students," we need to ascertain that these children attend a school. In this kind of foundation, the *abstractum*, that is, the epistemological category *school* ontologically founds the quality of the children that are not just children but also students. In this case, the foundation is from an *abstractum* to a *concretum*. The category "school" is fundamental for the children to be named students. Even though the students have their own individual meaning–content, they can only exist as real students if they are instantiated in the categorial object "school," that is, if they are one of the characteristics of the school. "The apprehension of a sensuous feature as a feature, or of a sensuous form as a form, points to acts which are all founded, and in this case as relational kinds of acts" (Hua XIX, VI, Section 47, 792; En. tr. 110). Similarly, citizens are citizens because there is a society, living beings are living beings because there is an environment, and so on.

Whereas ontological foundation moves from the *abstractum* to the *concretum*, the opposite happens in epistemological foundation. In this case, the primary object of sensuous intuitions is fundamental for categorial acts. For example, I need students in order to acknowledge the existence of a school, citizens to acknowledge a government, and living beings for the environment. Without these ontological structures, the school, for example, would be just an anonymous building. In this kind of foundation, what is foundational identifies what is founded as a whole. "When I say 'this', I do not merely perceive, but rather on the basis of the perception a new act of intending-this is established that is directed to it and is dependent upon it, despite its difference" (Hua XIX, II, 170; En. tr. 683). A dualistic interpretation of the human being either as a bodily (res extensa) or a spiritual (res cogitans) substance misses the categorial and ontological interconnectedness of the two because it separates the two substances from each other; hence, the ontological and epistemological foundations do not inform each other's layers of meaning and being.

The epistemological and ontological foundations of independent and nonindependent objects are not just abstract ways to explain the interconnection between parts and whole but represent concrete alternative ways to think of life in a relational way. Individuals are not dichotomic islands who connect occasionally with each other on a bodily or spiritual level, but they are organisms whose parts are interwoven with the environment in which they live through a co-foundational dynamic system. We are individuals because there is a collectivity to which we belong as its parts; otherwise, we could as well be called flesh. This collectivity is because we recognize it as such in its whole. Similarly, the environment exists not as an external being that floats somewhere independently from us but as an environment that is exactly around (*environ*) something or someone; environment, as well, is a highly relational concept. Our being as human organisms, too, is because of our dynamic connectedness to a relational whole. Any ontological negation (being deliberately careless toward the environment) of this foundation or any reasoning that is oblivious of this inter-connection (denying relational problems such as climate change) is highly da-maging for individuals and their organismic lives. The environment as an ontological and epistemological category is fundamental for us to be human beings. Reasoning about our society and environment in terms of applied mereology could help us set ourselves free from reductionistic interpretations of nature as something external from us (more on this in the next chapter) which seems to invite a dualistic interpretation of life.

II. A Problematic Application

How does this interconnection of living beings become one? How can we ac-tually explain and see the unity of a living organism from a spatial point of view? Although the application of the theory of parts and whole in an extra-mathematical field is highly problematic because of the time-spatial nature of its entities (Calosi and Graziani, 2014), significant attempts have been made in this direction. For instance, in his *Axiomatic Method in Biology* of 1937, J. H. Woodger sought to apply the formal theory of parts and whole to the field of biology in order to formalize relational biological notions such as DNA, cells, and so on. Since applied mereology takes into account spatio-temporal entities, a mer-eotopology is necessary to fully appreciate the relational qualities of those entities: their primitive relations, boundaries, and locations (what was defined as passive syntheses in the previous chapter). In this way, the mereological analysis would formalize the essential structural properties of these entities—such as con-nectedness, compactness, regularity, and spatial coincidence—that are essential to describe the nature of living relations.[4] According to Smith (1999), a further property should be added in order to fully describe the formal ontological characters of the world in which we live, that is the concept of "niche" or en-vironmental settings (Smith and Varzi, 1999).[5] By niche, they mean the function exercised by a particular place or subdivision of the environment that is occupied by an organism or a population within an ecological community (Whittaker and Lewin, 1975). Hutchinson (1978, 159) encouraged us to think of the environ-mental niche as "a volume in an abstract space determined by a range of physical parameters pertaining to food, climate, predators, parasites, and so on," in that sense indicating a specific range of place. Similarly, Aristotle's *Physics* defined a place as "neither a part nor a state of it, but is separable from it. For, place is supposed to be something like a vessel" (209b26f).[6] According to Aristotle, a place is a problematic function in terms of boundaries; in fact, it is around its body in a containing manner so that the body can relate to its place in a defining way, such a gas inside a bottle or water inside the ocean. The external boundaries of the thing coincide with the internal boundary of the surrounding space. What we think separates us from others, what we assume marks out the difference from us and the environment is, in fact, the bridge that makes us part of what is other and makes the other part of what is us.

Understanding the continuity between boundaries and the thing itself might help to overcome a dualistic worldview that has led to painful individualism and growing detachment from the environment. Our boundaries define us as much as our extension does. A meaningless and careless behavior toward others and the environment directly affects us and the quality of our lives. Doing bad toward others is explained by ignorance—Socrates believed—this is even truer if one understands life in organismic terms. As we will see in more detail in Chapter 5, there is no clear-cut distinction between inside and outside,[7] subject and object, and any attempt to reduce one's Lebenswelt (life-world) to it is at best reductionist. On this point, the eco-psychologist Roger Barker used the examples of Wagner's opera, a lecture on Hegel, or a garage sale. Wholes of these types are physical-behavioral units which are natural spontaneous and dynamic units, not regulated by any investigators and come together in a whole according to a nesting hierarchy of such wholes. These wholes are as real and as scientifically provable as rain and sandy beaches are experienced (Barker, 1968, 11). An environmental set or niche has the functional or relational role to contain and define the self-assembling nested hierarchy of parts and whole, as being itself an independent part of that whole. Other examples of these wholes occurring can be a chick embryo constructed according to nested hierarchy of organs, cells, nuclei, molecules, atoms, and subatomic particles which are simultaneously both circumjacent and interjacent, both whole and part, both entity and environment. "An organ—the liver, for example—is whole in relation to its own component pattern of cells, and is a part in relation to the circumjacent organism that it, with other organs, composes; it forms the environment of its cells, and is, itself, environed by the organism" (Barker, 1968, 154). In this sense, *the formal property of environmental sets puts in question the traditional distinction between subject and object that is central to traditional scientism and a certain reification of living beings* (see on this point Chapter 1).

II.1 What is an Object?

I believe that the organization of knowledge in subjects and objects of studies has favored a dualistic way of explaining life that separates individuals from each other and internal from external life. Moreover, a scientistic application of this view has been at times oblivious of the intrinsic value of life itself because it has reduced living beings to external objects whose value could be recognized by science. For this reason, I will discuss the notion of objects as "heuristic fictions" (Wolfe, 2010) or "convenient phenomenological nodes" (French, 2014), while addressing the problem of objectivity from a physical and biological perspective. For example, in the philosophy of physics, there is a sharp distinction between "object" and "individual,"[8] although this distinction is not always helpful to describing bodies in quantum physics. The philosopher of science French (2006, 2014) proposed for both disciplines to move the focus on the latter, the individual. It is possible, in fact, that an object-oriented metaphysics would risk metaphysical underdetermination in quantum physics when it is to decide whether particles as objects should be regarded as individuals or not, as in the case of entanglement, for example; or, likewise, in biology where it still persists that a lack of general consensus in theoretical debates about fitness, adaptation, sociality, and the evolution of sex prevents scientists from becoming aware of the slight differences between the "objects" that they are talking about (Clarke, 2013, 414).

To this purpose, French drew a mereological definition of what an individual (as an independent part) is in such a way that it could satisfy both physics and biology. Following the Quinean precept according to which "to be is to be a variable," an object is in physics what satisfies the system of laws that are required for that object to be recognized as such by us. As I have showed in my previous work (2015), the legality that we acknowledge to that object, that is, the system of values that makes that table a table (e.g., its being a surface useful to sit at and write on) constitutes the condition of possibility for the essence of that given object to be so and to be named by us as such. Objects are a system of values which work for us as variables that we put in place to make that interconnectedness of elements understandable and functioning for us (an epistemological and ontological foundation). Hence, a law-constituted definition of objects describes them as what satisfies the law.

French (2014) proposed interpreting it as "governance, in the sense that laws are standardly taken to 'govern' the entities that fall under them" (French, 2016, 374). Yet, it is very difficult to establish what marks out the quality of these standards given the wide variety of the standards. Alternatively, he proposed interpreting the notion of "satisfaction" here by appealing to the idea of dependence (Lowe, 2009); this would mean that an object for us is what depends on the relevant laws and their possibility to be satisfied according to the given variables.

On the other hand, according to French, in biology an object is what "(1) has 3D spatial boundaries, (2) bears properties, and (3) is a causal agent (see Wilson, 2013), to which many would be inclined to add (4) is countable and (5) is genetically homogenous (which amounts to what Dupré insists is the further presumption of genomic essentialism)." Yet, this last point is difficult to satisfy because there are biological objects whose main components are nonindependent colonies, such as the humongous fungus or the Hawaiian bobtail squid[9] whose presence covers a wide amount of space in a systemic way through colonies (see, e.g., the symposium "Heterogeneous Individuals," held at PSA, 2010, Montreal). Therefore, Pradeu (2012) offered an immunological alternative to the definition based on the fact that the genetic homogeneity of the object is guaranteed by the immune system that controls variation in growing colonies of bacteria (Pradeu, 2012). Similarly, Connolly listed the character of what he called entangled humanism:

> ancient bacteria imprisoned in human cells (mitochondria) (…) incorpo-rated drives nested within and between us (…) modes of interspecies symbiosis and disease jumps (…) cultural relations with innumerable species with perspectives of their own (…) numerous imbrications with the planetary, partially self-organizing capacities of climate, glaciers, ocean currents (…) and species evolution. (2017, 169)

Accepting this view yields, according to French, a conception of the biological object in terms of a system, that is: "a set of interconnected heterogeneous con-stituents, interacting with immune receptors, where such heterogeneous organisms express the highest level of individuality by virtue of the immune system acting to eliminate lower-level individuals as variants"[10] (2014, 312). This definition, though, implies that the spatial and temporal connection within organisms and lineages are always stable, which is not the case. Thus, Clarke (2012) has addressed this problem in a very interesting way by suggesting that "a biological organism is any collection of living parts that possesses individuating mechanisms, where an individuating mechanism is a mechanism that either limits an object's capacity to undergo within-object selection … or increases its capacity to participate in a between-object selection process" (Clarke, 2013, 427). Thus, an individuating mechanism is any mechanism that increases capacity for between-unit selection, relative to within-unit selection. Such mechanisms act as the causal basis or realizer of the disposition to change at the between-organism level, rather than at the within-organism level (or higher) in response to natural selection. Based on this idea of individuating mechanism that allows the between- and within-unit to work, biological individuals would then be defined as "all and only those objects that possess both kinds of individuating mechanism" (Clarke, 2013, 22).

There are numerous examples of noncellular entities whose individual life-histories mirror this individuating mechanism of working between-unit (their lives are achieved through contributing to the lives) and within-unit (the life histories of the larger entities in which they collaborate, and this collaboration constitutes their claim to life). But this definition of objects can be extended to individual life histories of paradigmatic organisms such as animals or plants and communities of entities from many different reproductive lineages (Dupré and O'Malley, 2009, 15). Objects are the stable moments of an interaction.

As Dupré remarked: "Individual organisms … are an abstraction from a much more fundamental entity" (Dupré and O'Malley, 2007, 842), and objects are no more than "temporarily stable nexuses in the flow of upward and downward causal interaction" (842). It would then be possible to reassign objects to the more modest sphere of "heuristic fictions" (Wolfe, 2010) or "convenient phe-nomenological nodes" (French, 2014) that allow the mechanism of biological organisms to function by possessing the required stability at the required level. From a biological perspective, the legality mentioned above and its satisfaction can be explained through this "truthmaker," that is, this moment of stability within the fluidity of movements.

III. Theory of Parts and Whole: The Critical Debate about Priority[11]

Now that the notions of object and individual have been explained in their legality according to an organismic perspective that sheds light on the dynamic continuity of life and its interconnectedness, in this section, I will focus on how we recognize this continuity in "heuristic fictions" (Wolfe, 2010) or "convenient phenomenological nodes" (French, 2014) that we call objects or individuals. I will go through the foundational problem and address Kant's above-mentioned question: "how is it possible for several substances to coalesce into one thing (*unum*), and upon what conditions it depends that this one thing is not a part of something else?" (Kant, 1905, 389). Phenomenology addresses this problem through the theory of parts and whole.

According to Nenon (1997), there are two forms of foundation that explain the coming together of parts and whole: one ontological and one epistemological. As described before, in the ontological one, the relationship is described as a form of instantiation of being (sensuous), while the second one is described as moments of truth (categorial). In a nutshell, "the question of foundation is reduced to the questions of the most primitive components of acts of consciousness and these components are taken to be those which are identified in the direct sense perception of individual object" (1997, 98). This coincidence comes from the fact that it is always the lower complex of acts that founds the higher one. Lower and higher levels are copresent, and they occur together in the same act in an undifferentiated way. For example, judgments are based on perceptions in the same way as the notion of "human being" is founded on its concrete body. Nenon (1997), with reason, wrote that sensuous and categorical as a whole cannot be reduced to each other because they are two different forms of objects (we discussed this same problem of reducing ideal to real, concepts to percepts in Chapters 1 and 3). "The concrete objects of sense perception, independent objects that are made of sensibly perceptible properties, are what he calls 'real' objects. The other objects, be they categorial objects in the usual sense such as collections, disjunctions or the *Sachverhalte* to which judgments are directed, or universal objects such as redness constituted on the basis of objects given in the primary acts of the sense perception" (Nenon, 1997, 109). Both foundations extensionally coincide with each other—although an intentional tension remains between the two of them—because the foundation is a matter of priority and originality of elements. In the case of the ontological foundation, the entity as a whole enjoys a kind of priority over any of its constituent parts, for they exist in it (…). In the case of the epistemological interpretation of foundation by contrast, an element that is capable of being given as a simple real thing, a lower-order object enjoys priority over a higher-order object founded upon it, even if the lower-order object is only a part of what it means to be this object. (1997, 112)

Differently from Nenon, Fine (1995) considered the foundation as reducible to a foundation of pieces. In agreement with Null (2007) according to whom "every [part] is foundationally connected (…) with every [part]" (37–69), Fine considered the pieces as the sum of the moments that make the object. Correira (2004) and Mohanty (2008) disagreed with Fine on this point because according to them the founded object is something that cannot exist without the definite object. Thus, the whole is not founded on its parts because they would not be self-sufficient; the whole needs the parts in order to exist and similarly the parts need a whole in order to be parts. They both coexist in their own way, and the way in which they assemble does not necessarily result in a sum, as crystals in a snowflake do not assemble together in any predictable summation. There is a law of essence or the law of species that Correira cited according to which the whole is the whole because of the parts that it employs in order to exist. In Section 21 of the third *Logical Investigation*, Husserl wrote: "A is founded upon B if an A can by its essence not exist unless B also exists." A is founded upon B and any B moments not because of the sum of B moments,—this sum in fact would be the same—but because it exists through its B moments. The whole A exists only if B exists. Here existence, be it ontological or epistemological, is what makes the whole a whole. In this case, the essential law of species seems to describe a circle that comes in support of the interpretations of the foundation of Nenon, Correira, and Mohanty.

III.1 The Circle of Founding and Founded: Continuing the Critical Debate

This co-foundational circle can help us to understand how the theory of parts and whole can be conducive to explaining the constitution of individual identity and self as a dynamic circle of founding and founded through and within time. For now, in this section, I will focus on the debate around the ontological or epistemological nature of the founding act which can be summarized in the questions: What does make the whole a whole? Is it the actual coming together of the being into a Being? Or is it the epistemological act with which we acknowledge that unit of meaning as a self-standing being that makes the whole a recognizable Being?

According to Stapleton (1983), Husserl decided to introduce reduction (more on this in Chapters 1 and 3) mainly due to the ontological problem raised in the theory of parts and whole.

> The transcendental reduction is merely a variation and an extension of the logical reduction in which eidetic rationality completes itself by following out the theory of wholes and parts from the LI to the conclusion that transcendental consciousness alone can be conceived as the ultimate *"concretum,"* that which is truly self-sufficient in the order of being. (quote in Crowell, 1997, 14)

To explain this difficult passage differently from Stapelton, Crowell argued that the transcendental question is a question of *being* a meaning. According to this interpretation, transcendental consciousness exists as a unit of validity or *Seinsgeltung* (1997, 23). The reduction is motivated by the need to recover the *Seinsgeltung* of the world (1997, 24), and this unit of validity exists as a condition of the possibility for knowing the world (1997, 26). For Crowell, the ontology of meaning represents the normative connection between being and meaning. In contrast, Stapelton regarded this gap as a logico-ontological one (Crowell, 1997, 25). Husserl's notion of "founding" is not exclusively epistemological because it is not only the categorial that determines the sensuous. "The condition for the possibility of the objects' existence lies in their necessary correlation with other objects" (Stapleton quoted in Crowell, 1997, 25). Constitution is a logical phenomenon that is "unintelligible from a worldly perspective since worldly concepts presuppose (…) an ontological concept of reality" (Stapleton quoted in Crowell, 1997, 11). The logical pieces integrate the *concreta* in the emotional (as *Gemüt*) animation and understanding of the *concreta* itself (Stapleton quoted in Crowell, 1997, 116).

According to Hickerson (2007, 105), the riddle of foundation can be solved through an Aristotelian reading that is, to a certain extent, indebted to James' theory of fringes. According to Hickerson, James emphasized that the things or events that exist in reality are treated as characters or phenomena emptied of their contents. Things are given to us as actual forms devoid of their actual contents. Things are given to us in the form of pieces, that is, as properties instantiated in a mental act. They belong to the object, and the ideal object, the *Object überhaupt,* as an atemporal and universal existence, could not exist independently of these properties. For this reason, it is vital to keep the distinction between *abstracta* and *concreta*, pieces and moments, in place since they are radically different from each other and yet are codependent parts of the same whole.[12] Their temporal structure is radically different; meanings are atemporal ideals, while concreta are perceived by us as temporal qualities. That is why we cannot say that foundation moves from the piece to the whole so that the piece founds the whole through the moments, or the moments found the whole through the pieces. Any foundation is, in fact, a double game in which the pieces can be objectified because of the moments, but at the same time the moments can be triggered because of the pieces. All this is possible because the pieces are actual ontological instantiations within the phenomenon. This means that every meaning has a theoretical, atemporal structure that is normative in itself and is embedded in any moment of the essence. This is what triggers the circle of founding and founded.

III.2 The Role of Time in Identity Foundation

The pieces to which we refer when we theorize in mereology are ideals or abstracta, that is, not spatio-temporal entities. This nature explains the circularity of their foundation given the complexity of their temporality. In fact, when we try to think of the correlation of parts and whole including the variable of time, their circularity becomes more difficult to follow.

In Husserl's phenomenology, there are at least three ways to understand and explain time; all of them, I will show, are very helpful for fleshing out the foundational problems and their application, for example, in the medical encounter, as well as the actions that humans decide to take toward each other.

To understand these three dimensions, we need to locate them aside the three forms of intentions that I described in Chapter 3. While active intentionality entails position-taking (Stellungnahme) and meaning-giving (Sinngebung) activity (Hua 3, 207), passive intentionality is a synthetic process that takes place mainly in the environment as it relates to us at two egoless layers: those of spontaneous and nonspontaneous syntheses (Hua 33). The spontaneous syntheses bring together the percepta of our experience according to a principle of homogeneity, while the non-pontaneous ones name these data. Through the layers formed by these syntheses, we constitute the material core around which the meaning-giving activity of active intentionality revolves. The transition from egoless synthetic processes to egoic meaning-giving (Sinngebung) activity is characterized by practical intention. In fact, the sphere of irritability (Hua, 33, text 1), the layer of affections and reactions, represents the lowest level of affections from which the ego emerges and reacts to the irritating affecting matter by deciding what position it is going to take (Hua, 33, text 1, 5, 6, 9, 10). This reactive emergence is rooted in the volitional body (Hua-Mat 4, 186) which bridges nature (passive syntheses) and spirit (active intention). The ego reacts to matter by deciding whether to accept and validate that matter as its own. Some of the material content provided to the ego will remain in the form of passive syntheses; others will be organized through values and meanings. While the realm of passivity provides heretofore formless matter with a logical or graspable form, the realm of activity is the constitutive pole through which a given number of synthetic layers are comprised in a graspable meaning. The pieces of matter that make us who we are are determined within the categorial whole that we call subject, or in psychological terms identity, and in the ontological whole that the categorial whole would recognize as my body. The whole-subject decides (practical intentionality) to move toward a self-constituting act in recognizing the interconnection between passive syntheses and its own activity as a self-reflecting subject. The bridge between active intention and passive synthesis is represented by practical intentionality, the "Ich will und Ich tue" (I want and I do) which operates by means of the volitional body in order to awaken (Hua Mat IX, 128–129, 133) the ego to its present matter. This circularity is equivalent to the ontological and categorial foundation of parts and whole but with the inclusion of the variable of time.

I argue that the cofounding relationship between passive, active, and practical intentionality describes a threefold sense of time: living present, timeless time, and linear time. The layer of passive matter is the "*founding* stratum" (Hua I, Section 44) around which the awoken ego gravitates in order to realize itself (i.e., determining the matter in a graspable meaning). While the matter is a living present as it presents itself in the form of a concrete decision that the volitional body has to make in relation to that presence (e.g., the stimulus of hunger presents itself to the volitional body that then decides whether to acknowledge the stimulus or not), the decision we make in relation to this presence takes place in a timeless time but is organized according to a linear time whose meanings are understandable according to a logic of befores and afters, causes and effects.

The layer of passive matter represents our environment from which we emerge (practical intention) as subjects of an active intentional act that assigns meanings and values to that environment. The concreteness of the environment (concreta) represents what founds and is copresent to the meanings and values (abstracta) with which we determine and recognize ourselves as living beings (whole). This foundational stratum cannot be thought of in terms of a before-after, but as a relational core (in Chapter 3, noetic-noematic core) that entertains a threefold relationship with time and matter. The time that knits together the passive syntheses of the material world is a living present, the eternal moment whose structure is explained in the series of protentions and retentions. This living present of consciousness is the *substratum,* the original flow or the light through which what comes to evidence is luminous (Hua XIV, 45, 301). This "*lebendige Gegenwart* (living present) is an impressional stream"[13] which continuously fills intentions/ protentions. "It is a creative primal presenting" (Husserl cited in Hart, 2009, 25, 26). This form of time constitutes the core of immanent, hyletic time[14] that organizes itself in the mundane form of time perceived by the subject in a chain of before-afters. When a particularly painful clinical encounter takes place, for example, receiving a lethal diagnosis as Kay Toombs recounts in her book (1992), the living present instantiates a materiality of ourselves that does not coincide any more with the one of the self we used to be right before the diagnosis. The ego that awakes from that living present is a new one and its world, too, is completely different. For this reason, ethical professionals should be particularly careful about the approach to the temporal sense of identity that arises after such a diagnostic encounter. The co-foundation that gives rise to the identity during the clinical encounter is highly unstable and problematic.

In phenomenology, time is not a category or a predicate, but is a *systatical*[15] *function.* Systatical is a term borrowed from physics to indicate a synthetic activity that organizes data in dynamic categories. The first founding relationship between parts and whole takes place on this living present level (the concreteness of the matter). The egoless parts of ourselves organize with each other in such a way that our sense of self in and for the world changes constantly at any meaningful awakening. From this point of view, human linear time brings formless matter (living present) into existence in an ongoing synthesis (eternal present) of being and meanings that human beings organize in a linear time according to a before and after.

IV. The Foundation of Personal Identity in Time

The primordial I that awakens from the living present organizes the moments of itself in first of all an "Ich kann–Ich tue" (I can–I do) that can decide to act in many different and teleologically directed ways (Hua-Mat IX, 128–129). This I as a "wache Ich" (awoken I) in a moment of time (Zeitpunkt) functions in time (Hua-Mat IX, 133), which means it decides to renew the source of its habits or the horizon of its being with its momentous choice ("jetzigen Wahl," Husserl, 2012, 133). As a matter of fact, the subject and its world are given as a fixed picture, but one which is at the same time living and changing.[16] So Ich tue!' ("I act then!") is the most primitive principle that the bioethicist can recognize on the theoretical and normative level in the relationship between individuals with each other and the environment. The *Ich kann* (I can) is such because it can act and therefore be, otherwise it would not be an *Ich* in the first place. This integration has been famously described by William James (1890) as extended or "specious present," by Henri Bergson (1950) as "duration," and by Husserl (1991) as "inner time consciousness." To explain it briefly, the mere succession of conscious moments, as such, could not establish the experience of continuity. It is only when these moments mutually relate to each other in a forward and backward directed intention that the sequence of experiences is integrated into a unified process—this relationality is the most primordial definition of environment. Husserl conceived this as the synthesis of *protention* (indeterminate anticipation of what is yet to come) and *retention* (indeterminate conservation of what has just passed) which shows itself into a *presentation* of what it is in front of us now. As Merleau-Ponty remarked, "I am not myself a succession of 'psychic' acts, nor for that matter a nuclear I who brings them together into a synthetic unity, but one single experience inseparable from itself, one single 'living cohesion', one single temporality which is engaged, from birth, in making itself progressively explicit, and in confirming that cohesion in each successive present" (Merleau-Ponty, 1962, 363). The notion of time and that of the self are strictly interwoven.

Locke was one of the first thinkers to recognize the importance of memory in the constitution of one's identity. He criticized the Cartesian dualism by stating how memory is the necessary glue to build the sense of self as memory incarnates the separate moments of awakening of the subject according to a linear causality in which it becomes impossible to separate *res cogitans* from *res extensa:* "That which seems to make the difficulty is this, that this consciousness being interrupted always by forgetfulness (…) and we sometimes, and that the greatest part of our lives, not reflecting on our past selves, being intent on our present thoughts, and in sound sleep having no thoughts at all (…)—doubts are raised whether we are the same thinking thing, i.e. the same substance or no"[17] (Locke, Essay, Book II, Chapter XXVII, Section 10; cf. Locke, 2006, 420).

For this reason, psychopathologies that involve a disturbed sense of time like schizophrenia (Riutort, 2003; McLeod et al., 2006; Fuchs, 2016) would create a disruptive sense of identity as parts and whole would come together through a different pathway of time. As Jordan and Vinson (2012) remarked, for example, "the dynamics of a single-cell organism allow it to sustain relation at the rather immediate level of context at its cell wall, humans are able to sustain relation with abstract contexts such as today, tomorrow, and next year. By abstract contexts, we mean contexts that are not available in one's immediate present—what are traditionally referred as ideas (…) Thus, for example, the idea to 'get a college degree' has the power to constrain the contexts one finds oneself in over a roughly four-year period (e.g., the particular college one attends, the courses one takes, and the rooms in which those courses take place)" (Jordan and Vinson, 2012, 246). Schizophrenics have, often, the problem of retaining these abstract ideas, in Husserl's language the synthesis between protention and retention, which leads to the impossibility of creating an immediate level of context in which they can place themselves and their lives. This might lead to a sense of depersonalization for schizophrenic patients who feel fragmented in time despite having adequate memories at their disposal, as in the following case: "BI feels as parts of a whole person, but never at the same time. It is difficult to explain (…) I constantly have to ask myself 'who am I really?' (…) Most of the time, I have this very strange thing: I watch myself closely, like, how am I doing now and where are the 'parts' (…) I think about that so much that I get to nothing else. It is not easy when you change from day to day. As if you were a totally different person all of a sudden" (de Haan and Fuchs, 2010, 329). A person suffering from schizophrenia does not always find their way to wholeness because of a disturbed functioning of the three-layered temporality. This is how a person affected with schizophrenia would describe the relationship of his/her identity with time:

> Time is also running in a strange way. It falls apart and progresses no longer. There arise only innumerable dissociated now, now, now—quite crazy and without rules or order. It is the same with myself. From moment to moment, various "selves" arise and disappear entirely at random. There is no connection between my present ego and the one before.
> *(Description given by a female schizophrenic patient of Bin Kimura in*
> *Kobayashi, 1998, 114)*

The co-foundation of parts and whole that takes place within the embodied space of one's identity and its environment is quite complex. From moment to moment, the various fragments of selves that are there in the living present are organized according to a linear time structure. The volitional body that has the task of connecting this living present with a linear meaning fails its purpose. The moments of one's person remain scattered in the living time which explains the sense of fear, paranoia, and restlessness that schizophrenic patients can nurture in relation to their own environment. They have memories at their disposal, but they do not make sense to them, no co-foundation occurs either on an ontological or on a categorial level. The meanings that are assigned are always provisional and disconnected from each other with the result of a fragmented ego that cannot initiate any successful determination of meaning.

"The flow of the consciousness that constitutes immanent time not only exists but is so remarkably and yet intelligibly fashioned that a self-appearance of the flow necessarily exists in it, and therefore the flow itself must necessarily be apprehensible in the flowing. The self-appearance of the flow does not require a second flow; on the contrary, it constitutes itself as a phenomenon in itself" (Husserl, 1966, 83). The self is built on this timely and dynamic co-foundation of being and meaning. This means that retrospection and memory span are the decisive bridge for constituting the sense of individual identity: the diachronic unity of the person is bound to the potential act of explicit remembering (Shoemaker and Swinburne, 1984; Noonan, 1989). In fact, as Butler (1736) and Reid (1785) noticed, a vicious circle is lurking in Locke's account: if my identity has no basis in my bodily life, it will vanish as soon as I am unable to remember my earlier states and attribute them to myself. Hence, the continuity of being oneself is based on bodily existence in a twofold sense (Jonas, 1966; Varela et al., 1991; Thompson, 2007; Di Paolo, 2009): (1) as the continuity of the life process of organismic self-preservation and self-reproduction (autopoiesis) and (2) as the continuity of embodied self-experience, ranging from unconscious over prereflective to reflective conscious states, which is to be regarded as a manifestation of the life process as a whole (and not as a mere product of the brain).

IV.1 Self as an Organism among Organisms

The way in which the I becomes myself through mereological recollection shows how even our identity is a part-whole organism like others. In this sense, even the way in which we build ourselves and make sense of who we are can be explained in mereological terms. While a certain way of interpreting Platonic and Cartesian dualism might have led us to believe that our true self lies intact in an abstract isolated place, life seems to show us the opposite. Our self is a systemic dynamic being whose contents and boundaries change according to the combination of environment and time in which we live and with which we interact. According to Damasio's theory, a "protoself," or a primary sense of self, arises from a complex of neural activation patterns in the upper brainstem "which map, moment by moment, the state of the physical structure of the organism in its many dimensions" (Damasio, 1999, 154). The human brain is a born cartographer because "Maps are constructed when we interact with objects or our bodies as a person" (Fuchs, 2010, 64). Of course, there is an essential structure that belongs to us, as an independent piece that combines with a whole while being a whole in itself, but its ontological and epistemological nature demands different fulfillments or combinations on the basis of the previous experiences. The self is not exclusively a result of cognitive sophistications and reflections; rather it arises with the affective and motivational instincts that serve the organism's vital needs (Fuchs, 2010, 113). The challenge of "selfhood" qualifies everything beyond the boundaries of the organism as foreign and somehow opposite: as "world," within which, by which, and against which it is committed to maintain itself. Without this universal counterpart of "other," there would be no "self" (Jonas, 1968, 242–243).

From a biological point of view, Varela, Rosch, and Thompson (1991) described human beings as self-organizing systems: whole as a condition of all its parts (body a condition for the brain, heart, etc.). The human body is a system itself whose being is a condition for its parts to become themselves as a meaningful unit of being. The fulfillment of the body as an individual, that is as an independent piece, is the functioning of the parts of which the whole is the condition. In that sense, the natural identity of the body is fulfilled through self-preservation which consists of its continual self-reproduction down to the individual parts which outside of the organism soon decay into their components (within 1 year, 98% of the molecules in a human body are replaced and organically speaking we are renewed bodies, see Margulis and Sagan, 1995, 23). The ways in which this self-preservation is attained are always different according to the environment in which the organism lives. Accordingly, the layer of passive syntheses, that is, the organic body demands from us actions and meanings that always change according to this very basic condition that our body needs to fulfill (I would call this passive intentionality as I described it in the previous chapter). In his *Critique of Judgement*, Immanuel Kant considered "the natural purpose" (*Naturzweck*) of a living being to be fulfilled when "its parts (as regards their being and their form) are only possible through their reference to the whole." Conversely, however, "its parts mutually depend upon each other both as to their form and their combination, and so produce a whole by their own causality" (Kant, 1914, Section 65, 276–277). The name that Varela gave to the foundational movement of this system is *autopoiesis*, which literally means creating (ποιείν) oneself (εαυτό) through our own actions. This is how Varela described human beings as autopoietic systems:

> A living system is constituted by a semipermeable membrane that delimits it from the environment, while at the same time allowing for the metabolic exchange by which the system constantly regenerates itself. At the most

basic level, the system is a single living cell whose metabolic network continuously (re-)produces its membrane, thus creating the boundary which sets it apart from its chemical surroundings. Hence, an autopoietic system can be defined as a system, which continuously produces the components that specify it, while at the same time realizing it (the system) as a concrete unity in space and time, which makes the network of production of components possible.

(Varela, 1997, 75; see also Weber and Varela, 2002)

IV.1.1 Self and the Environment

The notions of space and niche, as I described above, along with the criticism of the notion of "object" in biology, seem to fit perfectly into this definition of human being as an autopoietic system. The human being as a unit in space and time sets boundaries that define its being both as independent and part of the chemical surrounding of its environment.

If we follow Varela's definition of a living system, it becomes evident how the notions of identity and self are strictly dependent on the environment of which the organism is a part and to which it contributes as a whole. The organism is the environment, although our sense of self and identity are often so dualistically biased that we cannot perceive any continuity between the two to the point that the world appears to us as an external being from which we feel completely detached. (In my forthcoming *The Role of* Bio-*Ethics in Emotional Problems*, I will discuss how this sense of disconnection between the self and the environment is the source of problems such as narcissistic traits, emotional numbness, and anxiety.) As we saw before with the definition of *niche*, the human being, as a living system, delimits a space/time content whose boundaries are part of other systems that are adjacent with the previous system. Thinking of our being as an isolated island separated from the rest of the environment would mean to miss the full picture of what we are and losing the concrete terrain of passive intentionality from which we can produce meanings and values. A living being is part of the components produced by the system and it is its realization of this system in a concrete unity in time and space that can produce meanings and values understandable for itself and others. For this reason, Husserl attributed to living organisms "double sensations" (Husserl, *Doppelempfindungen*; Husserl, 1973a, 378) which mark a *point of conversion* ("*Umschlagspunkt*," in Husserl's term) of subjectivity into objectivity, and vice versa. From this point of view, the lived body is never only subject and never only object; rather, it is a "subject-object" (Husserl, 1952, 195) or it is both *Leib* (living body) and *Körper* (biological body).[18] The first-personal experiential givenness is manifest in the very having of the experience. "It is a givenness that one obtains even when we are not explicitly aware of it (…). A conscious mental state (…) is simultaneously self-disclosing or self-revealing" (Zahavi, 2017, 198).

Survival depends on the ability to transform this interdependence into meanings so that the merely physical surroundings can continuously become a set of meanings and values available to us. Being a person does not consist of adhering to a mental construct, but it is being part of experiential facts and the way in which they interact with the environment. If we impoverish the environment, we impoverish our chance to be ourselves. Another way to prove this from a biological point of view is the fact that at birth the human brain is 25% the size of the adult brain (against 50% in a chimpanzee and 70% in a macaque); the growth of the remaining 75% is socially informed (Portman, 1969; Trevarthen, 2001).[19] The brain is a socially, culturally, and biographically shaped organ (see "interactive brain" Di Paolo and De Jaegher, 2012; De Jaegher and Di Paolo, 2016; "social neuroscience" Cacioppo et al., 2002; Decety and Ickes, 2011; Cozolino, 2014). Each stimulus the brain receives is an opportunity for interaction and mediation with an infinite number of possibilities since it is continuously caught in a circular loop (Thompson, 2005; Noe, 2009).

> Looped circuit where the body communicates to the central nervous system and the latter responds to the body's messages. The signals are not separable from the organism states where they originate. The ensemble constitutes a dynamic, bonded unit (…) this unit enacts a functional fusion of body states and perceptual states, such that the dividing line between the two can no longer be drawn (…) the signals conveyed would not be about the state of the flesh but literally extensions of the flesh.
>
> *(Damasio, 2010, 273)*

The central nervous system (CNS) develops in such a way as to centralize and internalize the characteristics from the environment through mediation and selection. These actions are characterized by a sensorimotor interface which processes in a sensory way the needs from the environment and fosters the exchange between organism and environment (Van Dijck, 2008; Fuchs, 87). Dewey described this process through the notion of "the reflex arc" (1896, 359):

> We begin not with a sensory stimulus, but with a sensorimotor coordination, the optical ocular (…). In a certain sense it is the movement, which is primary, and the sensation which is secondary, the movement of the body, head and eye muscles determining the quality of what is experienced. In other words, the real beginning is with the act of seeing: it is looking, and not a sensation of light … [In audition] the sound is not a mere stimulus, or mere sensation; it again is an act (…). It is just as true to say that the sensation of sound arises from a motor response as that the running away is a response to the sound. (1896, 137, 138)

The same process is explained by Husserl with the term *kinesthesis*. Our life, both in its meaning and being, starts with our ability to interact with the environment. Realizing to *be* the environment is the very first way to express our being alive: seeing the light and then the sensation, meaning, and value that the act brings with itself is the very basic arc process with which we build our sense of self both as an ontological instantiation and as meanings.

As we will see in my forthcoming *The Role of* Bio-*Ethics in Emotional Problems*, Chapter 1, one of the big problems with emotional disorders such as anxiety, emotional numbness, or narcissistic traits is that they are rooted in a radical detachment of the individual from their environment. The individual perceives him/herself as an alien or an isolated island separated from the rest of the world. This belief is reinforced by the reductionistic way in which society is organized: habitation (Chapter 2), workload (Chapter 4), social exchanges (Chapter 1), and medical care (Chapters 1 and 2) reinforce the sense of detachment and isolation that the emotionally *disturbed individuals feel by leading them to behave not anymore as an organism but as a tumoral cell*. As Panksepp noticed, "it is the interaction with the environment that creates the necessary conditions of experiencing this environment. (…) The higher brain, namely neocortex, is born largely tabula rasa, and all functions, including vision (…) are programmed into equipotential brain tissues" (Panksepp, 2012, 8).

The circular and vertical causality explained by Fuchs in his diagram illustrates the mereological foundation of the organism according to a vertical and horizontal causality.

The verticality proceeds from the simplest to the most complex organization, that is, from molecule to cells, from organs to organism.[20] The horizontal causality regulates, instead, the exchange between the organism and the environment; this exchange is structured according to the needs that connect organism and environment, that is, perception and movement, homeostasis, and metabolism. The life of an organism arises through the very basic interactions of its components with the environment. As I will explain in more detail in Chapter 5, what is initially internalized is not an object per se, but the relation that the organism has with the object. "What is internalised, thus, is the mutually regulated sequences of interactions within the definite temporal setting" (Beebe and Stern, 1977, 52). This interaction is a kinesthetic experience, meaning, it is built upon the organism's ability to move (kynesis) parts of its system (the eyes, for example) and perceive (aisthesis) the sensation produced out of this movement. Feelings, emotions, and obligations arise and acquire a meaning because of this possible relation between organismic movement, sensation, and environment. Emotions are the important bridge that allows communication between the concreteness of our body and the abstracta of our meanings. As Colombetti remarked, emotions should be conceptualized as a faculty of the whole embodied and situated organism. Evaluations arise in this organism in virtue of its embodied and situated character, and the whole organism carries meanings as such—not by way of some separate

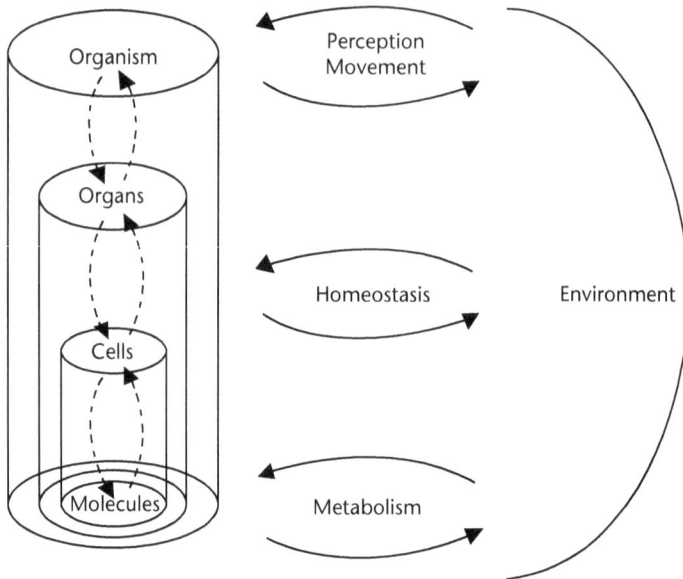

FIGURE 4.1 From Fuchs, T., *The Ecology of the Brain*.

abstract cognitive-evaluative faculty (Colombetti, 2010, 146). *The function creates its cerebral organ* (Brodmann, 1909): "the crucial function of *consciousness* in this context is to establish an integrated superordinate process—conscious experience or *Erleben*—which enables a specific type of adaptivity, namely *learning*" (Fuchs, 224). This basic form of interaction is the essential ground for conscious experience to be;[21] missing the elaboration of the basic aesthetic response to the movement means to put in motion a schizoid process of dissociation that profoundly hurts the organism as it separates it from the ability to connect with the content of its own experience. The body and subjective awareness of the body, including visceral awareness, instantiates the 'self' and provides the intermediary by which the nervous system interacts with the external world (Cameron, 2001, 708).

IV.2 The Social Resonance System

An example of the coexistence of ontological and epistemological foundations of the self and the environment is the social resonance system. Hans Jonas (1903–1993) was one of the first thinkers who understood the importance of the social persistence of the organismic connection between living beings and environment through time. His imperative of responsibility for future generations aimed at the preservation of a world fit for an organismic cohabitation. In his philosophy of life (1966), Jonas stressed the importance of the identity between organisms and human beings. The term *self*, he explained, indicates the most elementary instance of life as it emerges from this internal identity (Jonas, 1968, 242). Following Jonas' emergence perspective, our identity is not an abstract cognitive construction, but is a whole which has a property that its parts would not have on its own. Identity emerges in social, biological, cultural, and biographical resonance with the environment as an epistemological as much as an ontological category.

According to weak emergence theory: "The brain causes certain 'mental' phenomena, such as conscious mental states, and these conscious states are simply higher-level features of the brain. Consciousness is a higher level or emergent property of the brain in the utterly harmless sense of 'higher-level' or 'emergent' in which solidity is a higher level, emergent property of H_2O molecules when they are in a lattice structure (ice)" (Searle, 1992, 14–15). According to strong emergence theory, there is the primacy of the whole which functions against their components that cooperate according to a vertical and horizontal causality (Fuchs, 2010). According to Deacon (2006, 116), whole organisms do not emerge from a disparate assembly of their parts but by the differentiation of their parts from one another. *Supervenience* can be a good term here to describe how these parts are not just joined to each other but their assembly occurs as something novel and unexpected (Horgan, 1992).[22] Although they grow by cell multiplication, these cells divide and differentiate from prior, less differentiated precursors. Both in development and in phylogeny, whole precedes parts (Deacon, 2006, 116). Emergent wholes have contemporaneous parts, but these parts cannot be characterized independently from their respective wholes (Kronz and Tiehen, 2002, 345). In both cases, the elementary instance of life that emerges from this intercorporeal resonance is such that the other is literally felt with one's own body (see Fuchs and De Jaegher, 2009; Fuchs, 2017d).

IV.2.1 Pregnancy as an Example of a Social Resonance System

What is stated above becomes even more evident in pregnancy when the first proto-conversation between mother and child occurs (Trevarthen, 2011). These proto-conversations give space to an affective synchronization (Stern, 1985; Thronick, 2003) that is developed through nine months of pregnancy while creating intercorporeal memory (Fuchs, 2003) which builds the primordial schemes of "being with" structured in sensorimotor, emotional, and temporal manners (Stern, 1985). This form of affective and biological resonance establishes an implicit relational knowing, preverbal encoded knowledge (Stern, 1998b) for the identity of the future baby and for the mother. Similarly, the ongoing resonance between the organism and the vegetative, endocrine, and autonomous brain is the basis for developing the feeling of being a body or as Damasio put it "the feeling of being alive"—missing this resonance increases the chances of emotional and personality disorders that would result in an alarming lowering of the sense of vitality. Being alive means having a functioning social resonance system whose units' tasks are embedded in an *intersubjective space of shared action and meaning*. In Wild System Theory (WST), a recently developed approach to bodies and meaning, bodies are considered as self-sustaining energy transformation systems that are able to sustain relations with dynamics occurring at multiple, nested time-scales simultaneously (e.g., neurons, neural networks, brains and behaviors). From this perspective, the relationship between organisms and environments can be seen as a mutual modulation and processing of the information that they both detect in each other.

This point of view is consistent with Merleau-Ponty's definition of intercorporeality as "being about" and "being within" each other. Merleau-Ponty's philosophy (1962) defined *bodily subjectivity* as "being-towards-the-world" (*être-au-monde*) through the medium of the lived body. The social resonance made it possible, through this shared intersubjective space, to transform meanings, intentions, and affective states into organ functions. As Fuchs remarked (2018, 233):

> while being subject to the natural laws of causal relation, they are simultaneously constrained by the superordinate influence (downward determination) of these integrated activities. In particular, they are subject to the bodily, emotional, and intellectual capacities, which an individual has appropriated throughout his learning history. Their superordinate determination is manifested in each concrete realization of such capacities. In other words, *only living organisms as a whole, and not their constituent parts, are the sufficient causes of some physical occurrences in the world.*

When parts of this system undervalue the whole, social dysfunction occurs. Narcissism, for example, as I will show more in detail in my forthcoming *The Role of* Bio-*Ethics in Emotional Problems*, leads parts of this whole to exploit more resources than are needed for personal benefit; the tragedy of the commons is a perfect example of this problem.

IV.3 "The Feeling of Being Alive"

The systemic and organismic view of life proposed by Potter (1971) finds its confirmation in the idea of a social resonance system. In this sense, Potter agreed with Damasio (1995, 150) when he described the interactive regulatory processes between organisms and environment as "the feeling of life itself, the sense of being" (Damasio, 1995, 150). According to different gradation, the feeling of being alive corresponds to a *basic bodily self-affection* or a *minimal form of subjectivity* (Fuchs, 2012b). The deep roots for the self, including the elaborate self which encompasses identity and personhood, are to be found in the ensemble of brain devices which continuously and unconsciously maintain the body state within the narrow range and relative stability required for survival (Damasio, 1999, 31). Being aware of these roots reinforces our sense of being alive. This awareness comes through self-affection, that is, our ability to reflect on what affects our being. Self-affection is the condition for the whole body to feel itself as part of life as it expresses itself in the environment and as part of the environment. As Colombetti remarked "[E]motion should be conceptualised as a faculty of the whole embodied and situated organism. Evaluations arise in this organism in virtue of its embodied and situated character, and the whole organism carries meaning as such—not by way of some separate abstract cognitive-evaluative faculty" (Colombetti, 2010, 146). The body is the theater of these emotions which can be distinguished as primary or secondary. The primary emotions, such as fear and anger, are innate and arise in response to situations in which subcortical-limbic structures such as the amygdala or periaqueductal gray are triggered. These responses are registered in the somatosensory regions of the right brain hemisphere (insula, parietal lobe) thus generating feelings as conscious experiences of the coordinated responses (Damasio, 1995, 155). Secondary emotions, such as shame, sadness, or envy, seem to be mediated by perceptions, thoughts, and imaginations connected with prior emotional experiences. "By means of the amygdala and the cingulate gyrus they, in turn, activate a cascade of bodily reactions, which is again registered by somatosensory brain regions" (Damasio, 1995, 155) that resonate with the coordinated experience in the prefrontal cortex. Gut feelings are an emotional body memory that influence our decisions because of this resonance with the primary experience. A decision does not stem from lightning volitions. Decisions are ultimately directed by unconscious emotional processes in the limbic system, and the actions are then triggered by the premotor areas of the brain before the person becomes conscious of this. The brain only deceives us into believing we are acting and responsible persons, whereas we can in fact only ratify its decisions in hindsight. A decision comes with time according to its three layers. It is somato-psychically and psychosomatically influenced. Imaging, suspension of impulses, horizon of possibilities, inner dialogue (engaging with motives and reasons), and emotional congruency generate this integral causality as self-determination which brings the person to choose what resonates with their own identity. As remarked in the section before, time is one of the main constituents that allows this feeling to flow. As Locke wrote: "yet it is plain, consciousness, as far as ever it can be extended (…) unites existences, and actions, very remote in time, into the same person, as well as it does the existences and actions of the immediately preceding moment: so that whatever has the consciousness of present and past actions, is the same person to whom they both belong (…) That with which the consciousness of this present thinking thing can join itself, makes the same person, and is one self with it, and with nothing else" (Locke, l.c., Sections 16/17). Feeling alive means to be one within one's own body and its primary and secondary emotions as they result from the interactions between the parts of the organism and its environment.

V. CRISPR-Cas9—What Would a Victory Look Like?

How could the cohabitation of parts and whole be safe and harmonious if we were capable of modifying the very structure of ourselves and others? What kind of criteria would we decide to choose? What would a victory in this technology look like?

CRISPR-Cas9 is a genome editing technique that started emerging in 2012. Its scientific use has rapidly expanded because of its results and the cheap budget required to perform it. This technique uses "an RNA guide molecule to bind to complementary DNA sequences, which simultaneously recruits the endonuclease Cas9 to introduce double-stranded breaks in the target DNA. The resulting double-stranded break is then repaired, allowing modification or removal of specific DNA bases" (Cribbs et al., 2017). The cheap, quick, and easy use of this technique has contributed to a rapid growth of online tutorials that show how anyone from home can receive a kit and use this technique to do gene-editing at home.

While this technique seems to work with genetic and nongenetic problems even for patients who are still in their infancy or youth, the risk of bio-hacking and an irresponsible use of this technique is a real possibility in the near future (see, e.g., the case of the Chinese doctor He Jankui and his illegal practice on twins made genetically resistant to HIV). Consequently, the legal and ethical frameworks that would allow for harmonious intersubjective access to this technique have yet to be fully discussed. Should this technique be applied to preimplantation human embryos (Liang et al., 2015)? It is true that its potential is such that people suffering from rare genetic disease can finally be assisted and helped. The problem that phenomenology can help to solve is how do we define a disease and to what extent is a disease an unexpected and an unaccepted intersubjective normality? The examples of Down syndrome or dwarfism are good cases for showing how what is perceived as a problem for the whole is not always perceived as such from the parts involved.[23] What genomic traits would we accept to expound from the whole of our intersubjective world? Which criteria would apply in these decisions? Hauskeller's thesis (2013) is that what would make human life better is a very philosophical debatable question. What one would like to enhance, such as physical strength, intelligence, emotional stability, a long lifespan, predispositions to feel happy, and so forth, are not isolated variables but they belong to a complex interconnection of traits whose impact on other people and their society is unforeseeable. Not only dwarfism or Down syndrome but also emotions and feelings such as solidarity or gratitude can become endangered by the evolution and democratization of this technique. Sandel wrote: "Here, then, there is the interconnection between solidarity and giftedness. A lively sense of the contingency of our gifts—an awareness that none of us is fully responsible for his or her success—saves a meritocratic society from sliding into the smug assumption that success is the crown of virtue, that the rich are rich because they are more deserving than the poor" (2007, 91). If human mastery of the genomic traits was to become an accepted way to assure a better life, the sense of entitlement, already worrisome in our society, would only grow and make humbleness and gratitude obsolete feelings. Instead of furthering human progress, we may end up heavily contributing to a degradation of society.

In March 2015, a group of scholars, among them the Nobel laureates David Baltimore and Paul Berg, proposed to work on the alteration of the genome in order to avoid problems for future generations. In May, the U.S. National Academy of Sciences (NAS) and National Academy of Medicine (NAM) announced an "international summit to convene researchers and other experts to explore the scientific, ethical, legal, and policy issues associated with human gene-editing research" (Scheufele, 2014).

Once again, I believe that in order to avoid repeating the horror and misuse of science in Nazi Germany (Li, 2004), we need to consider the impact that these discoveries would have on our emotions and interaffective lives.

For example, if sexism and male entitlement are still intersubjectively accepted, unethical and unwise medical practices can still be perceived as normal. In fact, even though the views of eugenics held by the Nazis were later discredited, the sterilization of women with intellectual disabilities, on social and therapeutic grounds, was still legal practice in a number of European countries and in North America until the mid-twentieth century (Thomson, 1992). Useful regulations can be put into practice if we have the courage to look at social phenomena as they unfold in front of us and we give ourselves time to question their interaffective layers. Today, we have several regulatory bodies, including the WHO, UNESCO, and the Declaration on the Human Genome and Human Rights, that can be used to regulate gene-editing. There are conventions that are legally binding but strongly rely on the legal system of each country, such as the "Oviedo Convention" (the Council of Europe's Convention for the Protection of Human Rights and Dignity of the Human Being with regard to the Application of Biology and Medicine: Convention on Human Rights and Biomedicine), and professional regulatory bodies (such as the HFEA in the United Kingdom and the FDA in the United States) that are heavily involved in the deliberations.[24]

Hence, what would a victory in this field look like? Being able to not lose track of the life-world as an interaffective and intersubjective whole can be the first step toward "a victory." Science and technology can improve our lives, but we need to not forget our humanity. For example, the use of contraception and assisted reproduction gave women and men a responsible way to become parents and enabled a growing economic and social independence that was impossible only a half-century ago. Yet, this autonomy does not mean that parents delegate entirely to their children the responsibility to represent meanings for their lives or to tackle their fears of mortality. Technology should not be the replacement for responsibility and emotional maturity. Similarly, the Internet has led to an increase in the number of "friends" one can call one's own, but it has often impoverished the emotional meaning of friendship and shrank the privacy space in which we can enjoy that friendship. Gene-editing is a socio-scientific issue (SSI) and as such each decision we make in that respect comes from a deliberative process. As Habermas remarked (1999), our deliberative actions are connected to three different but complementary planes of existence: the objective perspective that regards all natural, social, and subjective items/themes as subject matter; the subjective perspective that includes the inner world of feelings, ideas, opinions, and attitudes; and the social world that does not simply exist, but is construed and legitimated (Habermas, 1999). These perspectives are noncontradictory, but distinctly interconnected with each other and they all should be considered legitimate in the deliberative process because they all encourage productive communication practices of scientific citizenship, including discussion, perspective taking, questioning, and consideration of different types of evidence when coming to a decision. Becoming responsible for our "scientific citizenship"[25] (Mejlgaard et al., 2010) requires both competency in scientific knowledge and active participation in deliberating the future of scientific public issues according to these realms.

Conclusion

In this chapter, I argued against reductionism and substance dualism by showing the continuity of life as an organism in physics, biology, and psychology. Using Husserl's theory of parts and whole and its complex application of ontological and epistemological foundations, I explained how the structural difference of time constitutes one's notion of identity that is vitally interconnected with the notion of environment. Ultimately, I discussed a provisional definition for what it means to feel alive and expounded on its causality.

More specifically, the epistemological and ontological foundations of parts and whole with which we recognize that something *is* and we sense its being there proves to be an alternative way to think of life in a relational way. In fact, individuals, defined as nodes of systemic truth, are not dichotomic islands who connect occasionally with each other but are organisms whose parts are interwoven with the environment in which they express their liveliness as a functioning cooperating system.

Understanding the fluidity and continuity of the boundaries between individuals and their environment helps to overcome a dualistic view of the distance that separates our bodies from what we recognize as external. The formal property of environmental sets puts in question the traditional distinction between subject and object that is central to traditional scientism and a certain reification of living beings. This object or that body that I recognize as separate from others is in continuity with them, and there is no space for a strict separation because, as we showed with Aristotle and others, the notion of space itself involves a continuity between entities. Speaking of individual organisms or objects is an abstraction (Dupré and O'Malley, 2007, 842). Objects are no more than "temporarily stable nexuses in the flow of upward and downward causal interaction" (Dupré and O'Malley, 2007, 842) that we use to facilitate our understanding of reality. It was important for this chapter to show the continuity between organism and environment, parts and whole, and self and identity. Our sense of self and identity is often so dualistically biased that we cannot perceive any continuity between the two to the point that the world appears to us as an external being from which we feel completely detached, like remote islands that struggle to communicate with each other. Thinking of our being as an isolated island separated from the rest of the environment would mean to miss the full picture of what we are and lose the concrete terrain of passive intentionality from which we can produce meanings and values. A living being is part of the components produced by the system, and it is its realization of this system in a concrete unity in time and space that can produce meanings and values understandable for itself and others. Survival depends on the ability to transform this interdependence into meanings so that the merely physical surroundings can continuously become a set of meanings and values available for us. Being a person does not consist of adhering to a mental construct, but it is being part of experiential facts and the way in which they interact with the environment. If we impoverish the environment, we impoverish our chance to be ourselves.

Notes

1 In literature, "mereology" is also devoted to the study of system decomposition as in General Systems Theory (Mesarović et al., 1970; Winther, 2011). It is not until Leśniewski's *Foundations of the General Theory of Sets* (1916) and his *Foundations of Mathematics* (1927–1931) that we arrive at a general formulation of the theory of part-relations; yet, since Leśniewski's work was largely inaccessible to nonspeakers of Polish, we have to wait for the publication of Leonard and Goodman's *The Calculus of Individuals* (1940), partly under the influence of Whitehead, to read about mereology as a matter of interest for modern ontologists and metaphysicians.

2 The roots of mereology in antiquity can be traced back to the Presocratics and continuing throughout the writings of Plato (especially the *Parmenides* and the *Theaetetus*), Aristotle (especially the *Metaphysics*, but also the *Physics*, the *Topics*, and *De partibus animalium*), and Boethius (especially *De Divisione* and *In Ciceronis Topica*). Mereology occupies a prominent role also in the writings of medieval ontologists and scholastic philosophers such as Garland the Computist, Peter Abelard, Thomas Aquinas, Raymond Lull, John Duns Scotus, Walter Burley, William of Ockham, and Jean Buridan, as well as in Jungius's *Logica Hamburgensis* (1638), Leibniz's *Dissertatio de arte combinatoria* (1666) and *Monadology* (1714), and Kant's early writings (the *Gedanken* of 1747 and the *Monadologia physica* of 1756).

3 James M. Clark and John V. Skinner, eds. and trans., Treatises and Sermons of Meister Eckhart, New York: Octagon Books, 1983. (Reprint of Harper and Row ed., 1958/ London: Faber & Faber, 1958.)

4 On individual integrity, see, for instance, Cartwright (1975); on artifacts, see Simons and Dement (1996); on events, see Hacker (1982).

5 The ontological marks of environmental settings or niches as Aristotle and Barker might conceive them can be explained as follows: "(1) An environmental niche takes up space, it occupies a physical-temporal locale, and is such as to have spatial parts. Within this physical-temporal locale is a privileged locus—a hole—into which the occupant of the niche fits exactly. (2) Environmental niches are unitary. A typical niche enjoys a certain natural completeness or rounded-offness, in contrast to its arbitrary undetached parts and to arbitrary heaps or aggregates of niches. (3) An environmental niche has an outer boundary: there are objects which fall clearly within it, and other objects which fall clearly outside it. (4) Environmental niches may have actual parts that are also environmental niches, and they may similarly be proper parts

of larger, circumcluding environmental niches. (5) An environmental niche is not simply a location in space; rather, it is a location in space that is constrained or marked by certain functional properties of temperature, foliage density, federal jurisdiction, etc. (6) An environmental niche may overlap spatially with other environmental niches with which it does not share common parts" (Smith, 199, 248).

6 "We say that a thing is in the world, in the sense of in place, because it is in the air, and the air is in the world; and when we say it is in the air, we do not mean it is in every part of the air, but that it is in the air because of the surface of the air which surrounds it; for if all the air were its place, the place of a thing would not be equal to the thing—which it is supposed to be" (Aristotle, *Physics*, 211a 24–8).

7 See on this point, for example, Scheler's effective critique of inner space (Scheler, 2008, 23–24).

8 See Guay and Pradeu (2016, 389): "this conceptual distinction became manifest in the physics context with the development of the logic and metaphysics of 'nonindividual' objects, and, as far as I know, there has been no such similar development in the philosophy of biology."

9 See Guay and Pradeu (2016, 384): "The life history of the bobtail squid ... shows a very short life span, reaching sexual maturity at 2 months and dieing [sic] anywhere between 3 and 10 months. It is a semelparous species, reproducing once in its lifetime. It has been suggested that E. scolopes have a high level of neural complexity, on par with more behaviorally advanced cephalopod molluscs."

10 See Wilson (2013): "Alternatively, one might adopt a 'tripartite account,' according to which an organism is (1) a living agent (2) that belongs to a reproductive lineage, some of whose members have the potential to possess an intergenerational life cycle, and (3) has minimal functional autonomy" (see also Wolfe, 2010).

11 There is significant critical debate regarding this theory; see Banega (2012). "Formal ontology as an operative tool in the theories of objects of the life-world: Stumpf, Husserl and Ingarden," *Symposium: The Canadian Journal of Continental Philosophy*, 16(2): 64–88 in which formal ontology as it is presented in Husserl's Third Logical Investigation is interpreted as a fundamental tool to describe objects in a formal sense. In this paper, the author uses Stumpf's Über den psychologischen Ursprung der Raumovorstellung (1873) to explain the notion of representation; Pilar Fernández Beites. (2007). "Teoría de Todos y Partes: Husserl y Zubiri," *Signos Filosóficos*, 60(17): 63–99, in which the author proposes that an ontology which is able to satisfy the current philosophical necessities has to be understood as a theory of parts and wholes like that developed by Husserl. Comparison is made between this latter theory and Zubiris' theory of substantivity. De Monticelli's (2003) article "On Ontology," *Croatian Journal of Philosophy*, 3(2): 171–186 compares two approaches to ontology. One originated within the analytic tradition and encompasses two diverging streams, philosophy of language and (contemporary) philosophy of mind which lead to "reduced ontology" and "neo-Aristotelian ontology" Blecksmith and Null. (1990). "Matrix representation of Husserl's part-whole-foundation theory," *Notre Dame Journal of Formal Logic*, 32(1): 87–11; Boi. (2007). Phénoménologie et méréologie de la perception spatiale, de Husserl aux théoriciens de la Gestalt. In Boi, Kerszberg, and Patras (eds.) *Rediscovering Phenomenology: Phenomenological Essays on Mathematical Beings, Physical Reality, Perception and Consciousness (Phaenomenologica)* (English and French Edition). Springer, 33–66; Casari. (2007). *On the Relationship Between Parts and Wholes in Husserl's Phenomenology*. In Boi, Kerszberg, and Patras (eds.) *Rediscovering Phenomenology: Phenomenological Essays on Mathematical Beings, Physical Reality, Perception and Consciousness (Phaenomenologica)*. Springer. 67–102; Ettore Casari. (2000). "On Husserl's theory of wholes and parts," *History and Philosophy of Logic*, 21(1): 1–43; Crespo. (1995). "En Torno a Los 'Estados de Cosas:' Una Investigación Ontológico-Formal," *Anuario Filosófico*, 28(1): 143–158; Crosson. (1962). "Formal logic and formal ontology in Husserl's phenomenology," *Notre Dame Journal of Formal Logic*, 3(4): 259–269;

Drummond. (2009). La limitation de l'ontologie par la logique. Methodos 9; Drummond. (2008). Wholes, parts, and phenomenological methodology (Logische Untersuchung). In V. Mayer (ed.) *Edmund Husserl: Logische Untersuchungen*. Akademie Verlag Berlin. 35–105; Dubosson. (2008). "L'ontologie des Objets Culturels Selon Husserl," *Studia Phaenomenologica*, 8: 65–81; Lampert. (1989). "Husserl's theory of parts and wholes: the dynamic of individuating and contextualizing interpretation— Übergehen, Abheben, Ergänzungsbedürftigkeit," *Research in Phenomenology*, 19(1): 195–212; Libardi. (1994). "Applications and limits of mereology. from the theory of parts to the theory of wholes." *Axiomathes*, 5(1): 13–54.

12 Every intentional act corresponds to a mental object animated by sensations. As explained in Chapter 3, intentionality is whatever is perceived through changes in an actual (*reellen*) content. Sensations represent, through passive syntheses, this real content that is given to the subject and intentionality is exactly what makes us able to perceive the *reellen* and give it to us in the form of a whole (in Chapter 3 this was described as the passage from passive to active intentionality). This form of intentionality is triggered by emotional awakening (practical intentionality). We are struck by sensuous pieces (passive intentionality) and this makes our ego (active intentionality)—as Langrebe remarked (1981)—a sensuous one.

13 Edmund Husserl, Späte Texte über Zeitkonstitution (1929–1934). Die C-Manuskripte, Hrsg. von D. Lohmar, "Husserliana Materialen VIII" (Dordrecht, 2006), 110: "This primal impressional flowing present of the concrete originally presence has then the following quite universal structure: (1) the phenomenological residuum of the proper perceivable side of mundane realities etc., namely the sensation-hyle, the originary hyle in its own temporalization; (2) theI with all open and concealed egological components, belonging there: all components of the worldly apprehension, all components of the worldly 'reference,' of what is essentially according to a horizon (Horizontmäßig), of the worldly representations and so on."

14 Hua-Mat VIII, 84: "Temporalization of the concrete present as impressional present of persisting unities and pluralities (...) [it] is the first and more original temporalization of the time-mode present, and then of the time-mode past."

15 I borrowed this term from Gebser (2011). See also on time and self, Lohmar (2010) and Simeonov (2015).

16 "Here, it is not only what is intentional (das Intentionale) that is a temporal object (zeitlicher Gegenstand), but also the intending experience (das intendierende Erlebnis), this last one also a 'pole' itself, and all these poles lie on coinciding time series (sich deckende Zeitreihen), and all these time series in their unity of coincidence make up the whole experiencing (Erleben), the stream of experiencing" (Hua XXXIII, 279).

17 See Locke, 2006, l.c., Section 9: "in this (i.e. consciousness) alone consists personal identity, i.e. the sameness of a rational being: and as far as this consciousness can be extended backwards to any past action or thought, so far reaches the identity of that person."

18 See study on self-palpation (Taipale, 2014, 49), or the way in which we relate to each other in a personalistic and naturalistic attitude (Fuchs, 75), or Plessner's (1975) explanation of eccentric attitude as capacity of human beings to relate to themselves.

19 The selective processes are generally completed by the end of the third year (Markowitsch and Welzer, 2009, 87), in the youngest brain region, the prefrontal cortex, the highest synaptic density is not reached before the age of 5. Its nal structure is only completed around the 25th year of age (Sowell et al., 1999; Fuster 2001).

20 See Meyer et al. (2017, 368): "At the chemical level, self-sustaining work has been referred to as autocatalysis (Kauffman, 1995), the idea being that a self-sustaining chemical system is one in which reactions produce either their own catalysts or catalysts for some other reaction in the system. At the biological level, self-sustaining work has been referred to as autopoiesis (Maturana and Varela, 1980)—again, the

idea being that a single cell constitutes a multiscale system of work in which lower-scale chemical processes give rise to the larger biological whole of the cell which, in turn, provides a context in which the lower-scale work sustains itself and the whole it gives rise to (Jordan and Ghin, 2006, 2007). Hebb (1949) referred to the self-sustaining nature of neural networks as the 'cell assembly,' the idea being that neurons that fire together wire together. Jordan and Heidenreich (2010) recently cast this idea in terms of self-sustaining work by examining data that indicate the generation of action potentials increases nuclear transcription processes in neurons which, in turn, fosters synapse formation. At the behavioral level, Skinner (1976) referred to the self-sustaining nature of behavior as operant conditioning, the idea being that behaviors sustain themselves in one's behavioral repertoire as a function of the consequences they generate. Streeck and Jordan (2009) recently described communication as a dynamical self-sustaining system in which multi-scale events such as postural alignment, gesture, gaze, and speech produce outcomes that sustain an ongoing interaction. And finally, Odum (1988) and Vandervert (1995) used the notion of self-sustaining work to refer to ecologies in general."

21 Fuchs (2017, 221): "The conditions for all life processes are always the respective functions. The routes and actions of a human being are never directed by consciousness as such. They are directed and enacted by the conscious human being as a whole, including all its physiological and brain processes. The role of consciousness: (1) To produce a unit of intermodal action space with integral gestalt units ("apple," "grasping"). (2) To be intentionally and actively directed towards relevant objects ("perceiving the apple," "hunger," "desire"). (3) To transcend the momentary present, either anticipating what is about to come ("reaching for the apple"), or retaining what has just been experienced. (4) To provide a sense of self-awareness which integrates the organism's current state with regard to its own self-preservation as well as in relation to external objects ("satisfying my hunger by eating the apple").

22 As it concerns the debate on whether the notion of supervenience helps or not to avoid reductionism, I defer to Horgan, David Lewis, and especially Jaegwon Kim.

23 Several sources and social movements on this point. For example, BBC's documentary *A World without Down Syndrome?* or the activities promoted by the nonprofit "Little People of America."

24 There is a ban on human germline modification by many European countries (Montgomery et al., 2016) and in the United States, and any edited embryos for pregnancy require permission from the U.S. Food and Drug Administration. Similarly, in China, any clinical use of gene-editing must be permitted by the Chinese Ministry of Health. The recent report by NAS/NAM classifies gene-editing using CRISPR-Cas9 on the basis of purpose and heritability: *purpose* being therapeutic interventions (treat or prevent disease) or enhancement and *heritability* involving somatic or germline cells. From a public point of view, the report observes that the majority agrees with the use of genome editing in both somatic (64%) and germline cells (65%) for therapeutic purposes but not for enhancement applications (National Academy of Science, 2017). However, it is important to note that basic research objectives in gene-editing techniques are also closely tied up with therapeutic/enhancement interventions thereby adding a layer of complexity for the principle *purpose* of the technique.

25 Gross (1994), Sadler (2004, 2009), Bauer (2007), and Grooms (2014) showed the importance of promoting science by emphasizing ethical and scientific concerns in order to increase productive engagement of socio-scientific issues (SSI). They suggest that it is useful to teach science by sharing active, communicative habits of citizenship, habits which bring the public into discussion. These researchers tailored techniques and shared some recommendations for teaching effective skills in science communications in the classroom.

Bibliography

Aristotle. (1928). *The Works of Aristotle*. Vol. 8, Metaphysica. Trans. D. Ross. Oxford, Clarendon Press.

Aristotle. (1932). *Politics*. Ed. and trans. Horace Rackham. Cambridge, MA: Harvard University Press.

Aristotle. (1949). *Categoriae et liber de interpretation*. Ed. L. Minio-Paluello. Oxford: Clarendon Press".

Banega (2012), "Formal Ontology as an Operative Tool in the Theories of Objects of the Life-World: Stumpf, Husserl and Ingarden". *Symposium: The Canadian Journal of Continental Philosophy* 16(2): 64–88.

Bauer M. W. Allum, N. Miller, S. (2007). "What can we learn from 25 years of PUS survey research? Liberating and expanding the agenda". *Public Underst Sci*. 16: 79–95.

Beebe, B., Sterne, D. (1977). Engagement-disengagement and early object experiences. In: N. Freedman, S. Grand (Eds.) *Communicative structures and psychic structures*, 35–55. New York: Plenum Press.

Bergson, H. (1950). *Time and free will: An essay on the immediate data of consciousness*. Trans. F. L. Pogson, 6th edition. London: George Allen & Unwin.

Blecksmith, Null, (1990). "Matrix Representation of Husserl's Part-Whole-Foundation Theory". *Notre Dame Journal of Formal Logic*, 32 (1):87–11

Boi, K. (2007). "Phénoménologie et méréologie de la perception spatiale, de Husserl aux théoriciens de la Gestalt". In Boi, K. Patras (eds.), *Rediscovering Phenomenology: Phenomenological Essays on Mathematical Beings, Physical Reality, Perception and Consciousness*, Dordrecht: Springer. 33–66.

Brodmann, K. (1909). *Vergleichende Lokalisationslehre der Großhirnrinde, in ihren Prinzipien dargestellt auf Grund des Zellenbaues*. Leipzig: Barth.

Butler J. (1736). *Of Personal Identity*. Berkeley: University of California Press.

Calosi, C., Graziani, P. (2014). *Mereology and the Sciences*. Dordrecht: Springer.

Cacioppo, J. T., Berntson, G. G., Adolphs, R., et al. (2002). *Foundations in Social Neuroscience*. Cambridge, MA: MIT Press.

Cameron, O. G. (2001). "Interoception: the inside story—a model for psychosomatic processes". *Psychosomatic Medicine* 63: 697–710.

Cartwright, R. (1975). 'Scattered Objects', in Lehrer, K. (ed.), *Analysis and Metaphysics*, Dordrecht: Reidel, 153–71.

Casati, R. Smith, B, and Varzi, A. C. (1998). 'Ontological Tools for Geographic Representation', in N. Guarino (ed.), *Formal Ontology in Information Systems*, Amsterdam and Oxford: IOS Press, 77–85.

Casari, E. (2007). *On the Relationship Between Parts and Wholes in Husserl's Phenomenology*. In Boi, Kerszberg & Patras (eds.), Rediscovering Phenomenology: Phenomenological Essays on Mathematical Beings, Physical Reality, Perception and Consciousness (Phaenomenologica). Springer. 67–102

Casari, E. (2000). "On Husserl's Theory of Wholes and Parts". *History and Philosophy of Logic* 21 (1):1–43.

Crespo, (1995). "En Torno a Los "Estados de Cosas": Una Investigación Ontológico-Formal". *Anuario Filosófico* 28 (1):143–158.

Crosson (1962). Formal Logic and Formal Ontology in Husserl's Phenomenology. Notre Dame Journal of Formal Logic 3 (4):259–269

Clarke, E. (2012). "The Organism as a Problem in Biological Ontology". Talk given at the Objects, Kinds and Mechanisms in Biology Workshop, Leeds, April.

Colombetti, G. (2010). Enaction, sense-making, and emotion. In: J. Stewart, O. Gapenne, E. Di Paolo (Eds.) *Enaction: Toward a new paradigm for cognitive science*, 145–164. Cambridge, MA: MIT Press.

Connoly, W. (2017). *Facing the Planetary: Entangled Humanism and the Politics of Swarming*, Duke University Press.

Cozolino, L. (2014). *The neuroscience of human relationships: Attachment and the developing social brain*. New York: Norton & Co.

Crowell, S. (1997). *Normativity and Phenomenology in Husserl and Heidegger*, Cambridge University Press.

Damasio, A. (1995). *Descartes' error: Emotion, reason and the human brain*. London: Picador.

Damasio, A. (1999). *The feeling of what happens: Body and emotion in the making of consciousness*. New York: Harcourt Brace & Co.

de Haan and Fuchs. (2010). "The Ghost in the Machine," *Psychopathology*, 43, 5, 327–33.

Deacon, T. (2006). "Emergence: the whole at the wheel's hub". In: P. Clayton, P. Davies (Eds.) *The re-emergence of emergence: e emergentist hypothesis from science to religion*, 111–150. Oxford: Oxford University Press.

Decety, J., Ickes, W. (2011). The *social neuroscience of empathy*. Cambridge, MA: MIT Press.

Descartes, R. (1993). *Meditations on first philosophy*. Haldane, E. Ross, G. R. T. (trans.) New York: Routledge.

Descartes, R. (2015). *The passions of the soul, and other late philosophical writings*. Moriarty, M. (trans.) Oxford: Oxford University Press.

Dewey, J. (1896). The refleex arc concept in psychology. *Psychological Review* 3: 357–370.

Di Paolo, D., De Jaegher, H. (2012). e interactive brain hypothesis. *Frontiers in Human Neuroscience* 6: 163.

Di Paolo, E. (2009). Extended life. *Topoi* 28: 9–21.

De Jaegher, D., Di Paolo, E., Adolphs, R. (2016). "What does the interactive brain hypothesis mean for social neuroscience? A dialogue". *Philosophical Transactions of the Royal Society* B, 371: 20150379.

De Monticelli, R. (2003) "On Ontology". *Croatian Journal of Philosophy* 3 (2):171–186.

Dupré, J. Maureen O' M. (2007). "Metagenomics and Biological Ontology". *Studies in the History and Philosophy of Science C: Biological and Biomedical Sciences*, 28: 834–846.

Drummond (2009). La limitation de l'ontologie par la logique. Methodos 9;

Drummond (2008). Wholes, Parts, and Phenomenological Methodology (III. Logische Untersuchung). In V. Mayer (ed.), Edmund Husserl: Logische Untersuchungen. Akademie Verlag Berlin. 35–105

Dubosson (2008). L'ontologie des Objets Culturels Selon Husserl. Studia Phaenomenologica 8:65–81

French, S. and Décio K. (2006). *Identity in Physics: A Historical, Philosophical, and Formal Analysis*. Oxford: Oxford University Press.

French, S. (2014). *The Structure of the World: Metaphysics and Representation*. Oxford: Oxford University Press.

Fuchs, T. (2010). Phenomenology and psychopathology. In: S. Gallagher, D. Schmicking (eds.) *Handbook of phenomenology and the cognitive sciences*, 547–573. Dordrecht: Springer.

Fuchs, T. (1989) "Phenomenology and the Metaphysics of Presence", in *Phaenomenologica*, 115, The Hague, Martinus Nijhoff.

Fuchs, T. (2016). "Self across Time: The Diachronic Unity of Bodily Existence". Phenomenology and the Cognitive Sciences, 15. Published online first.

Fuster, J. M. (2001). "The prefrontal cortex—an update: time is of the essence". *Neuron* 30: 319–333.

Gebser, J. (2011). *Ursprung und Gegenwart. Zweiter Teil: Die Manifestationen der perspektivischen Welt.* Flensburg Fjord: Novalis Verlag.

Grooms J, Sampson V, Golden B. (2014). "Comparing the effectiveness of verification and inquiry laboratories in supporting undergraduate science students in constructing arguments around socioscientific issues". *Int J Sci Educ.*, 36: 1412–1433.

Habermas, J. (1999). *Wahrheit und Rechtfertigung. Philosophische Aufsätze*, Frankfurt a.M.: Verlag.

Hacker, P. M. S. (1982). 'Events and Objects in Space and Time', *Mind* 91, 1–19.

Hart, J. "The Person and the Common Life", in *Phaenomenologica* 148, Dordrecht/Boston/London, Kluwer Academic Publishers, 1998.

Hauskeller, M. (2013). *Better Humans? Understanding the Enhancement Project*, Durham: Acumen Publishing.

Hebb, D. O. (1949). *The Organization of Behavior: A Neuropsychological Theory.* New York: Wiley.

Horgan, T. Timmons, M. (1992). "Troubles on Moral Twin Earth", *Syntheses*, 92, 221–260.

Husserl, E. (1921/1973). *Zur Phänomenologie der Intersubjektivität.* Texte aus dem Nachlass. Zweiter Teil. 1921-28, ed. by Kern, I. The Hague, Netherlands, Martinus Nijhoff. (Hua XIV)

Husserl, E. (1922/1984). *Logische Untersuchungen. Zweiter Teil. Untersuchungen zur Phänomenologie und Theorie der Erkenntnis*, Halle: 1901; rev. ed. 1922, ed. by Panzer, U. The Hague, Netherlands, Martinus Nijhoff. (Hua XIX)

Husserl, E. (1913/1950). *Ideen zu einer reinen Phänomenologie und phänomenologischen Philosophie.* Erstes Buch: Allgemeine Einführung in die reine Phänomenologie, ed. by. Biemel. W. The Hague, Netherlands, Martinus Nijhoff Publishers. (Hua III)

Husserl, E. (1919/2002). *Natur und Geist. Vorlesungen Sommersemester 1919*, ed. by Michael Weiler, Dordrecht, Netherlands, Kluwer Academic Publishers. (Hua-Mat. IV)

Husserl, E. (1916/2012). *Einleitung in die Philosophie. Vorlesungen 1916-1919*, ed. by Hanne Jacobs. Dordrecht, Springer, 2012. (Hua-Mat. IX)

Husserl, E. (1917/2001). *Die 'Bernauer Manuskripte' über das Zeitbewußtsein (1917/18)* ed. by Bernet, R. Lohmar, D. Dordrecht, Netherlands: Kluwer Academic. (Hua XXXIII)

Husserl, E. (1907/1973). *Ding und Raum. Vorlesungen 1907.* ed. by Claesges, U. The Hague, Netherlands: Martinus Nijhoff. (Hua XVI)

Husserl, E. (1929-34/2006). *Späte Texte über Zeitkonstitution (1929–1934). Die C-Manuskripte.* Ed. by Lohmar, D. New York: Springer (Hua-Mat. VIII)

Husserl, E. (1921/1952). *Ideen zur einer reinen Phänomenologie und phänomenologischen Philosophie. Zweites Buch: Phänomenologische Untersuchungen zur Konstitution.* Ed. by. Biemel, M. The Hague, Netherlands: Martinus Nijhoff. (Hua IV)

Husserl, E. (1931/1973). *Cartesianische Meditationen und Pariser Vorträge.* Ed. by Strasser. The Hague, Netherlands: Martinus Nijhoff. (Hua I)

Husserl, E. (1918-26/1966). *Analysen zur passiven Synthesis. Aus Vorlesungs- und Forschungsmanuskripten, 1918-1926.* Ed. by Fleischer, E. The Hague, Netherlands: Martinus Nijhoff. (Hua XI)

Hutchinson, G. E. (1978). *An Introduction to Population Ecology.* Yale University Press, New Haven, CT.

James, W. (1884). What is an emotion? *Mind* 9: 188–205.

James, W. (1890). *e principles of psychology*. New York: Henry Holt and Company.

Jonas, H. (1968). Biological foundations of individuality. *International Philosophical Quarterly* 8: 231–251.

Jonas, H. (2001). *The phenomenon of life: Toward a philosophical biology* [1st edition 1966]. Evanston, IL: Northwestern University Press.

Jordan, J. S., and D. Vinson. (2012). "After Nature: On Bodies, Consciousness, and Causality." *Journal of Consciousness Studies* 19(5–6):229–250.

Jordan, J. S., and M. Ghin. (2007). "The Role of Control in a Science of Consciousness: Causality, Regulation and Self-Sustainment." *Journal of Consciousness Studies* 14(1–2):177–197.

Jordan, J. S., and M. Ghin. (2007). "The Role of Control in a Science of Consciousness: Causality, Regulation and Self-Sustainment." *Journal of Consciousness Studies* 14(1–2):177–197.

Jordan, J. S., and B. Heidenreich (2010). "The Intentional Nature of Self-Sustaining Systems." *Mind & Matter* 8(1):45–62.

Kant, Immanuel (1902): *Kants gesammelte Schriften*. Preussischen Akademie der Wissenschaften (vols 1-22), Deutschen Akademie der Wissenschaften (vol. 23), Akademie der Wissenschaften zu Göttingen (vols 24-9). Berlin: Walter de Gruyter. (AK.)

Kronz, F. M., Tiehen, J. T. (2002). Emergence and quantum mechanics. *Philosophy of Science* 69: 324–347.

Lampert (1989). "Husserl's Theory of Parts and Wholes: The Dynamic of Individuating and Contextualizing Interpretation —Übergehen, Abheben, Ergänzungsbedürftigkeit". *Research in Phenomenology*, 19 (1):195–212;

Leśniewski, S. (1916). *Podstawy ogólnej teoryi mnogości. I*, Moskow: Prace Polskiego Koła Naukowego w Moskwie, Sekcya matematyczno-przyrodnicza; Eng. trans. by D. I. Barnett: 'Foundations of the General Theory of Sets. I', in S. Leśniewski, *Collected Works* (ed. byS. J. Surma *et al.*), Dordrecht: Kluwer, 1992, Vol. 1, 129–173.

Leśniewski, S. (1927–1931). 'O podstawach matematyki', *Przegląd Filozoficzny*, 30: 164–206; 31: 261–291; 32: 60–101; 33: 77–105; 34: 142–170; Eng. trans. by D. I. Barnett: 'On the Foundations of Mathematics', in S. Leśniewski, *Collected Works* (ed. byS. J. Surma *et al.*), Dordrecht: Kluwer, 1992, Vol. 1, 174–382.

Leonard, H. S. Goodman, N. (1940). 'The Calculus of Individuals and Its Uses', *Journal of Symbolic Logic*, 5: 45–55.

Liang, P., Xu, Y., Zhang, X., Ding, C., Huang, R., Zhang, Z., Lv, J., Xie, X., Chen, Y., Li, Y., Sun, Y., Bai, Y., Songyang, Z., Ma, W., Zhou, C., & Huang, J. (2015). "CRISPR/Cas9-mediated gene editing in human tripronuclear zygotes". *Protein & cell*, 6(5), 363–372.

Li, H. L. Fujimoto, N. Sasakawa, N. Shirai, S. Ohkame, T. Sakuma, T. et al. (2015). "Precise correction of the dystrophin gene in duchenne muscular dystrophy patient induced pluripotent stem cells by TALEN and CRISPR-Cas9". *Stem Cell Reports*, 4(1):143–54.

Libardi (1994). "Applications and Limits of Mereology. From the Theory of Parts to the Theory of Wholes". *Axiomathes*, 5, (1):13–54.

Locke, J. (1813). *An essay concerning human understanding*. London: Cummings & Hilliard and J.T. Buckingham.

Lohmar, D. (2010). *On Time. New Contributions to the Husserlian Phenomenology of Time*, Dordrecht-Boston-London, Springer.

Lowe, E. J. (2009). *More Kinds of Being*. Oxford: Wiley-Blackwell.

Margulis, L., Sagan, D. (1995). *What is life?* New York: Simon & Schuster.

Markowitsch, H., Welzer, H. (2009). *e development of autobiographical memory*. London: Psychology Press

Mcleod, E. Chmura, G. Bouillon, S. Salm, R. Björk, M. Duarte, C. Lovelock, C. Schlesinger, W. Silliman, B. (2011). "A blueprint for blue carbon: Toward an improved understanding of the role of vegetated coastal habitats in sequestering CO2". *Frontiers in Ecology and the Environment*. 9. 10.

Merleau-Ponty, M. (1960). Le philosophe et son ombre. In: *Signes*. Paris: Gallimard.

Merleau-Ponty, M. (1962). *Phenomenology of perception*. Trans. C. Smith. London: Routledge.

Merleau-Ponty, M. (1968). *The visible and the invisible: Followed by working notes*. Trans. C. Lefort. Evanston, IL: Northwestern University Press.

Merleau-Ponty, M. (2010). *Institution and passivity: Course notes from the Collège de France. (1954–1955)*. Evanston, IL: Northwestern University Press.

Mejlgaard, Niels & Stares, Sally. (2009). "Participation and competence as joint components in a cross-national analysis of scientific citizenship". *Public Understanding of Science*, 19

Mesarovic, M. D. Mesarovic, D. Macko, Y. Takahara (1970). *Theory of hierarchical multilevel systems*. Academic press, New York.

Montgomery, J. Caney, S. Clancy, T. Edwards, J. Gallagher, A. Greenfield, A. (2016). *Council on Bioethics Report:Genome editing*.

National Academy of Sciences and National Academy of Medicine Human Genome Editing (2017). *Science, Ethics, and Governance*. Washington (DC): National Academies Press.

Noë, A. (2009). *Out of our heads: Why you are not your brain, and other lessons from the biology of consciousness*. New York: Hill & Wang.

Noonan, W. J. (1989). *Personal Identity*. London: Routledge

Nenon, T. (2002). "Freedom, Responsibility, and Self-Awareness in Husserl". *New Yearbook for Phenomenology and Phenomenological Philosophy*, 2 (1):1–21.

Odum, H. T. (1988). "Self-Organization, Transformity, and Information." *Science*, 242:132–139.

Pilar, F. B. (2007). "Teoría de Todos y Partes: Husserl y Zubiri". *Signos Filosóficos* 60 (17):63–99.

Plessner, H. (1975). *Die Stufen des Organischen und der Mensch* (1st edition 1928). Berlin: De Gruyter.

Portmann, A. (1969). *Zoologie und das neue Bild des Menschen*, 3rd edition. Reinbek: Rowohlt.

Pradeu, T. (2012). *The Limits of the Self: Immunology and Biological Identity*. New York: Oxford University Press.

Reid T. (1785). *Essays on the Intellectual Powers of Man*. Edinburg: John Bell; 1785. pp. 317–318. London: G.G.J. and J. Robinson.

Riutort, M. Cuervo-Lombard, C. Danion, J.-M. Peretti, C.-S. Salamé, Pi. (2003). "Reduced levels of specific autobiographical memories in schizophrenia". *Psychiatry research*, 117, 35–45.

Symposium "Heterogeneous Individuals," held at PSA 2010, Montreal

Sadler, T. D. Zeidler, D. L. (2004). "The morality of socioscientific issues: construal and resolution of genetic engineering dilemmas". *Sci Ed.*, 88:4–27.

Sadler, T. D. (2009). "Situated learning in science education: socio-scientific issues as contexts for practice". *Studies Sci Educ.* 45:1–42.

Sandel, M. (2017). *The Case against Imperfection*, Harvard: Harvard University Press.

Scheufele, D. A. (2014). Science communication as political communication. Proc Natl Acad Sci USA, 111.

Scheler, M. (2008). *The Nature of Sympathy*. Piscataway, N.J.: Transaction.

Shoemaker, S. Swinburne, S. (1984). *Personal Identity. Great debate in philosophy.* London: Blackwell.

Smith, B. and Varzi, A. C. (1999). 'Fiat and Bona Fide Boundaries', Philosophy and Phenomenological Research, *Nous*, 33, 214–38.

Simeonov, P. L. (2015). "Yet another time about time. Part I: An essay on the phenomenology of physical time", *PubMed*, 119, 3, 271–87.

Simons, P. M. and Dement, C. W. (1996). 'Aspects of the Mereology of Artifacts', in Poli, R. Simons, P. M., *Formal Ontology*, Dordrecht, Boston, and London: Kluwer Academic Publishers, 255–76.

Skinner, B. F. 1976. *About Behaviorism*. New York: Vintage.

Sowell, E. R., Thompson, P. M., Holmes, C. J., Jernigan, T. L., Toga, A. W. (1999). "In vivo evidence for post-adolescent brain maturation in frontal and striatal regions". *Nature Neuroscience* 2: 859–861.

Stapleton, T. (1983). *Husserl and Heidegger. The Question of a Phenomenological Beginning*, Albany, State University of New York.

Stern, D. N. (1998). "The process of therapeutic change involving implicit knowledge: Some implications of developmental observations for adult psychotherapy". *Infant Mental Health Journal* 19: 300–308.

Stern, D. N. (1985). *e interpersonal world of the infant: A View from Psychoanalysis and Developmental Psychology*. New York: Basic Books.

Stumpf, C. (1873). *Über den psychologischen Ursprung der Raumvorstellung*, Leipzig.

Taipale, J. (2014). *Phenomenology and embodiment: Husserl and the constitution of subjectivity*. Evanston, IL: Northwestern University Press.

Thompson, E. (2005). "Sensorimotor subjectivity and the enactive approach to experience". *Phenomenology and the Cognitive Sciences* 4: 407–427.

Thompson, E. (2007). *Mind in life: Biology, phenomenology, and the sciences of mind*. Cambridge, MA: Harvard University Press.

Thomson M. (1992). "Sterilization, segregation and community care: ideology and solutions to the problem of mental deficiency in inter-war Britain". *Hist Psychiatry*, 3, (12):473–98.

Toombs, K. (1992). *The Meaning of Illness*, Dordrecht: Springer.

Trevarthen, C. (2001). "The neurobiology of early communication: intersubjective regulations in human brain development". In Kalverboer, A. F. Gramsberg, A. (eds.) *Handbook of brain and behaviour in human development*, pp. 841–881. Dordrecht: Kluwer Academic Publishers.

Tronick, E., Als, H., Adamson, L., Wise, S., Brazelton, T. B. (1978). "The infant's response to entrapment between contradictory messages in face-to-face interaction". *Journal of the American Academy of Child Psychiatry*, 17: 1–13.

Uexküll, J. von (1920), *Streifzüge durch die Umwelten von Tieren und Menschen: Ein Bilderbuch unsichtbarer Welten*, Berlin: Springer-Verlag.

Van Dijk, J., Kerkhofs, R., Van Rooij, I., Haselager, P. (2008). Special section: can there be such a thing as embodied embedded cognitive neuroscience? *Theory & Psychology*, 18: 297–316.

Vandervert, L. (1995). "Chaos Theory and the Evolution of Consciousness and Mind: A Thermodynamic-Holographic Resolution to the Mind–Body Problem." *New Ideas in Psychology* 13(2):107–127.

Varela, F. J. (1979). *Principles of biological autonomy.* New York: Elsevier.

Varela, F. J. (1996). Neurophenomenology: a methodological remedy for the hard problem. *Journal of Consciousness Studies* 3: 330–349.

Varela, F. J. (1997). Patterns of life: intertwining identity and cognition. *Brain and Cognition*, 34: 72–87.

Varela, F. J. (1999). Present-time consciousness. *Journal of Consciousness Studies* 6: 111–140.

Varela, F., Thompson, E., Rosch, E. (1991). *The embodied mind: Cognitive science and human experience.* Cambridge, MA: MIT Press.

Weber, A., Varela, F. H. (2002). Life a er Kant: natural purposes and the autopoietic foundations of biological individuality. *Phenomenology and the Cognitive Sciences* 1: 97–125.

Whittaker, R. H., and Lewin, S. A. (1975). "Niche Theory and Applications", in *Ecology*, 3, Stroudsburg, PA: Dowden.

Winther, R. G. (2011). 'Part-Whole Science', *Synthese*, 178: 397–427.

Woodger, J. H. (1937). *The Axiomatic Method in Biology*, London: Cambridge University Press.

Wolfe, C. (2010)." Do Organisms Have an Ontological Status?" *History and Philosophy of the Life Sciences*, 32: 195–231."

5
INSIDE/OUTSIDE

Introduction

In this chapter, I am going to discuss another important consequence of substance dualism on our Lebenswelt (life-world). The painful way in which we organize our lives is still based on a quite rigid separation of the inner life from the bodily one. In the first chapter, I showed how the Galilean reaction to a religious interpretation of science and the Cartesian systematization of Galilean intuitions led to the separation of nature from the human soul, the body from its mind. This systematization divided human reality into two spheres of power: the bodily and the spiritual; the former pertained to science and politics and the latter to religion and later psychology. This strict separation between an inner and outer world served its purpose in a time of need for religious and political emancipation, yet today this form of organization has led to a schizoid society where individualism, antagonism, and solitude seem to prevail over cooperation and solidarity. Looking at mind and body as an inseparable organism within the bigger organism of nature and integrating this understanding into our daily lives can raise the quality of our lives and the quality of our care toward the environment.

For this reason, this chapter will focus first on the dichotomy of inside/outside that is reflected in the relation of the self with reality, and it will examine the way in which animals and nature are considered within this dichotomy. Then, it will propose the notion of interaffectivity to reduce the space between the two, and it will describe practical exercises that are used in case disturbances of interaffectivity impede the enjoyment of this closeness. Finally, it will discuss how in health care the inability to look at the continuity of the human organism with natural organisms has led to painful misdiagnosis and lack of care.

I. The Challenge of the Self and Reality

Cartesian dualism has encouraged a view of an impermeable body that is strictly separated from the self and its environment although located very close to it. As Descartes (1993, 93) wrote, "I am not lodged in my body as a pilot in a vessel, but I am very closely united to it." The reality of my existence is in my cogito, and the body that incarnates this cogito operates through senses that I cannot fully trust because they transcend my knowledge. I am a stranger in my own home.

As I mentioned before, this separation negatively impacted several areas of our lives, especially in the decades that preceded and ensued the Second World War. Feeling like a stranger in our own body reflected a sense of estrangement toward the public life which was felt as external and foreign to private interest. The declining interest toward public health as a discipline was accompanied by a view of health and disease as "individualized" (Morris and Saunders, 2017) and independent from the environment which was no longer considered to be a decisive component for health. Although attempts were made to foster an idea of well-being rooted in a permeable body that entertains a hosmotic relationship with the environment, they did not succeed in replacing the dualistic interpretation of human life. These new views encouraged the development of an ecological mind and the growth of a socio-ecological perspective;[1] Haekel, for example, introduced the word *ecology* in 1866, and after this, Bateson (1972) and Neisser (1988) elaborated on the notion of ecological subjectivity. Much later in 1990, scholars diffused the urgency of a social ecology (Bookchin, 1996), yet, as Jonas remarked, the sense of selfhood was still presented in Western society as a foreign being that goes beyond the boundaries of the organism:

> The challenge of 'selfhood' qualifies everything beyond the boundaries of the organism as foreign and somehow opposite: as 'world', within which, by which, and against which it is committed to maintain itself. Without this universal counterpart of 'other', there would be no 'self.'
>
> *(Jonas, 1968, 242f)*

The self exists because there is another against, within, and by which it is committed to be itself. The notions of space and niche, as examined in Chapter 4, were rarely used to overcome this mindset. Being healthy meant being located in a healthy body. This perspective strictly separates the spiritual inside of the individual from the outside of the individual body; as Jonas wrote, the selfhood is always a challenge because its presence entails a separation from what is not the self. Still today, the self is commonly perceived as an abstract construct that is nowhere to be seen as it dwells in a mysterious space inside of us which has been referred as an "out of the brain" illusion or a ghost in the machine. Metzinger, for example, compares the self to a pilot in a flight simulator that "continuously constructs and updates an external model of reality" based on a naive and often inexact interpretation of internal reality (2009, 107). Rorty explained the reason for this dislocation with a joke: "If the body had been easier to understand, nobody would have thought that we have a mind" (Rorty, 1970, 239).

I consider this mindset particularly harmful in bioethics because it impacts human psychological well-being (as I will explain in the following chapters) and accordingly the environmental care that humans are capable of dedicating to the planet. Living a life detached from one's own body and the environment not only fosters a lack of vitality for the individual who loses connection with the body, its main source of energy (Lowen, 1983), but it also encourages a careless behavior toward the impact we can have on our collective body, the environment. Loosening the connection between body and mind lessens personal and environmental vitality as we lose the sense of the impact that our embodied self has on itself and the things with which it interacts. An approach to the mind/body problem that emphasizes the permeability of this synolon (as in Aristotle's σύνολον to mean the "concrete whole" of matter and form) and its degrees of unity can help to overcome this growing problem.

Wilson's (2002) strategy, for example, as it has been expressed in his "Six Views of Embodied Cognition," shows the "growing commitment to the idea that the mind must be understood in the context of its relationship to a physical body that interacts with the world" (625). Understanding how "the persistent life of subjectivity may be related to the continuity of organic or biological life as its necessary basis" (Fuchs, 2016) is important for overcoming a strict Cartesian dichotomy and a consequent substance dualism. The subtle membrane that is seen in between the self and the body has generated the illusion "of the body here detecting the surrounding environment out there" (Gendlin, 2012, 144). This illusion still encourages dissociations which makes the cognitive "in between" space a pragmatic and distributive one as it posits the distribution of cognitive action and sensorimotor enquiry out there (Stuart, 2015).

I.1 Kinesthesia and the Embodied Self

According to phenomenology, our self, and life as we know it, starts with movement and the perception (αἴσθησις) of this movement (κῑνησῐς), kinesthesis. Husserl explained this point with the following words:

> The possibilities of transition are *practical* possibilities, at least when it is a question of an object which is given as enduring without change. There is thus a freedom to run through the appearances in such a way that I move my eyes, my head, alter the posture of my body, go around the object, direct my regard toward it, and so on. We call these movements, which belong to the essence of perception and serve to bring the object of perception to givenness from all sides insofar as possible, *kinestheses*.
>
> *(Husserl, 1973, 83–84)*

As this passage explains, the perception of our movement is the practical possibility for the external object to come into existence for me and to become part of who I am as intentional content of my experience (see Chapter 3). This movement which represents the essence of my perception serves to build the core structure of the reality in which I am going to experience further objects. In that sense, my kinesthesis is never only a singular event, but it is a systemic action profoundly embedded in the context in which it originally takes place. Enkinaesia, the embedded movement, is the way to show how the intercorporeal structure of our reality is there from the very beginning. "Cognition" is "the relational process of sense-making that takes place between the system and its environment" (Thompson and Stapleton, 2009, 26); "cognition belongs to the 'relational domain' in which the system as a unity relates to the wider context of its milieu" (2009, 26).

This way of approaching life sheds immediate light on the continuity between the self, its bodily movements, and its environment. In phenomenology, any interpretation of the individual self as dwelling in a mind separately from the movements of its own body would lead to seeing that individual as completely stuck and cut off from the main source of meanings in life, thus generating problems on several levels: emotional, environmental, and medical. In phenomenology, it would be counterintuitive to build a notion of well-being and care based on a schizoid interpretation of our own being that separates being from meanings, body from spirit, and individuals from the environment. We are our space as it unfolds from the perception of our movements. For this reason, Merleau-Ponty, following Husserl's teaching in *Natur und* Geist (1919), wrote:

> We say therefore that our body is a being of two leaves, from one side a thing among things and otherwise what sees them and touches them; we say, because it is evident that it unites these two properties within itself, and its double belongingness to the order of the "object" and to the order of the "subject" reveals to us quite unexpected relations between the two orders.
>
> *(1968, 137)*

The distance that separates my body from my being that body is only cognitive. Our ability to reflect on ourselves as things among other things is often biased by this cognitive distance that we apply to concepts such as nature, animals, and beings. Yet, if we suspend our judgment on what is natural, then we can find nature in ourselves and our being in nature. Phenomenology describes the epoché (see Chapter 3) as suspending judgment on the categories of nature and concrete beings in order to gather the essential truth about us as the phenomenon we are observing. Using Merleau-Ponty's words:

> Whenever I try to understand myself, the whole fabric of the perceptible world comes too, and with it comes the others who are caught in it (…) For [others] are (…) my twins or the flesh of my flesh.
>
> *(Merleau-Ponty, 1968, 15)*

Whenever I try to understand who I am, the world comes to life in me and takes its shape through me to the point that this same world becomes my flesh; its whole fabric manifests itself in the actions I decide to take and in the person I have been and I will become. Understanding this point might make each individual more responsible for the decisions they make in their life. The dreading sense of not counting or not making a difference negatively impacts intersubjective well-being. Any attempt to confine oneself within an insubstantial paradise would only double the distance and make the emotional pain of having deserted one's real self stronger and more difficult to handle.

> It belongs to what is taken for granted, prior to all scientific thought and all philosophical questioning, that the world is—always is in advance—and that every correction of an opinion, whether an experiential or other opinion, presupposes the already existing world, namely, as a horizon of what in the given case is indubitably valid as existing, and presupposes within this horizon something familiar and doubtlessly certain with which that which is perhaps canceled out as invalid came into contact.
>
> *(Husserl, 1954, 110)*

The world is the context that in our natural life we tend to take for granted—that the world exists underneath my feet and a reality is around me to accompany all my actions is a fact that I do not always question for the sake of my own sanity. Yet, the world and its reality are the most challenging horizon around and within which we build our sense of self and others; the meaning that the world and reality acquires for us shapes who we are for ourselves and others. In that sense, philosophy has challenged these terms in order to understand what meanings they actually carry for us. Merleau-Ponty (1945) used the term *interworld* to denote the socially shared quality of the world, where the meaning that the world acquires for me and its materiality are inseparable from each other. George Herbert Mead (1932, 1938) referred to this meaningful and socially shared space of face-to-face interaction as the *manipulatory area* to indicate the impact we have in our interaction with it. Alfred Schutz (e.g., Schutz and Luckmann, 1973, 42), similarly, regarded *the world within reach* as nothing less than "the kernel of the reality of the life-world." Every opinion and value we assign to others and ourselves is based on this interaction with the world; taking this world for granted without questioning the cognitive and axiological value that it has for us would undermine our sense of what is real and favor a detachment from reality. Eagleman (2015), for example, who explained the self in terms of brain and its neuronal activity, affirmed that the reality of the world is shocking as it is "colorless, odourless, tasteless silence" (Eagleman, 2015, 37).[2] For him, "Who we are is found within its intricate ring patterns of electrochemical impulses" as reality is the result of this computational process of our neuronal machinery.

Differently from Eagleman, I believe that the brain is an *organon* (from Greek, Όργανον which means instrument) which allows our self to become itsself in the world via the perception (aisthesis) of its own bodily movements (kinaeseis) in the world. As Feuerbach wrote: "It is neither the soul which thinks and senses (…), nor the brain; for the brain is a *physiological abstraction*—an organ removed from the totality, separated from the skull, face, and body as a whole (…). However, the brain is only an organ of thought as long as it is connected with a human head and body" (1985, 177). The perception of our movement (kinesthesia) in the environment is the most fundamental and psychologically meaningful property that we can take as a reference point for our own identity as embodied individuals within the environment.

The perception of the environmental stimulation is imposed on the passive receiver (Reed, 1988) and generates the meaning and values on which the receiver, as an agent, builds its own sense of reality in a situated context (Varela et al., 1991). The subjective space of bodily experiences is intertwined and they mutually modify one another, each situation in which the embodied mind expresses itself can generate a shift in one's own or other's meanings (Merleau-Ponty, 1945). To give an example of the outcome from this detachment, I can cite the words that a depressed person used to explain their own perception of reality and the shift that takes place in it:

> When we were outside I realized that my perception of things had completely changed. Instead of infinite space, unreal, where everything was cut off, naked and isolated, I saw Reality, marvelous Reality, for the first time the people whom we encountered were no longer automatons, phantoms, revolving around, gesticulating without meaning; they were men and women with their own individual characteristics, their own individuality. It was the same with things. They were useful things, having sense, capable of giving pleasure. Here was an automobile to take me to the hospital, cushions I could rest on. (…) for the first time I dared to handle the chairs, to change the arrangement of the furniture. What an unknown joy, to have an influence on things; to do with them what I liked and especially to have the pleasure of wanting the change.
> *(Sechehaye, 1970, 105–106)*

"What an unknown joy, to have an influence on things"—this person said. Depression, as much as other emotional problems, has the power to rescind the connection between body and mind, external and internal space, and movement and its perception. Our brain, per se, does not have any criterion to distinguish external reality from internal reality. Any threat we perceive is a real threat. If I feel anxious about something that is going to happen in the future, my body would secrete the same amount of cortisol as if this event is truly happening (Vos et al., 2012), similar to a fire alarm that suddenly rings while I am at work doing my regular job. The movement that I perceive is always the beginning point of my constitution of reality and this constitution is what makes me who I am every day. To continue on with this example, if my cortisol level is always high because I suffer from anxiety it is very likely that in the long run my digestive system will suffer from inflammation or I lose my period, because my body is busy fighting the threat and is not programmed to invest energy in the renewal of the cells or the repair of the tissues. Chronic inflammation would drain even more of my energy and foster the vicious circle of my depression (Felger, 2019). The reality of my being would more likely be a gloomy one because I would lack the energy to feel my influence on things and I would perceive it as far away from me.

It is a very difficult task to describe the perception of our own movements (kinesthesia) within a detached environment. As Merleau-Ponty wrote: "Truth does not merely 'dwell' in the 'inner human;' or rather, there is no 'inner human,' the human being is in and toward the world, and it is in the world that we know ourselves" (Merleau-Ponty, 1945, lxxxiv). Any separation from the self and the world would make the truthfulness of one of the two disappear. "My body is wherever there is something to be done" (Merleau-Ponty, 1945, 224). The body is my self and myself is the reality in which my body moves; for this reason, we can speak, like Bateson, of an extended or "*ecological subjectivity*" (Bateson, 1972; Neisser, 1988) because any attempt to separate the situated embodied self from its actions and its meanings would empty the essence of that reality. As Merleau-Ponty remarked, the spatiality of the lived body is not "a *spatiality of position*, but a *spatiality of situation*" (1962, 100). This means that the objective space of the physical organism and the subjective space of bodily experience are intertwined and mutually modify one another. Even the spoken word with which I communicate is not a hollow aspatial representation of the speaking subject, but it instead conveys the style of the person who communicates it, the world that the speaker embodies, and the content that the word evokes (Merleau-Ponty, 1945, 213). As Stuart remarked, "cognition" is "the relational process of sense-making that takes place between the system and its environment" (2009, 26). A close examination of the cognitive relational domain which draws experiencer and world together can be helpful to prove how the separation perceived between subjects and body, or self and environment, is the painful outcome of habitual misconception more than a scientific fact.

I.2 The Development of the Individual: The Impossible Demarcation Line

In *The Trouble of Being Born* (2013), the philosopher Cioran (1973) presented the quite pessimistic view somewhat diffused among existential philosophers and psychotherapists according to which the ultimate concern of our existence is loneliness: "we are born alone and we die alone" (Yalom, 1980). For as much as we can get close to another human being, our existential uniqueness is such that an actual proximity and continuity would be impossible. The persistence of life in combination with the environment can be possible only through approximation because the sense of not-belongingness is, in fact, an ultimate necessity built up in our being. Accordingly, Cioran continued:

> The same feeling of not belonging, of futility, wherever I go: I pretend interest in what matters nothing to me, I bestir myself mechanically or out of charity, without ever being caught up, without ever being somewhere. What attracts me is elsewhere, and I don't know where that elsewhere is.
>
> *(1973, 24)*

This belief arrives here at its most extreme consequences: life is so futile and disconnected from vitality that any action becomes a pretense and any place an elsewhere. In strong contrast to this point of view, I think that it is exactly the miracle of conception and birth that proves the opposite argument and helps us to dissolve the "habitual fog separating experiencer and world" (Varela, 1996, 337). There is, in fact, a growing number of studies that prove how the primordial exchange between mother and child is a form of intersubjective experience in which the "other" is literally felt with one's own body (see Fuchs and De Jaegher, 2009; Fuchs, 2017). This intersubjective experience is prepared by a proto-conversation between mother and child (Trevarthen, 2001); the fetus, for example, tentatively touches the placenta, umbilicus, and uterine wall with its hands at the eleventh week. "They make jaw movements and swallow amniotic fluid, expressing pleasure or disapproval at tastes injected into it by sucking and smiling or grimacing with disgust. Complex movements of the trunk, arms, and legs position the body, and may react to the mother's body movements or the contractions of the muscles of her uterus" (Lecanuet et al., 1995; Piontelli, 2002; Trevarthen and Reddy, 2007). This form of proto-conversation creates an affective synchronization (Stern, 1985) for which mother and fetus learn from each other how it feels to be part of the environment and how they can survive in it. By the end of the ninth month, the fetus has a fully developed affectivity that we might already call interaffective and intercorporeal (Gallagher, 2001; Fuchs and De Jaegher, 2009; Froese and Fuchs, 2012; Cuffari et al., 2015) because it goes beyond the limits of the proper body of the mother and the fetus alone. The two of them have built through the nine months schemes of being with each other

(Stern, 1985) that is based on the sensorimotor activities they undertook through time, the emotions that the sensation of the movement raised, and the inter-corporeal and interpersonal memory that they stored at the basis of these interactions (Fuchs, 2017). There is an implicit relational knowing and pre-predicative cognition (Stern, 1998) between the two that makes it impossible to draw a distinct line between the two. The inside-outside relationship between mother and child cannot be internalized as a subject-object relationship. "The model of what is internalised, thus, includes mutually regulated sequences of maternal-infant actions with a particular temporal patterning" (Beebe and Sterne, 1977, 52). As Piaget remarked (1936, 1947), infants develop a spatio-temporal sensitivity through a sensorimotor experience that generates a temporal pattern of befores-afters that later in life they can express through language. The im-mediate experience of movement inside the womb of the mother becomes a primary order to explicate their sense of reality, belongingness, and being. The mother and fetus relationship becomes an interpersonal resonance system for action schemes in which the language they develop ranges from movements to sounds (Malloch, 1999).

Bornemark mentioned the notion of "pactivity" (2018, 270) to explain how the actions that are undertaken by mother and fetus mutually impact each other and change each other time and time again. This impact is not to be limited to the theoretical realm only, but is a biological change, too. As studies have shown (Dawe et al., 2007), during the nine months of pregnancy, there is an actual cellular migration in which fetal cells can remain in the mother for decades. These fetal cells have the ability to cross the placenta and blood-brain barriers and affect the immune system of the mother.

From what has been stated so far, it is evident that the permeability of the body is such that it is almost impossible to individualize the organism and separate it from the environment. The mutuality of the two individualities is at work in the constitution of their being as an intersubjective and interaffective organism.

I.3 Are Outside Beings Stupid?: Aristotle and Descartes

It is very difficult to draw a line between human beings and nature even in our vocabulary. Some textbooks would use the distinction between organic and inorganic life to indicate the difference between inanimate and animate beings. Yet, since inorganic matter generally points to the molecular structure that lacks carbon-hydrogen bonds, it is evident how the human body, as well, can be organic and inorganic at the same time since parts of its bones, for example, are made of inorganic material.

Yet, we tend to distinguish "the nature out there" from "the mind (*Geist*) inside here." The intelligent and affective life of plants can be for us a mirror through which we understand the continuity and persistence of our life. Our mind is not separated from the body and life is expressed through this union. The idea that humans have an intelligence that is more developed than that of any other species has led us to mistakenly interpret our role as consumers and nature as our goods. We tend to feel superior to many other species and to see them as serving for our survival—as a matter of fact, small insects such as bees have been recently recognized as the most important living beings on earth for our survival (Royal Geographical Society of London, 2019). Aristotle, for example, conceded that both animals and plants have life, yet humans are the highest in the ranking of complexity since both animals and plants live for the sake of humans (plants live for the sake of animals, too).

> It is evident that "plants are for the sake of animals, and that the other animals are for the sake of human beings, domestic ones both for using and eating, and most but not all wild ones for food and other kinds of support, so that clothes and the other tools may be got from them"
>
> *(Book I, Part VIII of Politics).*

In the first book of *De Partibus Animalium*, Aristotle[3] excluded reason from among "the objects" of zoological investigation because reason (νοῦς) seemed to be a reflective practical quality (φρόνησις) belonging only to men (ἄνδρες). Parenthetically, I use the word *men* consciously because, according to Aristotle, women and children do not belong to this category. It is proper to plants and animals to perceive and change; it is proper to animals to move, but it is proper to men to perceive, change, move, and reflect on that movement (i.e., to have kinesthesia):

> However, it is not the case that all soul is a source of change, nor all its parts; rather, of growth it is the part which is present even in plants, of alteration the perceptive part, and of locomotion some other part, and not the rational; for locomotion is present in other animals too, but reasoning in none. So it is clear that one should not speak of all souls; for not all the soul is a nature, but some part of it, one part or even more.
>
> *(Aristotle, 641b4–1 0, cited in Lennox, 1999)*

The world of animals and plants is excluded from the world of humans because they do not possess reason (reason seems to dwell again in a higher level of reality). Similarly, Descartes argued that animals are like machines, although capable of sensations and perceptions. Hence, animals can react to external stimuli but are incapable of understanding why or unable to interrogate themselves as to why they have that reaction (Descartes, 1950).[4]

I.3.1 Conrad-Martius and the Intelligence of Life

Criticizing Descartes' dualism, Conrad-Martius inaugurated a trend of thinking that seemingly gave more justice to "the intelligence of life as it manifests itself

through plants, animals, or humans; bodies and souls have been artificially separated, yet they co-belong ontically," she wrote (1923, 75).[5] Body and mind
belong to each other: "I am my body. I am distributed inside it until the extreme
tips of my fingers" (Conrad-Martius, 1923, 70); body and mind develop together
through the same time and space. In *Bios and Psyche*,[6] Conrad-Martius explained
how living beings, without distinction, are animated from the intelligent
movement of life. Logos belongs to plants, too, and this can be appreciated by
observing their continuous attempts to make their way into the light in order to
be and develop.

> A narcissus seems to look at light from the point of view of someone who
> has a soul; that is, it presents itself, so to speak, in front of it from its soul,
> doesn't it? In that case, its being one and unique offers itself to the light in
> its purity and elegance. It seems to be the immediate reflection or
> projection of characteristic immanent scent, so to say, spiritual from which
> it irradiates itself toward the outside.
>
> *(2005, 368)*

According to Conrad-Martius, the intelligent life that brings humans to look for
food and aggregate with each other is not any different or more sophisticated than
the intelligence of plants that present themselves to the light.

I.3.2 Agamben and the Space of Exclusion

Taking a similar stance, Agamben, in his *The Open: Man and Animal*, showed
how human beings have presented themselves as anthropological machines whose
bios (reflective intelligent life) is distinct from zoe (unreflective animal life) in
order to favor their political and social survival (more on this in Chapter 1). He
showed how any attempt to create a taxonomy that draws a precise line of distinction between the two is arbitrary at best, although it might have seemed
scientific at the time:

> A serious scientific work such as Peter Artedi's *Ichthiologia* (1738) still listed
> sirens next to seals and sea lions, and Linnaeus himself, in his *Pan Europaeus*,
> classifies sirens—which the Danish anatomist Caspar Bartholin called *Homo
> marinus*— together with man and apes. On the other hand, the boundary
> between the anthropoid apes and certain primitive populations was also
> anything but clear. The first description of an orangutan by the doctor
> Nicolas Tulp in 1641 emphasizes the human aspects of this *Homo sylvestris*
> (which is the meaning of the Malay expression *orangutan*); and we must
> wait until Edward Tyson's treatise *Orang-Outang, sive Homo Sylvestris: or, the
> Anatomy of a Pygmi* (1699) for the physical difference between ape and man
> to first be posed on the solid grounds of comparative anatomy. Though this

work is considered a sort of incunabulum of primatology, the creature that Tyson calls a "Pygmie" (and which is anatomically dis-tinguished from man by thirty-four characteristics, from apes and monkeys by forty-eight) nevertheless represents for him a sort of "intermediate animal" between ape and man, to whom it stands in a relation symmetrically opposite to that of the angel.

To add more on this point, in an attempt to reduce the dualism between body and mind, animals and intelligent humans, Haeckel reconstructed in his *Anthropogenie* (1874) the history of "the men" and explained human beings as a moment of transition from animals, more precisely from Affen-Menschen (ape-humans) to humans. He considered language as the distinctive element for humans which meant that all those who do not have language are excluded from humanity and are an outside inanimate part of nature—this would mean that disabled people, infants, or injured human bodies are not considered to be humans. Certainly, this is a dismal picture that speaks volumes about the unethical experiments that took place during and after the Second World War.

Agamben's interpretation of this dichotomy strongly insisted on this exclusion mechanism: "The machine actually produces a kind of state of exception, a zone of indeterminacy in which the outside is nothing but the exclusion of an inside and the inside is in turn only the inclusion of an outside" (Agamben, 2004, 37). For this reason, all that becomes animalized can be excluded from society (38). As Agamben remarked, though, the space of exclusion that the human machines have created in order to survive is perfectly empty and continuously open to decisions. "That space is the space of bare life itself" (38). Hence, there is still some hope.

I.3.3 The Intelligence of Plants

The growing number of studies that prove the intelligence of plants can help us to see life as it manifests itself without dualisms and exclusions. Still today, "most of us usually think of plants more as objects than as organisms" (Baluška, 2009, 476). Yet, it is evident that plants have their own lives and behaviors (Schultz, 2002), separating plants from us or even from the environment because of our inability to understand their behavior would be meaningless and harmful. It would, in fact, encourage a consumerist attitude for treating external beings as commodities to consume, and it would enhance the sense of detachment from ourselves that is at the basis of the most common psychological disorders.

Baluska and colleagues (2019) even proposed attributing a brain to plants. They interpreted Darwin's words as a way to prove it: "It is hardly an exaggeration to say that the tip of the radicle thus endowed [with sensitivity] and having the power of directing the movements of the adjoining parts, acts like the brain of one of the lower animals; the brain being seated within the anterior end of the body, receiving impressions from the sense-organs, and directing the several "movements." According to the authors, this sentence conveys two important messages: first, that the root apex may be considered to be a 'brain-like' organ endowed with a sensitivity which controls its navigation through soil; second, that the root apex represents the anterior end of the plant body" (2019, 1121).

Baldwin's studies on tobacco plants seem to agree with this view and even move it a little bit further by attributing to plants the ability to make choices. He presented the case of a Peruvian species of tobacco plant (*nicotiana attenuata*) that makes its flowers smaller so as not to attract hawkmoths but colibri, giving it a better chance to germinate and escape herbivores. By the emission of a specific scent, they attract the enemy of their enemies, in this case caterpillars, in order to protect themselves (Wu and Baldwin, 2010). This seems to refute Aristotle's hierarchy and give plants not only the sensory power that he denied to them but also a reflective intelligence in the sense of problem solving through cooperation (Mancuso, 2013). As Simard (2016) explained, Darwin was wrong in thinking that beings in nature operate exclusively on the "survival of the fittest," they actually mutually cooperate. To this point, she brought the example of trees that communicate with each other "through the fungal web to trade nutrients with paper-bark birch trees over the course of the season." Mancuso, too, showed how trees in a forest organize themselves into far-flung networks, using the underground web of mycorrhizal fungi which connects their roots to exchange information and even goods. This "wood-wide web" (Avio, Pellegrino, Bonari, and Giovannetti, 2006; Crowther, 2019) allows scores of trees in a forest to convey warnings of insect attacks and also to deliver carbon, nitrogen, and water to trees in need.[7] Besides this web, rhythm (Mancuso and Shabala, 2007), too, seems to be a very important form of language with which plants communicate and support each other.[8]

Speaking of this space of exclusion as an intelligent living space and trying to understand this language is still a point of heated debate, but certainly the findings we have gathered so far would suggest that we adopt a humbler and more integrated perspective on ourselves and the environment. A perspective that goes beyond any dualism and reduction is the one on which a responsible bioethics can thrive.

II. Intercorporeality and Interaffectivity: Making a New Sense

Looking at bare life beyond a substance dichotomy might help us to see ourselves not as isolated individuals but as an organism that is intersubjectively connected to others and functions through a body-mind mechanism. I believe that the human community is based on the reciprocity of affective coexistence with other living organisms.

The notions of intercorporeality and interaffectivity (Fuchs and De Jaeger, 2009; Fuchs, 2016) are provided by phenomenology to explain this point. Fuchs and De Jaeger (2009) explained interaffectivity or mutual affection as "the individuals' experience of being moved, changed by each other in social encounters;" similarly, Loenhoff (2013) described it as the foundational dimension of living beings' interactions and coexistence (2019). Self-affection, as it is presented by Henry (1963), is the starting point for being a member of an apriori community with others; the kinesthesia, this very basic sensorimotor ability to perceive our own possibility of movement, sets in motion the experience of foundational patterns that we create in connection with others and that mutually affect each other during interactions. Experience starts with pre-reflective and pre-sensory (Stewart, 1973; Thompson, 2009; Stuart, 2015) engagement with reality. This form of engagement can be explained as a mind-feeling (Stuart, 2015) that describes the primordial mood of being, "a condition of sense for any encounter with beings, whether theoretical or practical" (Ratcliffe, 2002, 289). Differently from what Haeckel and others believed, it is not language that makes us humans but is the embodied preverbal ability to interact, which we have in common with other natural beings. As Merleau-Ponty (1945, xviii) wrote, "what makes us living being is this somato-sensory ability" to function in relation to each other in a form of operative intentionality that spontaneously connects the living breathing community with a form of mutual affective-effective co-engagement (Stuart, 2015). As Bohm remarked, "we got so habituated to the explicit order, and have emphasized it so much in our thought and language, that we tend to feel that our primary experience is of that which is explicated and manifest" (2018, 206). Life starts in the pre-predicative passive layers of our material being (see Chapter 3 on this point).

It is first the feeling of being connected that determines how we experience a person or another living being, and the quality of this experience will vary depending on the development of the interaction. Severing this connection means to undermine the well-being of the person and compromise their development (Fuchs, for example, showed the immediate connection between depression and interaffectivity, 2016). Interpersonal predicative understanding and functional development depend on the interaffective community (e.g., Gallagher, 2001; Hobson, 2002; Ratcliffe, 2007; de Jaegher and Di Paolo, 2007; Hutto and Myin, 2013) that we spontaneously develop from the very first movements of our lives. As explained in Chapter 3, passive intentional acts that result in thoughts or deeds do not happen because I cognitively command them so; they are sensuously and affectively moved by the organic matter, the organism of which we are part; it is this matter that gives us a shape before any controlling subjectivity has the will to impose its authority.

Merleau-Ponty therefore spoke of the passivity of our activity in these terms: "It is not I who makes myself think any more than it is I who makes my heart beat" (Merleau-Ponty, 1968, 221). Thinking as well as walking are organismic movements that stem from being in this interaffective and intercorporeal community—any disturbance in the functioning of this passivity creates or is an expression of psychosocial problems (on this see, for example, Muratori and Bizzari's studies on autism, 2019). Colombetti and Torrance (2009, 509) stressed the importance of this "basic level of feeling connected" to another person as that which forms a child's relations with others from a very early age. To quote Trevarthen (2001, 151), "expressions of the self 'invade' the mind of the other, making the moving body of the self resonant with impulses that can move the other's body too."

In *pairing association,* the characteristic feature is that, in the most primitive case, two data are given intuitively, and with prominence, in the unity of consciousness and that, on this basis—essentially, already in pure passivity (regardless therefore of whether they are noticed or unnoticed)—as data appearing with mutual distinctness, they *found phenomenologically a unity of similarity* and thus are always constituted precisely as a pair. If there are more than two such data, then a phenomenally unitary group, a plurality, becomes constituted (Husserl, 1950/ 1973, Section 51, 112/142).

As this passage shows, the pairing association of the matter gives a shape to the passivity of the being according to a distinct unit of similarity. In Chapter 3, we called this unit the noema (i.e., the content of the intentional act as it apprehends reality), and in Chapter 4, we explained its way of assembling through the theory of parts and whole. "In the noema of the act of perception, i.e., in the perceived, taken precisely as characterized phenomenologically, as it is therein an intentional Object, there is included a determinate directive for all further experiences of the object in question" (Husserl, 1919, 38). The functional intention that pushes living beings to move and interact with each other generates by nature a sense of reality that gives meaning to one's being and constitutes the apriori for all of our coming experiences. "Because we are in the world, we are condemned to meaning, and we cannot do or say anything without acquiring a name in history" (Merleau-Ponty, 1945, xxii). The basic affective interaction with the environment is bound to become a meaning for us, and that meaning will color our reality according to our unique perspective.

Some of the emotional disorders I am going to describe in my forthcoming *The Role of Bio-Ethics in Emotional Problems,* stem exactly from the lack of this coordination and the inability to reconnect with this basic function. Being unable to constitute meaning out of one's own life is becoming a diffused problem that points to the missing link with ourselves as basic organismic interaffective environment and with our volitional body as the organ that accepts and transforms affections into meanings and values (more on this in Chapter 3). As Nussbaum wrote in a collected book on bioethics and human dignity (2008), we have the "need to make sense of our existence as embodied rational beings who are in nature but not fully of it. We are driven by our end-setting nature to make sense of the world both in relation to ourselves and as a whole" (2008, 338).

II.1 Intercorporeal Therapeutic Experiments: Learning by Doing

An increasing number of intercorporeality-based approaches have been used to help people to overcome distressing states and ground their being upon a more solid base. Becoming aware of the hylonoetic nature of the mind by using modeling clay (Malafouris, 2013), for example, has revealed itself as a useful method to help individuals to feel like a part of their environment while reconnecting with their creative energy. As Dewey wrote: "Hands and feet, apparatus and appliances of all kinds are as much a part of it as changes within the brain" (Dewey, 1916, 13–14); the clay is not the only element to change under the creative impulse, the brain changes, too, for the better. Acknowledging the material and spiritual nature of our intelligence as a core point of our identity allows for a deeper connection with our center of vitality and accordingly well-being. The mind/body relationship should not be seen as inside/outside, either/ or, or physical/spiritual; both are integral parts of who we are as beings and agents. Modeling clay, as much as any other creative activity with which we shape any material that seems external to us, is a way to reinforce the continuity between the two. Things actively shape us and bring us together by providing channels of interaction: the materials we use and the things we make construct dependencies (paraphrasis of Hodder, 2012, 96).

MET (Material Engagement Theory, Malafouris, 2013, 2004) is the theory behind this interaffective approach strongly focused on the use of materials to improve the intersubjective bond between individuals with each other and with the environment. This theory focuses on reorienting the individual by emphasizing the connection between the creative act of the participants and the material qualities of the objects with which they enter into contact. According to this theory, we become the creative act and the actual material that takes shape from our own act of creation. This very simple activity is a powerful way to reflect on the continuity of our reality and recompose any harming dualism that separates the body from the mind. We recognize ourselves in the pot we modeled, the quilt we sewed, or the art we created.

This theoretical perspective becomes even more important when the material to which we refer is actually part of the human body and becomes essential for the functioning of that body. Today we have, in fact, numerous examples of how technology can both enhance and restrain the functioning of our sensory experience: the misuse of a social app or the proper use of a hearing device are both good examples of this. Technological inventions are part of who we are, whether we want them to be or not. Similarly to the pot we model through clay, a technological device can function either as a way to recognize myself as part of the environment or as a tool to disconnect from it. The technological material could be an underlying force for enhancing interaffectivity and intercorporeality by generating a sort of a "transactional body" (Shusterman, 2008, 214) with which we recognize ourselves through our functioning and our connection with others; or, it could work as a catalyst for reification and nihilism. In the case of the misuse of a social application, the facility with which one can connect with friends all over the world can easily become an empty obsession that negatively affects the quality of the time and space of the intersubjective community. Or, on the other hand, the proper use of a hearing device would change not only the way in which people would talk to me but also the way in which I perceive the world. Each technological invention needs to become a meaning for me in order to assure the continuity of my life. The unquestioned use of a material can lead to development of negative habits that, in the long run, would affect my identity and the characteristics of my environment. As Merleau-Ponty wrote:

> The communication or comprehension of gestures comes about through the reciprocity of my intentions and the gestures of others, of my gestures and intentions discernible in the conduct of other people. It is as if the other person's intention inhabited my body and mine his. (…) I do not understand the gestures of others by some act of intellectual interpretation; communication between consciousnesses is not based on the common meaning of their respective experiences, for it is equally the basis of that meaning. The act by which I lend myself to the spectacle must be recognized as irreducible to anything else. (…) The meaning of a gesture thus "understood" is not behind it, it is intermingled with the structure of the world outlined by the gesture, and which I take up on my own account.
>
> *(Merleau-Ponty, 1945, 185f)*

The meaning that the world acquires for us through the intentional activation of my attention toward others is "irreducible to anything else;" finding my self or discovering my ground means focusing on this reciprocity without which there is nothing to be discovered. To paraphrase Levinas, forms of co-engagement generated by tactile experiences of intercorporeality (Levinas 1987, 118) have the power to form meaningful lasting bonds that co-orient our lives in a meaningful way (Loenhoff, 2013). For example, cuddling on the sofa while watching a movie or playing games together are the ways the bond between parents and children can be formed. It is not about the movie we choose or the game we play but the space of the couch and the passive contact between each other's bodies that opens the door to gaining deeper conscience of being with others and resonates with the interaffective and intercorporeal bond that connects the child with its parents or caregiver. A caregiver's touch "is communicative and regulates the infant's perceptions, thoughts, feelings, or behaviors" (Hertenstein, 2002, 72). "Before children can talk they communicate via haptic and other nonvocal means, touch transmits valenced forms of emotion as well as specific information" (Hertenstein, 2002, 71). A very interesting sensory experiment practiced with people who suffer from different forms of social anxiety is banding.

FIGURE 5.1   Banding session, De Bellis, Roma.

As the figure shows, banding is a sensory experiment that uses sound and movement improvisation to connect people through industrial rubber bands, scarfs, or rugs (the material varies according to the degree of interconnectedness that the experiment is meant to express). Hahn began developing this technique in 2008 and over the years *banding* became a playful exploration of the ways in which people foreign to each other can come to know each other, overcome social anxiety, and learn to express themselves. The interviews collected after banding are particularly helpful for understanding the quality of the meaning that this experience is capable of producing:

> Afterwards I could very much feel everyone "in" me and "on" me, I could still feel their energy on me, within me, in my muscles, in my heart, in my feelings, in my sensibilities. This was a very pleasant sensation, and an experience that I think I had never had in quite that way, or probably in any way, for that matter. The closest thing I have experienced to *banding* would probably be dance improvisation, but *banding* puts others "into" me in a much more visceral and definite way than dance improvisation. It was fascinating how, even if someone was several people away from me, I could still sense their movement, and even their "energy" for that matter. It was like we were all part of a big spider's web, and no strand could be plucked without everyone else sensing it, knowing it. *Banding* seems a concrete metaphor for a performance group working together as a team. No one can "out-pull" anyone else, everyone must match everyone else's energy, and this should be a good thing, since anyone can bring more out of everyone by increasing their own individual pull.
>
> *(Hahn cited in Streeck et al., 2017)*

Sherrie Tucker's post-*banding* notes:

> At first I experienced choices. The choice to yield, to pull, the moments when I felt others yield or pull—then, we all became a body/organism and I stopped thinking in terms of what my own impulses were, which had been quite conscious—give, pull back, step over this one, lie down and roll with it—and tuned in to what the organism was doing. Then I noticed when subtle changes took place in patterns. I still anticipated snaps, the sonic-tactile ramifications of playing with rubber bands, and prepared to yield in these moments—but sensitivity to patterns felt different than choices, as listening is to sounding. It wasn't a passive experience to fold into the organism, but a different way of being. Senses attuned to bubbling and flowing, not to mention the smell of rubber, the unexpected pleasure of not consciously thinking through my steps and rolls in strands of rubber.
>
> *(Hahn et al., 2016, 158)*

Or Louise Campbell:

> The question, Me? You? Us? becomes at once appropriate but totally unanswerable. As I cannot feel any differentiation—I am me.you.us. I feel it. Your pulse rocks the band that nudges my ankle that glides across the floor that takes your belly with it. And down to the ground you go. And then I. And you. And I. And you. us. I. continually. It is at the point where: We have become the same project.
>
> *(Lindsay Vogt in Hahn et al., 2016, 153)*

The banding experiment is an excellent way to experience the intercorporeal and interaffective bond as it unfolds and to gain trust in the experience of being part of an interconnected world. According to Fuchs (2016) and Bizzari (2018), there are psychological and psychiatric disorders that arise exactly from the lack or disturbance of the interaffective and intercorporeal bond; banding, clay, and music can be ways to reinforce this bond.

In particular, integrative orchestras such as those in Rome (orchestra integrata, De Bellis) and in the United States (Me2) have given psychiatric patients an additional means to express their voice. In the past decade, Orff's approach to music (Orff Schulwerk) has become a meaningful example of how music can be a vehicle for interaffective bonding and therefore its expression. "Tell me, I will forget; show me, I remember; Involve me, I will understand" (Orff and Keetman, 1950)—this is the basic concept behind Orff's work. Children are involved in a fully accepting place to express their own voice through music. The teacher is part of their world and adapts to the playfulness of their space by using very simple forms of everyday activities with the purpose of creating sound together. This approach has been applied to psychiatric patients who managed to perform together in concerts for a consistent amount of years, thus significantly improving the quality of their life and loosening the emotional blockages that they normally experience.

Music provides the intersubjective context for relevant daily things to present themselves and acquire a meaning without representing a source of anxiety and concerns. The soothing quality of playing music together allows the creation of emotional bonds and then an emotional interconnecting space where daily life feels safer. "If ... one approaches the issue of meaning with the concepts 'context' and 'aboutness,' one seems more likely to come to the conclusion that all 'things' reside in context. If this is so, then all 'properties' are contextually dependent. No context—no things—no properties" (Jordan and Vinson, 2012, 238). Music becomes the actual movement through which personal lived experience can be seen and transformed into meanings and values. A "kinesthetic melody" can grasp phenomena in which "individual impulses are synthesized and combined into integral kinesthetic structures or kinetic melodies" (Luria, 1973, 176 quoted in Stuart, 2015, 171). Listening to music unfolds the sense of the implicate order of one's experience which enables a coherent mode of understanding the immediate experience of motion in terms of our thoughts and feelings (Bohm, 1980, 200–1). Being with others, as Knud Løgstrup (1956/1997) remarked, is principally a matter of being receptive to the fact that we have the potential to alter each other's world; music, clay, or bands become a vehicle to increase this perception.

III. Epidemiology

Another way to look at the problem of substance dualism is through epidemiological studies of health and well-being. By definition, epidemiology as the science of public health has focused on the interconnection between populations and environment for centuries: the study of the way in which the exposure to a certain environment affects one's well-being and the decisions that the society needs to make to favor good exposure and increasing health of the population are some of the main tasks of this discipline (Petticrew et al., 2004; de Meer, Baker, and Nieuwenhuijsen 2008).

Mervyn and Ezra Susser conducted a study on the different paradigms that characterized "epidemiological eras" in modern public health (Susser and Adelstein, 1975) which showed the growing understanding of the correlation, that today we take for granted, between poor areas and poor health.[9] Unhealthy working conditions, polluted air, and lack of sanitation were considered the main reasons for declining health among the poorest slice of the population (Rosen, 1993; Lang and Rayner, 2012). The sanitary revolution that took place after that discovery in the last third of the nineteenth century was considered the most beneficial and transformational act for the health in the society, even more than the change produced by the discovery of antibiotics (Ferriman, 2007). Hence, in the nineteenth century, there was a good level of awareness about the idea that the environment mattered for health and that the human body is permeable to it.

A socio-ecological perspective started spreading with the belief that understanding the connection between the disease and the environment would bring improvement for both and considering public health as connected to the environment would increase common well-being (see, e.g., Martuzzi, 2007). Yet, although, this conviction is still in place as a "precautionary principle," the willingness to act along those lines has diminished, probably because of the technologization of medicine and individualization of disease (Kessel, 2006; Brownson et al., 2009). The recent spreading of the COVID-19 pandemic proved this decline. The virus was able to spread so fast into a pandemic because, besides its harmful nature, most of the world's leaders were unprepared to stress the importance of the connection between environment and well-being (in the poor air quality, for example) and the interpersonal connection (i.e., every individual is responsible for the life of others). Managing the awareness of the permeability of our body could lead to political mistakes that impoverish the quality of care we can provide for each other. Foucault's (1975) analysis of isolation and punishment applied to medical disease, too. I believe he was right in reading the way in which society was treating disease as a social miasma, that is, political and social threat for contagion. The sick person was considered as the bearer of a stain that could have affected everyone; for this reason, the sick person was seen as a dangerous human being that had to be expelled from the common environment and isolated instead of a person in need that needs to be taken care of.

In the past century, the social stigma surrounding the AIDS epidemic was broken by a very simple gesture, a shake of a hand. In fact, the clamor raised when Princess Diana decided to shake the hands of AIDS patients without gloves initiated a virtuous circle of actions to reintegrate the sick people with the rest of the population. That simple tactile act of aggregation was seen as a quiet but powerful revolution toward the interaffective integration of people suffering from AIDS in their own environment.

Another interesting case of epidemiological study in which the interconnection between individuals and the environment was not taken into sufficient consideration is the Gulf War syndrome/illness. Veterans who served in the Persian Gulf War during 1990–1991 were exposed to pesticides, cyclosarin, and sarin emission of oil well fires and were prompted to take pills containing pyridostigmine bromide which strongly affected their neuronal system over the years. These veterans, differently from nondeployed ones, saw years after their discharge a dramatic decline in the condition of their health. Diagnosing the disease was very difficult for two reasons. One, the veterans lost touch with each other; even if they were all suffering from the same symptoms, they did not know that those symptoms were to be connected to a past common experience. The easiest way to look at the symptoms was by considering the disease as a present phenomenon that was manifesting itself in that moment in time. Second, there was a social and political reluctance to acknowledge those symptoms as an actual disease and take responsibility for its insurgence. Considering the blindness toward the correlation between individuals and environment and the absence of conscience toward the actions taken against the environment itself, the disease caused much suffering for the individuals and families involved. Fortunately, taking care of Gulf War syndrome has become relatively easier today, but there is still a wide number of diseases that are very difficult to diagnose because of our blindness toward the correlation of human life and environment.

Around the end of the twentieth century, more isolated voices started growing together in defense of reintegration of individual health and environment. Carson's case (1962) against the impact of DDT on the environment and its effects on human beings contributed, for example, to seeing with more clarity the connection between humankind and nature (Nash, 2007) and the unprecedented anthropogenic damage done to the global system and its implications for common health. A growing number of environmentalists (e.g., see Butler et al., 2005; Butler and Harley, 2010) and professionals from different disciplines are committing themselves to recompose the damage and to overcome the dualistic view with which humans have treated themselves and their own environment. This book is one of these attempts.

Conclusion

This chapter argued against a worldview that proposes a strict distinction between internal and external reality. Since substance dualism encourages a view of the body as impermeable that strictly separates the self from the body and accordingly from its environment, this chapter has discussed the notion of permeability of the body in order to show the continuity between the self and the environment. In preparation for my forthcoming *The Role of* Bio-*Ethics in Emotional Problems*, the goal of this chapter was to reduce the space between the two in order to overcome psychological disturbance coming from the separation of the body from its own mind and of the individual from its own environment.

Hence, I discussed the constitution of selfhood as it arises from kinesthesia, that is, our ability to perceive our movement and build meanings according to the way in which we relate to our senses. Accordingly, I have examined the case of pregnancy to show how difficult it is to draw a line between the internal space of my self and the external space of otherness. I explained how a pregnancy changes the body of the mother and how much the mother contributes to the constitution of the body of her children. In a similar fashion, I described how this form of mutual constitution takes place in the vegetative life of plants and trees. I criticized, then, the Aristotelian idea of the passive life of plants in favor of a humbler effort that should be made by us to understand their dynamic and intersubjective interactions. Hence, to this purpose, I described what is interaffectivity for human beings and how its lack can lead to psychological and ecological problems. Human community is built on interaffectivity and when our ability to interact with each other and with our environment is missing, we have problems with our feelings; we might not feel anything or feel too much, or we might isolate ourselves from others and our real self and hence risk being affected by psychological disorders that I am going to describe in the next three chapters (narcissism, anxiety, emotional numbness). This lack of a systemic view of life has led to an impoverished notion of well-being, which, even in public health, is described as isolated care administered to the individual separated from others and the environment. Clearly, this also leads to the systemic lack of care in medical fields such as epidemiology.

Notes

1 For example, see in ecological and philosophical biology von Uexküll (1920), Plessner (1970), Jonas (1968), and Maturana and Varela (1987), and on enactive approaches to life, as represented in particular by Varela et al. (1991), Thompson (2005, 2007), and Di Paolo (2005, 2009).
2 See also Fuchs and De Jaeger (2009, 25): "Things show themselves and enter into a relation with us in colors, sounds, and odors: Consciousness not as a phenomenal perspective but as an organism that is open to the world through intentionality."
3 For more around this debate, see Lennox, J. G. (1999). *The Place of Mankind in Aristotle's Zoology*. Cambridge: Cambridge University Press, 10–31; Charlton (1987). Aristotle on the place of mind in nature. In Allan Gotthelf and James G. Lennox (eds.), *Philosophical Issues in Aristotle's Biology*. Cambridge: Cambridge University Press; David M. Balme (1972; reprint, 1992). *Aristotle: De Partibus Animalium I and De Generatione Animalium I*. Oxford: Clarendon Press, 89, 92; Charlton, "Aristotle on the Place of Mind in Nature," 41 in Cynthia Freeland, "Aristotle on Perception, Appetition and Self-Motion," and Susan Sauvé Meyer, "Self-motion and External Causation," both in Self-motion from Aristotle to Newton, Mary Louise Gill and James G. Lennox (eds.) Princeton: Princeton University Press (1995), 33–63 and 65–80, respectively.
4 There is, of course, a wide literature that considers the veracity of these statements—see, for example, Harrison (1992).
5 "Die Ansicht über das Verhältnis von Leib und Seele hat in den letzten Jahrzehnten eine vollkommene Umwandlung erfahren. Fast allgemein wird jetzt anerkannt, dass Leib und Seele oder, wie man in diesem Fall besser sagt, Körper und Geist nicht mehr zu vereinigen waren, seit dem Descartes nicht nur zwei wesen verschiedene Substanzen aus ihnen gemacht hatte, sondern diese Substanzen auch je durch eine einzige Eigenschaft gekennzeichnet glaube, den Körper durch die Ausdehnung, die Seele durch das Denken: res extensa und res cogitans. Ein Ausgedehntes und nichts als Ausgedehntes, ein Denkendes und nichts als Denkendes—wie sollen diese zwei Dinge zu einer organischer Einheit im Menschen zusammengefügt warden! Wie soll das Eine auf das Andere wirken, das Eine Ausdruckfeld des Andere sein Können! Das Ausgedehnte ist ein schlechthin Äußerliches, aus sich Herausgegebenes, Verstreutes, Objectives; das Denken, oder, wie wir der historischen Entwicklung zufolge rechtmässig sagen können, das Bewusstsein ist ein unfassbar Innerliches, ganz Bei-sich-Seiendes, auf sich selbst Zurück-bezogenes, Subjectives" (1923, 75).
6 See, 98: Ibidem: "Wir wissen, dass jeder lebendige Organismus einen solchen Werkmeister voraussetzt, bzw. Mehrere Ober- und Unter Werkmeister, in letzter Instanz jedenfalls die Wesen Entelechie, die den Logos des ganzen Organismus

enthält. Nur dass hier der Werkmeister keine zweite Persönlichkeit innerhalb der ersten ist, kein psychisches Wesen oder mit möglichster Reduktion gedacht, kein 'Psychoid', das selber wieder plangemäß denken und handeln müsste, kein geheimnisvoller homunculus, der irgendwo im Organismus oder gar im Gehirn sitzt, sondern dass der Werkmeister des lebendigen Organismus der Artplan selber ist, der Art Logos. Dieser Plan, dieser Art Logos ist sozusagen ja sogar sehr eigentlich gesprochen, energetisiert. Er ist als solcher objektiv-ziel ursächlich wirkfähig. Er baut sich seinen Leib, inkarniert, verleiblicht sich in ihm. Er ist identisch mit dem, was wir die grundlegende entelechiale Seele nannten."

7 For a sense of the animated debate around this point, this piece from the *New Yorker* can be interesting: https://www.newyorker.com/magazine/2013/12/23/the-intelligent-plant; or this piece on "smart rocks" https://news.mst.edu/2014/07/researchers-study-smart-rocks-use-for-detecting-bridge-damage/.

8 See in Mancuso and Shabala (2007): "Observations about rhythmic movement in plants had been discussed already in the pre-Christian era. As early as the fourth century B.C., Androsthenes, scribes to Alexander the Great, noted that the leaves of *Tamarindus indica* opened during the day and closed at night" (Bretzl, 1903). Some early writers noticed single movements of parts of plants in a cursory manner. Albertus Magnus in the thirteenth century and Valerius Cordus in the sixteenth thought the daily periodical movements of the pinnate leaves of some *Leguminosae* worth recording (Albertus Magnus, 1260; for Cordus, 1544, see Sprague and Sprague, 1939). John Ray, in his "Historia Plantarum" toward the end of the seventeenth century (Ray, 1686–1704), commences his general consid- erations on the nature of plants with a succinct account of *phytodynamical* phenomena, but does not clearly distinguish between movements stemming from irritability and those showing daily, periodical rhythms; the latter, he writes, occur not only in the leaves of *Leguminosae* but also in almost all similar pinnate leaves. In addition to these periodical movements of leaves, he reports the periodical opening and closing of the flowers of *Calendula, Convolvulus, Cichorium*, and others. In 1729, the French physicist Jean Jacques d'Ortous de Mairan discovered that mimosa plants kept in darkness continued to raise and lower their leaves with a ~24-hour rhythm. He concluded that plants must contain some sort of internal control mechanism regulating when to open or close the leaves. Carolus Linnaeus studied the periodical movements of flowers in 1751 and those of leaves in 1755, but offered no mechanical explanation (Linnaeus, 1770). He contented himself with describing the external conditions of these phenomena in many species, classifying them and giving a new name—*sleep of plant*—to those periodic movements observed at night, considering that the plants had then assumed a position of *sleep*. Indeed, he did not use the word at all in a metaphoric sense, for he saw in this sleep of plants a phenomenon entirely analogous to that in animals. It should also be mentioned that he stated correctly that the movements connected with the sleep of plants were not caused by changes in temperature but rather by change in light, since these took place at uniform temperature in a conservatory. Knowing that each species of flower has a unique time of day for opening and closing, Linnaeus designed a garden clock in which the hours were represented by different varieties of flowers. His work supported the idea that different species of organisms demonstrate unique rhythms.

9 See John Snow (1813–1858) on the investigation of cholera (Vinten-Johansen et al., 2003); William Farr (1807–1883) also on cholera but more widely on medical statistics (Susser and Adelstein, 1975); Edward Jenner (1749–1823) on vaccination (Baxby, 2004); and Edwin Chadwick (1800–1890) (Chadwick, 1842).

Bibliography

Agamben, G. (2004). *The Open: Man and Animal*, F. Attel (trans.). Stanford: Stanford University Press.

Aristotle (1992). *De Partibus Animalium*, A. Gotthelf (trans.). Oxford: Clarendon Press.

Aristotle (1998). *The Politics*. Translated by C.D.C. Reeve. Indianapolis: Hackett Publishing.

Avio, L., Pellegrino, E., Bonari, E., and Giovannetti, M. (2006). "Functional diversity of arbuscular mycorrhizal fungal isolates in relation to extraradical mycelial networks", *The New phytologist*, 172, 347–357.

Balme, D. M. (1972). *Aristotle: De Partibus Animalium*. Oxford: Clarendon Press.

Baluška, F., Mancuso, S. (2009). *Signaling in Plants*. Holland: Springer.

Baluska, F., Reber, A. (2019). "Sentience and consciousness in single cells: How the first minds emerged in unicellular species", *BioEssays*, 41, 1800229.

Bateson, G. (1972). *Steps to an Ecology of Mind: Collected Essays in Anthropology, Psychiatry, Evolution, and Epistemology*. Chicago, IL: University of Chicago Press.

Baxby, D. (2004). Jenner, E. (1749–1823). In *Oxford Dictionary of National Biography*. Oxford: Oxford University Press

Beebe, B., Sterne, D. (1977). "Engagement-disengagement and early object experiences". In N. Freedman S. Grand (eds.). *Communicative Structures and Psychic Structures*. New York: Plenum Press, 35–55.

Bizzari, V. (2018). *"Sento quindi sono". Fenomenologia e Leib nel dibattito contemporaneo.* Milan: Mimesis Edizioni.

Bohm, D. (1980). *Wholeness and the Implicate Order*. London: Routledge.

Bookchin, M. (1996) *The Philosophy of Social Ecology: Essays on Dialectical Naturalism*. Montreal: Black Rose Books, 57–59.

Bornemark, J. (2018). "Anden mellan liv och vetenskap: Max Schelers fenomenologi". Hämäläinen-Karlström, P. (ed.). *Om anden: Filosofiska perspektiv på ande och andlighet*. Järna: Kosmos, 13–27.

Brownson, R. C., Fielding, J. E., and Maylahn, C. M. (2009). Evidence-based public health: A fundamental concept for public health practice, *Annual Review of Public Health*, 30, 175–201.

Butler, C. D., & Harley, D. (2010). Primary, secondary and tertiary effects of eco-climatic change: The medical response, *Postgraduate Medical Journal*, 86, 230–234.

Butler, C. D., Corvalán, C. F., & Koren, H. S. (2005). Human health and well-being in global ecological scenarios, *Ecosystems*, 8(2): 153–164.

Chadwick, E. (1842). *Report to Her Majesty's Principal Secretary of State for the Home Department from the Poor Law Commissioners on an Inquiry into the Sanitary Conditions of the Labouring Classes of Great Britain*. London: HMSO.

Charlton, W. (1969). "Aristotle on the place of mind", *Nature*, 41, 223–242.

Charlton, W. (1987). "Aristotle on the place of mind in nature", *Philosophical Issues in Aristotle's Biology*. In A. Gotthelf J. G. Lennox (eds.), Cambridge: Cambridge University Press.

Cioran, E. (1973). *Trouble of Being Born*. New York: The Arcade.

Colombetti, G.Torrance, S. (2009). "Emotion and ethics: An inter-(en)active approach", *Phenomenology and the Cognitive Sciences*, 8, 505–526.

Conrad-Martius, H. (2005). "Eine phänomenologiesche Sicht auf Natur und Welt", *Orbis Phaenomenologicus*, 5, 19–29, Verlag Königshausen und Neumann, Wüzburg.

Conrad-Martius, H. (1923). "Realontologie", *Jahrbuch für Philosophie und Phänomenologische Forschung*, 6, 159–333.

Crowther, T. (2019). "*The Ecologist who wants to map everything*", *Nature*, 573, 478–481.

Cuffari, E. C., Di Paolo, E., De Jaegher, H. (2015). From participatory sense-making to language: There and back again, *Phenomenology and the Cognitive Sciences*, 14, 1089–1125.

Dawe, G., Tan, X., Xiao, Z. (2007). "Cell migration from baby to mother", *Cell Adhesion & Migration*, 1, 19–27.

De Jaeger, H. and Di Paolo, E. (2005). "Toward an embodied science of intersubjectivity: Widening the scope of social understanding research", *Frontiers in Psychology*, 6, 227–234.

Descartes, R. (1950). "On animals", *The Philosophical Quarterly* Harrison, P. (trans.) 42(167): 219–227.

Descartes, R. (1993). *Meditations on First Philosophy*. E. Haldane, G. R. T. Ross (trans.) New York: Routledge.

Descartes, R. (2015). *The Passions of the Soul, and Other Late Philosophical Writings*. M. Moriarty (trans.) Oxford: Oxford University Press.

Dewey, J. 1916. *Essays in Experimental Logic*. Chicago: University of Chicago Press.

Di Paolo, E. (2005). "Autopoiesis, adaptivity, teleology, agency", *Phenomenology and the Cognitive Sciences* 4: 429–452.

Di Paolo, E. (2009). "Extended life", *Topoi* 28: 9–21.

Dienes, K. A., Hazel, N. A., Hammen, C. (2013). "Cortisol secretion in depressed and at-risk adults". *Psychoneuroendocrinology*, 38(6): 927–940.

Eagleman, D. (2015). *Incognito: The Secret Lives of the Brain*. New York: Pantheon Books.

Eagleman, D. (2016). *The Brain: The Story of You*. Edinburgh: Canongate Books.

Felger, J. C. (2019). "Role of inflammation in depression and treatment implications". *Handbook of Experimental Pharmacology*, 250, 255–286.

Ferriman A. (2007). "Sanitary revolution" as greatest medical advance since 1840". *British Medical Journal*, 334(7585): 111.

Feuerbach, L. (1985). "Wider den Dualismus von Leib und Seele, Fleisch und Geist". *Anthropologischer Materialismus. Ausgewählte Schri en I* . A. Schmidt (ed.), 165–191. Frankfurt: Ullstein.

Foucault, M. (1977). *Discipline and Punish: The Birth of the Prison*, New York: Random House

Freeland, C. (1995). "Aristotle on perception, appetition and self-motion," in *Self-Motion From Aristotle to Newton*, Gill, M. L. Lennox, J. G. Princeton, Princeton University Press, 65–80.

Froese, T., Fuchs, T. (2012). "The extended body: A case study in the neurophenomenology of social interaction", *Phenomenology and the Cognitive Sciences* 11, 205–235.

Fuchs, T. (2016). "Self across time: The diachronic unity of bodily existence", *Phenomenology and the Cognitive Sciences*, 15. Published online first.

Fuchs, T., (2017). "Intercorporeality and interaffectivity". *Intercorporeality: Emerging Socialities in Interaction*, C. Meyer, J. Streeck, S. Jordan (eds.), 3–24. Oxford: Oxford University Press.

Fuchs, T., De Jaeger, H. (2009). "Enactive intersubjectivity: Participatory sense-making and mutual incorporation.", *Phenomenology and the Cognitive Sciences* 8 (4): 465–486.

Fuchs, T., De Jaegher, H. (2009). Enactive intersubjectivity: Participatory sense-making and mutual incorporation, *Phenomenology and the Cognitive Sciences* 8, 465–486.

Gallagher, S. (2001). "The practice of mind: Theory, simulation or primary interaction?", *Journal of Consciousness Studies*, 8(5–7): 83–108.

Gendlin, E. T. (2012). "Implicit precision." In *Knowing Without Thinking*, Z. Radman (ed.), 141–166. Palgrave Macmillan.

Haeckel, E. (1904). *The Wonders of Life*. London: Watts & Co. 122–124.

Haeckel, Ernst (1874). *Anthropogenie, oder, Entwickelungsgeschichte des Menschen gemeinversthandliche wissenschaftliche Vortrage uber die Grundzuge der menschlichen Keimes- und Stammes-geschichte*. Leipzig: W. Engelmann.

Hahn, T. (2006). "'It's the RUSH': Sites of the sensually extreme.", *The Drama Review*, 50(2): 87–96.

Hahn, T. (2007). *Sensational Knowledge: Embodying Culture through Japanese Dance*. Middletown, CT: Wesleyan University Press.

Hahn, T. (2011). "Dancing with sensible objects (unpublished paper)". In *Presented at the Society for Ethnomusicology Conference*, Philadelphia, PA.

Hahn,T., Jordan, J. S. (2014)."Anticipation and embodied knowledge: Observations of enculturating bodies.", *Journal of Cognitive Education and Psychology*, 13(2): 272–284.

Hahn, T., et al. (2016). "Banding encounters—Embodied practices in improvisation." In *Negotiated Moments: Improvisation, Sound, and Subjectivity*, edited by G. Siddall and E. Waterman, 132–168. Durham, NC: Duke University Press.

Henry, M. (1963). *L'Essence de la manifestation*. Paris: PUF.

Hertenstein, M. J. (2002). Touch: Its communicative functions in infancy, *Human Development*, 45(2): 70–94.

Hobson, R. P. (2002). *The Cradle of Thought*. London: Macmillan.

Hodder, I. (2012). *Entangled. An Archaeology of the Relationships between People and Things*. Oxford: Wiley-Blackwell.

Hommel, B. J., Müsseler, G., Aschersleben, W., Prinz. (2001). "The theory of event coding (TEC): A framework for perception and action planning", *Behavioral and Brain Sciences*, 24(5): 849–937.

Husserl, E. (1919/2002). *Natur und Geist. Vorlesungen Sommersemester 1919*, ed. by M. Weiler. Dordrecht, the Netherlands, Kluwer Academic Publishers. (Hua-Mat. IV).

Husserl, E. (1936/1954). *Die Krisis der europäischen Wissenschaften und die transzendentale Phänomenologie: Eine Einleitung in die phänomenologische Philosophie*, Biemel, W. ed. Dordrecht: Kluwer. (Hua VI).

Husserl, E. (1907/1973). *Ding und Raum. Vorlesungen 1907*. Claesges, U. (ed.) The Hague, Netherlands: Martinus Nijhoff. (Hua XVI)

Hutto, D., Myin, E. (2013). *Radicalizing Enactivism*. Cambridge: MIT Press.

De Jaegher, H., Di Paolo, E. (2007). "Participatory sense-making: An enactive approach to social cognition", *Phenomenology and Cognitive Sciences*, 6, 485–507.

Jonas, H. (1968). "Biological foundations of individuality", *International Philosophical Quarterly*, 8, 231–251.

Jonas, H. (2001). *The Phenomenon of Life: Toward a Philosophical Biology* [1st ed. 1966]. Evanston, IL: Northwestern University Press.

Jordan, J. S., and D. Vinson. (2012). "After nature: On bodies, consciousness, and causality", *Journal of Consciousness Studies*, 19, (5–6): 229–250.

Kessel, A. (2006). *Air, the Environment and Public Health*. Cambridge: Cambridge University Press.

Lang, Tim, Rayner, Geof (2012). "Ecological public health: the 21st century's big idea? An essay by Tim Lang and Geof Rayner", BMJ, 345, e5466.

Lecanuet, J.-P., Granier-Deferre, C., Busnel, M.-C. (1995). Human fetal auditory perception. In *Fetal Development: A Psychobiological Perspective*. J.-P. Lecanuet, W. P. Fifer, N. A. Krasnegor, W. P. Smotherman (eds.). Lawrence Erlbaum Associates, Inc, 239–262.

Lennox, J. G. (1999). "Aristotle on the biological roots of virtue: The natural history of natural virtue. In *Biology and the Foundations of Ethics*. M. Ruse J. Maienschein (eds.). Cambridge: Cambridge University Press, 10–31.

Levinas, E. (1987). *Collected Philosophical Papers*. Dordrecht, the Netherlands: Nijhoff.

Loenhoff, J. (2013). "Multimodality and the senses." In *The Encyclopedia of Applied Linguistics*, edited by C. A. Chapelle. Somerset, NJ: Wiley

Lowen, A. (1983). *Narcissism*. New York: Macmillan Pub. Co.

Luckmann, T. (1973). "Phänomenologie und Soziologie". In W. M. Sprondel and R. Grathoff (eds.), *Alfred Schütz und die Idee des Alltags in den Sozialwissenschaften*. Stuttgart, Ecke: The President's Council on Bioethics, 196–206.

Luria, A. R. (1973). The frontal lobes and the regulation of behavior. In *Psychophysiology of the Frontal Lobes*. K. H. Pribram, A. R. Luria (eds.). Academic Press.

Løgstrup, K. (1956/1997) *The Ethical Demand*. University of Notre Dame Press.

Malafouris L. (2013). *How Things Shape the Mind: A Theory of Material Engagement*. Cambridge, MA: The MIT Press.

Malloch, S. (1999). "Mother and infants and communicative musicality". *Musicæ Scientiæ*, 3, 29–57.

Mancuso, S. (2013). *Plants Revolution*. Milano: Giunti.

Mancuso, S. Shabala, S. (2007). *Rhythms in Plants: Phenomenology, Mechanisms, and Adaptive Significance*. Holland: Springer.

Martuzzi, Marco (2007). The precautionary principle: In action for public health, *Occupational and Environmental Medicine*, 64, 569–570.

Maturana, H. R., and Varela, F. J. (1987). *The Tree of Knowledge: The Biological Roots of Human Understanding*. Boston, MA: Shambhala Publications.

Mead, G. H. (1934). *Mind, Self and Society from the Standpoint of a Social Behaviorist*. Chicago, IL: University of Chicago Press.

Mead, G. H. (1938). *The Philosophy of the Act*. In: C. W. Morris et al., University of Chicago.

de Meer, G., Baker, D., and Nieuwenhuijsen, M. J. (2008). "Environmental epidemiology: Study methods and application", *European Journal of Public Health*, 19, 3.

Merleau-Ponty, M. (1945). *Phenomenology of Perception*. London: Routledge.

Merleau-Ponty, M. (1968). *The Visible and the Invisible: Followed by Working Notes*. Trans. C. Lefort. Evanston, IL: Northwestern University Press.

Metzinger, T. (2004). *Being No One: The Self-Model Theory of Subjectivity*. Cambridge, MA: The MIT Press.

Morris, G., Saunders, P. (2017). "*The Environment in Health and Well-Being*". Oxford Research Encyclopedia of Environmental Science.

Muratori, F. B., (2019). V. "Autism as a disruption of affective contact: The forgotten role of George Frankl", *Clinical Neuropsychiatry*. 16, (4), 127–132.

Nash, Linda. (2007). *Inescapable Ecologies: A History of Environment, Disease and Knowledge*. California: University of California Press.

Neisser, U., Winograd, E. (Eds.). (1988). *Emory Symposia in Cognition, 2. Remembering Reconsidered: Ecological and Traditional Approaches to the Study of Memory*. Cambridge University Press.

Nussbaum, M. (2008). "Human dignity and political entitlements", In *Human Dignity and Bioethics: Essays Commissioned by the President's Council on Bioethics*, Published Online

Orff, C. Keetman, G. (1950) *Musik für Kinder I.* Mainz: Schott.

Petticrew, M., Whitehead, M., Macintyre, S. J., Graham, H., & Egan, M. (2004). "Evidence for public health policy on inequalities: 1: The reality according to policymakers", *Journal of Epidemiology and Community Health*, 58(10): 811–816.

Piaget, J. (1936). *Origins of Intelligence in the Child.* London: Routledge & Kegan Paul

Piaget, J. (1947). *La psychologie de l'intelligence.* Armand Colin.

Piontelli, A. (2002). *Twins. From Fetus Child.* London: Routledge.

Plessner, H. (1970). *Philosophische Anthropologie.* Frankfurt: Fischer.

Ratcliffe, M. (2002). "Heidegger's attunement and the neuropsychology of emotion", *Phenomenology and the Cognitive Sciences*, 1(3): 287–312.

Ratcliffe, M. (2007). *Rethinking Commonsense Psychology: A Critique of Folk Psychology, Theory of Mind and Simulation.* Basingstoke: Palgrave Macmillan.

Reed, E. S. (1988). "Applying the theory of action systems to the study of motor skills". Meijer, O. Roth, K. (eds.) *Studying Complex Motor Skills: The Motor–Action Controversy* Amsterdam: North-Holland, 45–86.

Rorty, R. (1970). "In defense of eliminative materialism", *Review of Metaphysics* 24, 112–121.

Rosen, G. A. (1993). *History of Public Health* (Expanded ed.). Baltimore, MD: Johns Hopkins University Press. Originally published 1958.

Royal College of Physicians. (2016). *Every Breath We Take: The Lifelong Impact of Air Pollution.* Report of a working party. London: RCP.

Sauvé Meyer, S. (1995). "Self-motion and external causation", In *Self-Motion from Aristotle to Newton*, M. L. Gill, J. G. Lennox. Princeton: Princeton University Press, 33–63.

Schultz, P. (2002). Environmental attitudes and behaviors across cultures, *Online Readings in Psychology and Culture*, 8(1).

Sechehaye, M. (1970). *Autobiography of a Schizophrenic Girl*, Paperback.

Shusterman, R. (2008). *Body Consciousness: A Philosophy of Mindfulness and Somaesthetics*, Cambridge: Cambridge University Press, 1–239.

Simard, S. W. (2016). "No plant is an island", *Nature Plants*, 2, 16146.

Stern, D. N. (1985). *The Interpersonal World of the Infant: A View from Psychoanalysis and Developmental Psychology.* New York: Basic Books.

Stern, D. N. (1998). "The process of therapeutic change involving implicit knowledge: Some implications of developmental observations for adult psychotherapy", *Infant Mental Health Journal* 19, 300–308.

Stewart, N. (1973). "Languaging the Body", *Performance Research*, 38, 42–53.

Streeck, Jürgen, ü, Christian, Jordan, J. (2017). *Intercorporeality. Emerging Socialities in Interaction.* Oxford: Oxford University Press.

Stuart, S. (2015). "The articulation of enkinesthetic entanglement." In *Inscribing the Body*, Ackermann, A. J., Bauks, M. 19–36. Wiesbaden, Germany: Springer VS.

Susser, M., & Adelstein, A. (1975). "An introduction to the work of William Farr", *American Journal of Epidemiology*, 101, 469–476.

Thompson, E. (2005). "Sensorimotor subjectivity and the enactive approach to experience", *Phenomenology and the Cognitive Sciences* 4, 407–427.

Thompson, E. (2007). *Mind in Life: Biology, Phenomenology, and the Sciences of Mind.* Cambridge, MA: Harvard University Press.

Thompson, E., Stapleton, M. (2009). "Making sense of sense-making: Reflections on enactive and extended theories", *Topoi* 28, 23–30.

Trevarthen, C. (2001). The neurobiology of early communication: Intersubjective regulations in human brain development. In A. F. Kalverboer and A. Gramsbergen (Eds.), *Handbook of Brain and Behaviour in Human Development*. Basel: Karger, 841–881.

Trevarthen, C. Reddy, V. (2007). "Consciousness in infants". Velmans, M. Schneider, S. (eds.), *The Blackwell Companion to Consciousness*, Blackwell. 41–57.

Tyson, Edward (1699). Orang-Outang, sive Homo Sylvestris: or, the Anatomy of a Pygmie Compared with that of a Monkey, an Ape, and a Man, Retrieved https://archive.org/stream/orangoutangsiveh00tyso/orangoutangsiveh00tyso_djvu.txt 20 October 2013.

Varela, F., Thompson, E., Rosch, E. (1991). *The Embodied Mind: Cognitive Science and Human Experience*. Cambridge, MA: The MIT Press.

Varela, F. J. (1996). "Neurophenomenology: A methodological remedy for the hard problem", *Journal of Consciousness Studies* 3, 330–349

Voegtline, K. M., Costigan, K. A., Pater, H. A., & DiPietro, J. A. (2013). "Near-term fetal response to maternal spoken voice", *Infant Behavior & Development*, 36(4): 526–533.

von Uexküll, J. (1920). *Streifzüge durch die Umwelten von Tieren und Menschen: Ein Bilderbuch unsichtbarer Welten*, Berlin: Springer-Verlag.

Vos, S. P., Huibers, M. J., Diels, L., et al. (2012). A randomized clinical trial of cognitive behavioral therapy and interpersonal psychotherapy for panic disorder with agoraphobia, Psychological Medicine, 42, 2661–2672.

Wu, J., Baldwin, T. (2010). "New insights into plant responses to the attack from insect herbivores", *Annual Review of Genetics*, 44, 1–24.

Yalom, I. D. (1980). *Existential Psychotherapy*. New York: Basic Books.

CONCLUSION

In 1969, humanity was struck by a moment of meaningful awareness. In their successful mission to the Moon, human beings saw for the first time the Earth in its entirety. The mission to the Moon was, in a certain sense, a mission for our planet. That day, in fact, the Earth stopped being an abstraction and became real for all of us. Until then, our Earth was an abstraction made real through maps and charts. The landing on the Moon made our Earth visible for all of us. April 22, 1970, was the first year humans celebrated Earth's birthday. This celebration became an occasion to be openly grateful for all the generous resources that the Earth provides for us and to cherish our being part of its beauty.

Yet, this book was born during one of the deepest crises that human beings have faced in decades. A very unsettling epidemic has spread throughout the world leaving a scar on the emotional geography of our human life. From Wuhan in China, a virus known as COVID-19 has spread throughout the world. I do not have the competence to write informative pages about the structure of this virus and the biological, as well as political, damage it has brought upon us. Certainly, I see how the content of this book is in line with the lesson we are hopefully learning from the spreading of this virus.

One of the major messages that the World Health Organization, worldwide political leaders, and medical authorities from all over the globe are trying to convey is the sense of collective responsibility that all of us have in containing the virus. Today, more than ever, we are learning at a very high cost that each one of us is responsible for our neighbor's well-being. If everyone became aware of their interconnectedness with others and how they are part of a complex system of life, then the virus would be easier to fight and our health care systems would not fear collapsing under the financial burden required to beat this virus. Yet, as I have explained in this book, these views are difficult to bring to the attention of the masses. The severe measures that we have had to take during this period of time to prevent the spread of the virus has shown us how it would be to live without the support of our environment. The monthslong lockdown to which most of the world population has been forced to live through has offered a practical example of what it means to cultivate a culture in which humans detach themselves from the environment. In these chapters, I showed some of the psychological disorders generated from the separation of individuals from their environment (more on anxiety, restlessness, narcissism, and emotional numbness in my forthcoming The Role of *Bio*-Ethics in Emotional Problems). Because of the spreading of the virus, the worldwide population has had to experience this detachment and its devastating emotional effects on their well-being. This shows how important it is for all of us to overcome our biases and care for our emotional connection with the environment.

Reductionism, individualism, and scientism are the biases on which I focused the most in this book. They have built around us a worldview that insists upon herding theories, survival of the fittest, *mors tua vita mea*, and mottos promoting discontinuity between individuals from each other and their surroundings. The empty shelves and the episodes of violence at supermarkets, the hoarding of masks and disinfectant gels by people not in urgent need, and the holidays at any cost are just a glimpse of where we are in the consideration we have for each other. Fortunately, this has been balanced by heartwarming examples of solidarity and cooperation.

This crisis will eventually end. Soon, we will have to choose what world we want to come back to and what kind of values we want to hold high for our well-being. During the crisis, the traumatic collective experience shattered the normality of our ethical lifeworld (*Lebenswelt*) and forced us to develop new customs, habits, and accordingly, a new (suspended) worldview: from the care we need to have in choosing an apple at the supermarket, being careful to touch the least possible so as to not spread the virus, to the forbidden joy of taking a small walk outside. This virus has forced us to rethink our smallest actions and to create new habits that have quickly become the basis of a new, unspoken ethical agreement for our social life—a life that seems to serve better our natural environment. As Chomsky and Butler[1] warned us, this pandemic crisis is just a glimpse of the real crises to come, those connected to climate change and nuclear war. We need to work toward a life-world that better serves a sustainable notion of well-being. We know that the Earth can continue without us—as we saw from the pandemic, the Earth thrives without us. For us to live a decent life, we need to become more emotionally mature and to understand life in its continuity with all living beings without falling into harmful binary ways of thinking that separate inside from outside, spirit from body, individuals from society, and persons from nature. Life needs to be cherished in all its forms. Bioethics can provide an ethical framework that goes in favor of the psychological, environmental, and social well-being of living beings as a whole. I would like to conclude this book with the poetic epitaph written on Raphael's tomb which summarizes my wish to find a way of living a life that is deeply respectful of and almost one with Nature:

> Qui è quel Raffaello da cui, fin che visse, Madre Natura temette di essere superata da lui e quando morì temette di morire con lui/Here lies Raphael, by whom Nature feared to be outdone while he lived, and when he died, feared that she would die with him.

Note

1 Retrieved from https://www.pressenza.com/it/2020/03/noam-chomsky-supereremo-la-crisi-del-coronavirus-ma-abbiamo-davanti-a-noi-crisi-piu-gravi/; https://www.versobooks.com/blogs/4603-capitalism-has-its-limits.

INDEX

For Product Safety Concerns and Information please contact our EU
representative GPSR@taylorandfrancis.com
Taylor & Francis Verlag GmbH, Kaufingerstraße 24, 80331 München, Germany